CRIMES IN ARCHIVAL FORM

CRIMES IN

ARCHIVAL FORM

HUMAN RIGHTS, FACT PRODUCTION,
AND MYANMAR

Ken MacLean

 UNIVERSITY OF CALIFORNIA PRESS

University of California Press
Oakland, California

© 2022 by Ken MacLean

Library of Congress Cataloging-in-Publication Data

Names: MacLean, Ken, author.
Title: Crimes in archival form : human rights, fact production, and
    Myanmar / Ken MacLean.
Description: Oakland,California : University of California Press,
    [2022] | Includes bibliographical references and index.
Identifiers: LCCN 2021037034 (print) | LCCN 2021037035 (ebook) |
    ISBN 9780520385382 (cloth) | ISBN 9780520385405 (paperback) |
    ISBN 9780520385412 (epub)
Subjects: LCSH: Human rights—Burma—Case studies. | Crimes
    against humanity—Burma—Case studies. | Victims of violent
    crimes—Burma—Case studies. | Burma—Politics and
    government—21st century.
Classification: LCC JC599.B932 M34 2022 (print) | LCC JC599.B932
    (ebook) | DDC 323.09591—dc23
LC record available at https://lccn.loc.gov/2021037034
LC ebook record available at https://lccn.loc.gov/2021037035

The author acknowledges permission from the poet and translator to
reprint Tee Noe, "I Do Need Peace," translated by Violet Cho and
first published in *Transnational Literature* 6, no. 2 (May 2014): 2–3.

Manufactured in the United States of America

31 30 29 28 27 26 25 24 23 22
10 9 8 7 6 5 4 3 2 1

I Do Need Peace

without notice
suffering came quick to greet us:
soldiers
rapid
they burnt our house
an annihilated place.

rice barns to ashes
our food lost
inhabiting the forest deep
as the enemy searched for us
in the basket, father took me away
my village
I can never see again.

—Tee Noe

CONTENTS

ACKNOWLEDGMENTS AND DEDICATION

Authors' acknowledgments typically include the admission that it is impossible to thank everyone who played a role in the book's completion. That is the case here. But rather than include a long, but inevitably partial, list of names (family, friends, colleagues, reviewers, editors, and so on), I wish to both recognize and to dedicate this work to the thousands of ordinary people whose traumatic experiences form the evidentiary core of my book. It is a troubling but unavoidable fact that books on human rights violations utilize these experiences to make arguments and to advance conclusions that the victims will never ever read or directly benefit from. Again, that is the case here. However, I hope the claims I make in the book will inform the future work of not only academics but also policymakers and human rights activists who seek to connect theory with practice in a manner that contributes to justice for all victims of state-sponsored violence.

ABBREVIATIONS

AAPP	Assistance Association for Political Prisoners
CBO	community-based organization
CIDKP	Committee for Internally Displaced Karen People
CoI	commission of inquiry
CSO	civil society organization
DKBA	Democratic Karen Buddhist Army
FBR	Free Burma Rangers
ICC	International Criminal Court
IDP	internally displaced person
IHRC	International Human Rights Clinic at Harvard Law School
ILO	International Labour Organization
INGO	international nongovernmental organization
ISO	International Standards Organization
KHRG	Karen Human Rights Group
KNLA	Karen National Liberation Army
KNU	Karen National Union
KORD	Karen Office for Relief and Development
KRC	Karen Relief Committee
MIMU	Myanmar Information Management Unit
ND-Burma	Network for Human Rights Documentation-Burma
NGO	nongovernmental organization

NLD	National League for Democracy
NRDC	Natural Resource Defense Council
NSAG	non-state armed groups
SLORC	State Law and Order Restoration Council
SPDC	State Peace and Development Council
TBBC	Thai-Burma Border Consortium
UNHCR	United Nations High Commissioner for Refugees
UNSC	United Nations Security Council

NOTES ON TERMINOLOGY

First, the question of whether to use "Burma" or "Myanmar" when referring to the country is a politically charged one, so I address it at the outset. Proponents of one or the other justify their positions by citing different moments in history, defining inclusiveness in conflicting ways, and invoking alternate linguistic practices.[1] These disagreements are global in addition to local in nature, according to Mark Duffield, the former director of the Global Insecurities Center. "Myanmar—or Burma—is an internationalized battlespace where the peoples' multiple masters have established competing regimes of truth and legitimacy," he argues. "Between and around these defining poles," represented by the armed forces and its supporters on the one hand and political exiles and human rights advocacy groups on the other, "lies a medley of different actors—government bureaucracies, ceasefire groups, noncease fire groups, businessmen, aid agencies, and donor governments—that are either trying to coerce, tax, or dispossess the people, or else, protect, educate, and better them."[2] I would much prefer to use the combined form, Burma/Myanmar, to visually remind readers that the country's name was disputed during the period covered in the book and, equally importantly, that these "battlespaces" continue to be a source of conflict today. (Though not discussed in this book, the 2021 coup exemplifies my point.) However, in recent years, Myanmar has almost entirely replaced Burma, even among people who resisted military rule for decades. I follow common usage, except where Burma appears in the source material, for this reason.

Second, in Myanmar, the standard name for non-state armed groups (NSAGs) is "ethnic armed organizations" (EAOs). However, the term elides the fact that many of the country's minority populations regard the state's national armed forces (Tatmadaw, which literally means "Royal Force") to be an EAO as well, on the grounds that it represents the interests of Burmans, the dominant ethnic group, at the expense of non-Burmans. I use the neutral label NSAGs to avoid erasing this widely shared view on the Tatmadaw.

Third, the Myanmar Information Management Unit (MIMU), which operates under the United Nations resident and humanitarian coordinator, has assigned unique "place codes" to approximately 75 percent of the country's villages. Each place code includes GPS locational data and an English transliteration of the village name based on a standardized system MIMU developed.[3] A village may lack an official place code for several reasons, however. Remoteness is a common one. But decades of armed conflict have also reshaped where people live and the names they give to places they reside, which may or may not be recognizable as villages from an administrative perspective. Additionally, many of the villages mentioned in this book are located in territory (formerly) controlled by a NSAG, which does not always want the precise GPS coordinates known to the government. Finally, different linguistic groups sometimes assign the same place different names, which further complicates matters. To minimize confusion and to avoid the introduction of errors, I use the place-names that appear in the original source material, the spelling of which in transliterated form is not always consistent both within and across fact-finding organizations.

Introduction

Finding a fact means determining that its existence
is more probable than its non-existence.
—American Law Institute

"When we first got the [satellite] photos, we had no idea they were prison
camps. The North Korean gulags are work gulags, but the prisoners are
forced to work and live in what look like North Korean villages. It wasn't
until we began interviewing former prisoners that we knew what we were
looking at," a senior scientist at the Natural Resources Defense Council
(NRDC) told me during an interview I conducted with him in 2008. The
scientist in question has a PhD in experimental physics and oversees the
NRDC's nuclear nonproliferation programs. The NRDC scientist was also
the technical adviser for a path-breaking human rights research project on
North Korea, which is why I contacted him.

At the time, I was involved in a mapping project that would employ satellite imagery for human rights verification purposes. The goal was to identify
the likely route of the Shwe Pipeline, which the then lead joint venture partner, South Korea's Daewoo International, had not yet publicly announced.
Once built, it would pump oil and natural gas from an offshore site in the
Gulf of Bengal across Myanmar to southwestern China—a distance of nearly
twenty-four hundred kilometers, with some sections of it passing through
areas contested by different non-state armed groups (NSAGs). The project
was strategically important. The pipeline would enable China to diversify
the routes it used to import oil and gas from the Middle East and to avoid
the Straits of Malacca, which is narrow, crowded with tankers, and easily
blocked if armed conflict were to break out. Cutting the transport distance
would significantly reduce time and costs as well. The joint venture project

would further provide much-needed hard currency to the State Peace and Development Council (SPDC), the military-led regime then in power. (Economic sanctions, imposed by several Western governments, made it very difficult for the regime to access such currency at the time.) Given the regime's terrible human rights record, advocacy groups were very concerned that pipeline construction would result in large-scale violations, including the forced relocation of villages without compensation and forced labor to cut construction costs, as had transpired with previous infrastructure projects.

EarthRights International (ERI), the nongovernmental organization (NGO) that I worked for at the time, set out to map the environmentally sensitive areas and population centers that were potentially at risk. To plot possible routes, we used a combination of satellite imagery, digital mapping tools, and an atlas of existing roads and rail networks, as well as information from advocacy groups, such as the Shwe Gas Campaign, that conducted research on the ground.

We planned to present the information to the South Korean Human Rights Commission in the hopes that this body could pressure Daewoo to pay for an independent third party to monitor construction using remote sensing (an assemblage of high-resolution satellite imagery, geographic information systems, and Google Earth, which combines them both). The financial cost of such "deterrent" monitoring, we maintained, was minimal when compared to the possible expense of a lawsuit, as had occurred in the recent past. Unocal and Total Oil had paid many millions of dollars each in 2005 as part of separate out-of-court settlements for their role in "aiding and abetting" human rights abuses during the construction of the Yadana and Yetagun Pipelines in the southeastern part of the country.[1]

The primary goal of my conversation with the NRDC scientist was to learn what we would have to bear in mind if we moved forward with the monitoring proposal. But his answers to my questions also inform the focus of this book, which concerns human rights "fact" production. In it, I examine different types of human rights documentation, the archival formations that result from them, and the effects both have upon transnational advocacy. All three types of documentation center on disparate efforts to prove that the country's armed forces (Tatmadaw) routinely committed crimes against humanity and, in many cases, war crimes, against civilians in southeastern Myanmar over of the course of decades. I devote special attention to the epistemological, methodological, and ethical issues that arise when we recognize the extent to which human rights "facts" are, in fact, fashioned rather than found, as the North Korean example will make clear.

My analysis of the investigative decisions made, field methods employed, analytical practices utilized, and advocacy strategies mobilized demonstrates how "fact" production occurs and why it matters to human rights claims. Sociologist Howard Becker, in a recent work on the philosophy of knowledge, makes an important point that applies here: "The word *accepted* in *accepted fact* reminds us that the evidence has to convince someone of its validity, its weight, to become evidence."[2] Persuasion, in other words, is an inescapable element of human rights documentation from the very start. ("Facts are argumentative practices," as another human rights philosopher bluntly put it.)[3] Becker's point is a useful reminder that it is not information per se that matters, but rather "what *kind* of information, produced by *whom*, and authorized by *what symbolic and material powers* that make it persuasive."[4] When a fashioned "fact" becomes accepted as fact, it does not mean that social constructivism has triumphed over positivism, however. The belief that one can be easily distinguished from the other in the context of human rights documentation is a specious one, as neither exists in complete isolation from the other. A process-oriented account thus enables us to examine the interplay between what happened in empirically verifiable terms and what is said to have happened. Focusing on the interplay, which may at occur at several different moments in the life cycle of a human rights "fact," disrupts conventional binary views that conceive of positivist approaches to human rights documentation as "true" and constructivist ones as, if not "false," then at best politically biased.

The point of departure for such an investigation begins with what is generally assumed to be a straightforward element fundamental to human rights praxis: fact-finding. In recent years, calls have grown stronger to establish more uniform "codes, rules, manuals, and guidelines" to help standardize human rights fact-finding practices, which remain quite diverse.[5] However, the increased interest in this area overwhelmingly overlooks the assumptions that underlie efforts to achieve greater standardization, and this neglect poses an opportunity to subject the current "turn to the factual" in human rights documentation to much-needed scrutiny.[6] Fact-finding, as conventionally understood, entails a determination of what transpired, who bears responsibility for it, and what kinds of action are recommended in response. Yet the means by which the conclusions are reached rarely receive critical reflection beyond informal conversations among practitioners. This situation is finally beginning to change, and this book adds to those efforts.[7]

According to human rights philosopher Frédéric Mégret, three debates about the nature of "facts" have emerged recently in the field of human rights documentation.[8] The first debate concerns the procedures that should be used to identify human rights facts.[9] While a welcome development, a narrow focus on procedural issues can obscure the extent to which purportedly factual statements are propositions—that is, assertions that expresses a judgment or opinion. Some facts, for example, may be true propositions, such as "informant A" personally witnessed army "officer X" order an attack on civilians. Other facts are plausibly true exemplifications; that is, they possess qualities or stand in relation to other facts yet are subject to interpretation and thus disagreement. Civilians, to offer another relevant example, are only civilians if they possess the qualities or relations that define a noncombatant under international humanitarian law. But in contexts of asymmetric warfare, such as insurgencies, distinguishing civilians from combatants when they outwardly resemble one another and may participate in some similar practices can be extremely difficult. Still other facts refer to states of affairs, in other words, the way the actual world must be in order to make a given proposition about the world true. In the case of "officer X," he can be deduced to be a war criminal because his actions, killing civilians, make him so. In sum, the first type of human rights "fact" is logical, the second is epistemological, and the final one is ontological in nature. Despite significant differences, all three types of facts unavoidably rely on what Mégret refers to as "mental operations that tie them together," which include "presumptions, deductions, inferences, and extrapolations."[10] As this book demonstrates, these operations are not incidental to human rights documentation. They are instead fundamental to it.

The second debate revolves around the credibility of a "fact" as conveyed by a witness. Typically, a witness is deemed to be credible if recognized by others as a source of reliable information regarding someone, an event, or a phenomenon. But other factors have a bearing on credibility, such as evaluations by others of witness confidence, accuracy, and intentions, all of which are, to a greater or lesser degree, subjective in nature. A witness, in other words, is judged on their performance, specifically the degree to which their comportment and statements align with the "formal and pragmatic dimensions" the context requires.[11] (A witness who "recites a myth in response to a lawyer's request for a factual account" would not be deemed credible in a court of law, for example.)[12] Trustworthiness, another key element of credibility, is similarly difficult to measure in objective terms, though an established track record of reliability can help buttress witness claims, as can official "proof," such as credentials and certifications in the case of experts. But the fact remains that the credibility of the witness is not solely defined by the witness; rather, it is determined, in large part, by others, which is why the "facts" are, especially in legal settings, subject to contestation.[13]

The third debate, Mégret explains, revolves around the impact human rights "facts" are intended to have on a specific audience, which in turn hinges upon the standards of proof required. Such standards vary depending on the purpose of the fact-finding and the thresholds different researchers rely upon (reasonable suspicion, sufficient evidence, and conclusive evidence, for example) to calculate the probabilities of each. However, these evidentiary thresholds are defined in nonuniform ways, which hampers comparative analysis across fact-finding methods and again invites conflicting interpretations of what the presented "facts" mean.[14]

I engage with all three of the debates that Mégret identified to analyze the fact-finding practices different organizations used to document state-sponsored violence in Myanmar, long considered a human rights pariah. My discussion of fact-finding, although focused on the situation in the southeastern part of the country, is relevant beyond it. Human Rights Watch is an excellent example due to its global reach and considerable financial resources. Human Rights Watch documents violations and conducts advocacy on abuses in more than eighty countries annually. Its researchers also conduct fact-finding on nearly a dozen other cross-cutting issues, such as women's rights, international justice, and military affairs. The work is made possible by private donations and foundation grants. In 2019, such funding enabled Human Rights Watch to spend almost US$63 million on its programming.[15] Human Rights Watch is among the largest nongovernmental producers of human rights "facts" in the world for these reasons. Yet no documents are publicly available on the types of training its fact finders receive and the research methodologies they use, two issues that raise questions about how documentation is carried out and the representativeness of the "truth" claims made.

The North Korea mapping project, mentioned earlier, which requires minimal contextual knowledge to understand what I mean by "fact" production, illustrates why organizational silences on such issues matter. Representatives of the US Committee for Human Rights in North Korea approached the NRDC scientist I interviewed in 2008. They asked whether he could help them interpret some high-resolution commercial satellite images of seven suspected "political penal-labor colonies" located in the country's remote mountainous areas near the border with the People's Republic of China. He regularly used satellite imagery to monitor nuclear programs, and he agreed to assist the research team with image analysis. But the NRDC scientist quickly found the process to be far more complicated than anticipated. The images, despite the impressive amount of detail they contained (roads, railways, rivers, fences, fields, and so on, down to one-meter resolution), were meaningless on their own for a simple reason. The research team could not readily distinguish real villages from "political penal-labor colonies" disguised as real ones—even with the information David Hawk, the report's lead author, had elicited from former prisoners and guards living in exile whom he had interviewed while preparing it. The informants had provided context concerning the history of the penal colonies and their inner workings. The details, however, did not solve the central problem the team faced: how to determine which buildings were used for what purposes when they outwardly looked the same, and whether the economic activities also visible in the images—primarily logging, mining, plantation agriculture, textile manufacturing, and cement production—were legitimate or performed though forced labor by political prisoners.

The problem persisted, the NRDC scientist told me, because the informants could not easily place themselves in the two-dimensional pictures. Confused, I asked what he meant. The informants, he explained, had always moved horizontally through these spaces, whereas we were asking them to tell us what they saw from a vertical perspective. To solve this problem, the report's research team decided to dramatically enlarge the images until each of them was twelve feet by three feet in size. They then pieced the separate images together. The result was a meta-image of the suspected political penal-labor colonies, one that added a third dimension to the composite whole, as it enabled the informants to walk around "inside" the villages, identifying the structures and the nature of the work carried out in them while they did so.

Geo-spatial and digital visualization technologies, such as the ones the NRDC scientist used while putting together the 2003 report *The Hidden*

Gulag, now provide an important method for documenting human rights violations in conflict zones from "afar."[16] Visual evidence, many NGOs assert, provides purportedly objective proof of state-sponsored violence, especially in remote areas, by making visible the material traces it leaves behind, such as charcoal scars where villages previously stood before armed actors burned them to the ground. The reality is considerably more complicated, however.[17] Nevertheless, visual evidence, when it corroborates eyewitness testimony, provides a powerfully persuasive tool, not only for identifying the size and scale of forced displacement but also for monitoring high-risk areas as a potentially preventative measure, which is what ERI sought to do with the Shwe pipeline mapping effort in Myanmar. Unfortunately the proposed pipeline monitoring project did not go forward due to a political shift in the leadership of the South Korean Human Rights Commission and the decision by Myanmar's military regime to grant China the rights to construct the US$2.5 billion project, which finally went online in 2015. Fortunately, large-scale abuses did not occur during the construction phase, though widespread complaints suggest that inadequate compensation to affected villagers for the land they lost to the project was a significant problem.[18]

Importantly, the effort to map North Korean political penal-labor colonies relied on a number of translations, each of which produced different types of "facts," which is why I used this example to introduce what I explore at length in this book. In this example, *translation* has two connotations. The literal process for transforming words expressed in one language into another and the technical process of moving something from one contextual place to another affect meaning-making. The "fact" of what happened required distinguishing the political penal-labor colonies from ordinary ones, and this outcome was produced through a number of steps. Very few of the steps were the result of advance planning, however. Instead, the researchers had to develop strategies on an ad hoc basis to overcome the problems they encountered along the way when trying to link informant testimonies with specific locations and particular practices.

The translation of the oral testimonies from the North Korean dialect into English was obviously the first challenge. Next, the researchers sought to connect the testimonies with the satellite images. When that effort failed, they created a meta-image that the former guards and prisoners could physically walk around "in." The process of moving through the two-dimensional visual representation of the political penal-labor colonies triggered their three-dimensional embodied memories of place. By connecting the two forms of sensory experience, the informants were able to identify the divergent functional purposes of structures that outwardly looked the same. Having done so, the researchers then rendered the specific buildings that the defectors identified into computer-generated schematic drawings depicting the spatial organization of forced labor within them. The end result was a path-breaking report that became "a textbook on political imprisonment in North Korea" and a key tool for international advocacy efforts in the years that followed.[19] But the process by which this occurred, as the NRDC scientist explained to me, was far from straightforward. The creative problem-solving approach the team devised, details of which did not appear in the report, was the condition of possibility for answering the central research question, as the satellite images and testimonies from defectors were insufficient on their own.

My summary of the process of identifying the North Korean labor camps broadly captures some of the complex issues that arise when we carefully examine how human rights–related "facts" are produced as well as found. This book explores these dynamics and their afterlives in the form of reports written, archives established, and the artifacts advocacy campaigns deployed. Close attention to these dynamics, I argue, foregrounds the importance of fact-finding, which continues to be an underexamined element of human rights practice despite its centrality to the entire project.[20] Why is this important? Foregrounding fact-finding in critical yet constructive ways prompts long overdue conversations about the possibilities and limits of human rights documentation as a mode of truth-seeking. Such conversations are particularly urgent in an era when the perpetrators of large-scale human rights violations exploit misinformation, weaponize disinformation, and employ outright falsehoods, including deepfakes, to undermine the credibility of those who document abuses and demand that they be held accountable for them in the court of public opinion and in courts of law. To respond to such attacks, practitioners and scholars alike need to be more transparent about and accountable for how human rights "fact" production works, why it is important, and when its use should prompt concern.

Here, it is worth quoting at length why such theoretical, methodological, and ethical labor is essential. John Van Maanen and Brian Pentland, in their work on the "rhetoric of records," explain:

Records are not factual, neutral, technical documents alone, although while serving legitimate ends they must appear this way, and while serving illegitimate ones even more so. They are designed—implicitly or explicitly—to produce an effect in some kind of audience, which itself actively uses records to interpret events. This is not to suggest conscious deceit or cynicism on the part of either record keepers or uses (although . . . this is certainly possible). Rather it is simply to acknowledge and open up for analysis the conditions under which organizational records are produced and used.[21]

Human rights "facts" are no different. In fact, given the often life or death stakes involved in human rights documentation and advocacy, the slowly growing call to open up these processes to examination is all the more pressing if efforts to hold perpetrators accountable is to succeed in an increasingly "post-truth" era.

HUMAN RIGHTS ARCHIVES

Transitional justice initiatives, although originally focused on questions of criminal accountability and dominated by legalistic approaches, have expanded since the 1990s into a multidisciplinary field of practice and scholarship.[22] Not surprisingly, the proliferation of official and unofficial transitional justice and truth-telling projects globally has contributed to a diverse array of human rights–related archival projects—all of them based on fact-finding in one form or another.[23] Many of the projects are practical in orientation and focus on the mechanics of documentation. The Lund-London Guidelines, perhaps the best-known example, outline international best practices for NGO-led fact-finding visits and reports.[24] Prepared by the International Bar Association in 2009 and updated in 2015, the purpose of the guidelines is to provide the "basis for improving the accuracy, objectivity, transparency, and credibility in human rights fact-finding by NGOs."[25] But many competing examples of best practices exist. The Human Rights Information and Documentation Systems International (HURIDOCS) posts how-to manuals online to help activists standardize their data collection methods, and it conducts peer-to-peer training to assist them in more effectively disseminating their findings.[26]

Benetech and the Human Rights Data Analysis Group, like HURIDOCS, support these efforts by making open-source software for information

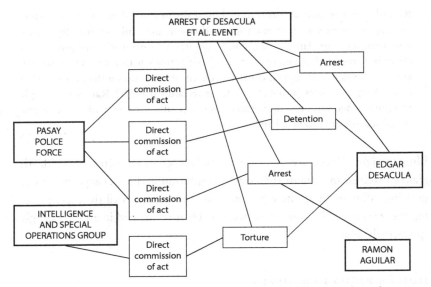

FIGURE I. Alternate graphical presentation of events. SOURCE: Human Rights Information Documentation Systems.

management, especially quantitative data, publicly available.[27] Archivists Without Borders offers yet another example. Its experts work globally to help professionals repurpose state archives, originally created and used by authoritarian regimes as "tools of control and repression," into ones that can "promote social justice and respect for human rights."[28]

These practitioner-oriented initiatives and the conflict-specific archives that result from them (e.g., the Truth and Reconciliation Commission of South Africa and the National Commission on the Disappearance of Persons in Argentina) have prompted a growing body of critical scholarship. This scholarship—*Archivaria* and *Archival Science* are the key English-language forums for such discussions—raises provocative questions regarding how power, memory, and ethics shape the creation and utilization of human rights archives.[29] Typically, scholars categorize these archives by what they contain, ranging from self-declared human rights archives (e.g., the Kigali Genocide Archive in Rwanda), to archival projects internal to human rights organizations (e.g., Amnesty International's Archive Project), to archives with human rights–related holdings (e.g., University of Texas–Austin's Human Rights Documentation Initiative).[30] These categorizations, while helpful, nevertheless narrowly frame archives as repositories that contain records relevant to criminal accountability and not as sites of knowledge production.

By contrast, Ann Stoler, whose scholarship crosscuts the disciplinary divisions that separate anthropology and history, advocates an analytical and methodological shift from "archive-as-source" to "archive-as-subject." Archives, including human rights ones, are cultural agents of "fact" production, of taxonomies in the making, and of state authority, she argues.[31] Michel-Rolph Trouillot, who also worked at the intersection of both disciplines, made a related point regarding the power of silences. Trouillot argued that silences—what is excluded or repressed—shape historical production at four key moments: "the moment of fact creation (the making of sources); the moment of fact assembly (the making of archives); the moment of fact retrieval (the making of narratives), and the moment of retroactive significance (the making of history in the final instance)."[32] Consequently, the distinction between "what happened" and "that which is said to have happened" is not always clear, according to Trouillot.[33] Silences do not simply foreclose other narratives, however. The four moments Trouillot identified, as the gerund "making" suggests, also produce "facts."[34] The moments do so, as historian Hayden White famously observed, because their content is to a significant degree shaped by the documentary forms used: in this case, the fact-finding methods NGOs employ to record violations, to compile the field data into searchable categories, and to make this information available to different audiences, most often packaged as reports.[35] In sum, these three scholars are centrally concerned with the politics of epistemology. To understand these politics, they explain, it is necessary to critically engage with methodology, that is, the making of archives themselves: their collection protocols, organizational logics, custodial practices, modes of access, and so on. Unfortunately, little of the scholarship on human rights archives explores these interrelated topics in depth, even though "every archive is the product of ongoing struggles over the production, politicization, and institutionalization of knowledge," to quote Renise Mawani, a scholar of law and society.[36] Indeed, most studies still merely portray these archives as repositories of evidence.[37]

Katherine Weld's book *Paper Cadavers* offers another good example of why such portrayals are problematic.[38] Weld put the practitioner-oriented human rights documentation manuals that prescribe best practices in archival information science in conversation with the critical academic literature on archives as discursive formations. This conversation emerged out of her research on the Guatemalan civil war (1960–1996). In 2006, an explosion at a military base in Guatemala's capital led to the unexpected discovery of the nearly eighty million documents the national police had generated during the war. The primary focus of Weld's project was to document the *processes* of documentation shaping the ongoing rescue, preservation, organization, and systematization of the materials into what one of her informants evocatively called an "archive of pain." "Archives of pain," Weld explains, are based largely on written documents such as case files, memos, and other forms of official correspondence, the contents of which delineate the microdynamics of state-sponsored terror.[39] By contrast, "archives as weapons" are based primarily on oral accounts. Victims' testimonies about their own experiences, as well as those of the dead and disappeared, who cannot speak for themselves, are the two most common examples.[40] Archives as weapons thus bear witness and are the claimed evidentiary point of departure for efforts to counter the state's narratives that justify violence or deny its involvement in it altogether.

These archives, Weld points out, operate according to different logics: repression on the one hand and rescue on the other. The two archives also rely on different forms of evidence (written vs. oral), as well as standards of proof, to support their conclusions. But the two archives and the competing accounts of the country's past cannot be read in isolation. Instead, Weld asserts, the archives must be put into dialogue with one another to understand the silences, omissions, and other types of patterned bias that structure them both.[41] Otherwise, she contends, it will remain impossible for people to challenge impunity, to seek restorative justice, to conduct truth and reconciliation proceedings, and to engage in successful memory projects.[42]

The archives as object and archives as subject debate, which I have summarized here, illustrates the two perspectives that dominate how archives in general are constructed, curated, and utilized. Both are relevant to understanding human rights "fact" production more broadly. The life-cycle approach, which emerged in the late nineteenth century, carefully documents the creation, receipt, classification, maintenance, and disposition of information in the form of records. The relationship of these records to one another is fixed according to the principle of *respect des fonds* and the subprinciples of order and provenance that follow from it. Trained experts manage these records, and they possess the ability to help (or hinder) the ability of others to access the archive that contains them.[43] As I suggested, human rights "facts" are customarily treated in this manner, as their evidentiary power emerges out of the extent of their verifiability. Proof, in other words, rests heavily on the degree to which a witness can convince others what violation(s) occurred, when, and where, and—to the degree possible— the identity of the person(s) that committed it/them. Proof further depends on the credibility of the organization that publicizes the account as well as the manner in which it does so, a relationship that contributes to what legal scholar Jennifer Mnookin calls "reputational knowledge."[44]

By contrast, the continuum approach, which emerged in the late twentieth century, confronts the challenge of managing records, especially digitized ones, in a rapidly changing technological environment. From this perspective, the relationship of these records to one another is not fixed . Rather, as Sue McKemmish, an expert in social informatics puts it, "records are always in the process of becoming."[45] By this she means that we need to develop more reliable and trustworthy ways to update archival descriptions as our views on the records they contain evolve over time, and an audit mechanism, often called metadata, to track these changes over time. The people involved in the construction of archival collections, McKemmish continues, must always consider "the unknowns of unspecifiable future needs," that is, the possibility that others will wish to use the records in ways not initially intended.[46] Such approaches, often called participatory archives, regardless of whether or not they are digital in form, encourage a reconceptualization of the rights of communities affected by violence. The goal, among those who share this view, is to create processes for community members to have a meaningful say in how records are acquired, managed, and made accessible to others.[47] The reconceptualization also has significant implications for transitional justice proceedings where suffering, be it personal or collective, becomes a form of property, prompting debates over who "owns" the information, a topic I revisit at the end of the book.

In sum, the life-cycle approach is most closely associated with the "archive as object" understanding of fact retrieval, and the continuum approach is more akin to the "archive as subject" as a consequence of the divergent ways different actors produce and utilize records after their creation. Both approaches— the former privileges a custodial relationship, the latter a stewardship model—have their respective strengths and weaknesses.[48] Increasingly, human rights archives exhibit aspects of both approaches, which—with my apologies to archivists everywhere—I have outlined in highly schematic and oversimplified terms. I situate this book at the intersection of these two approaches, which requires me to write both with and against the archival grain. On the one hand, I must craft a sufficiently coherent narrative for my account of the creation and utilization of the archives featured in the book to be intelligible to others. On the other hand, I have to unwrite this same narrative, to the degree possible, to illustrate how some human rights "facts" are fashioned rather than simply found, then convey the significance of this being the case. The reader can judge whether or not I have succeeded.

One additional explanatory note is needed before moving forward. "What's in a name?" asked Kenneth Price, the head of the Center for Digital Research in the Humanities, in 2009. Price set himself the task of distinguishing several widely used terms in the field, all of which he finds problematic given the complicated relationships of the past, present, and future to one another in contemporary textual studies. He explains: "*Project* is amorphous; *archive* and *edition* are heavy with associations carried over from print culture; *database* is both too limiting and too misleading in its connotations; and *digital thematic research collections* lacks a memorable ring and pithiness."[49] A great deal has changed since he posed his question, particularly in the field of digital humanities. Nevertheless, this definitional problem persists. How should we differentiate these concepts, and what are the consequences of how we do so? For the purposes of this book, three terms matter: *the archive, archives,* and *collections.*

The "archival turn" in many disciplines (history and law being the notable exceptions) owes much to social theorist Michel Foucault, who argued that the archive is a system that "governs the appearance of statements as historical events."[50] It does so, he explained, because it consists of "enunciative possibilities and impossibilities," by which he meant that the archive establishes the epistemological conditions for what can and cannot be said about events at a given moment in time.[51] From this perspective, the archive possesses a "historiographic function in addition to a preservationist one."[52] By contrast, archives and collections are housed in specific locations, traditionally physical edifices, but now more commonly on computer servers. Both archives and collections contain *records,* a generic term for recorded information. However, these records often differ significantly in terms of their "transactional and contextual nature, evidential qualities, intents, purposes, and functionality rather than physical characteristics," as archivists point out.[53] The differences reflect the radically different logics of archives when compared to collections. Archives seek to maintain elements of the contexts that produced the records. They are "about reference," as Penelope Papailias stated in her study of the poetics of recollection in modern Greece, which is why archival respect for provenance is essential and entrance to archives is regulated.[54] Collections, however, do not "revere tradition and its authority." Instead, she explains, "collections are set on shattering the inheritance of the past," which their creators do by removing materials from one context and ordering them in another, usually with the goal of public display.[55] I use all three of these concepts, as defined here, throughout the book to illustrate the interplay between facts produced and facts found in the context of human rights documentation and advocacy.

WHY MYANMAR?

For more than a quarter century, dozens of advocacy groups have documented large-scale human rights violations in Myanmar and then conveyed their findings to the relevant UN bodies, most commonly the General Assembly, Commission on Human Rights (now Human Rights Council), International Labour Organization (ILO), Committee on the Elimination of Discrimination against Women, and Security Council. The UN bodies have drawn and still draw upon the reports these advocacy groups submit to inform UN resolutions on Myanmar. Resolutions are a specialized genre of document that consist of a combination of polite acknowledgments, measured judgments on degrees of noncompliance with international human rights, refugee, and humanitarian law, and aspirational recommendations for rectifying the situation. As a consequence, preambulatory phrases (e.g., "declaring, "affirming," "having considered," and "noting) and operative ones (e.g., "further requests," "accepts," "endorses," and "reaffirms") predominate. The General Assembly and the Human Rights Commission issued nearly three dozen such resolutions on Myanmar between 1992 and 2008, the primary period of documentation covered in this book.[56] Special envoys and UN special rapporteurs also traveled to Myanmar more than forty times during these same years to gather information regarding the situation on the ground, to convey messages from the secretary-general to high-ranking military officials, and to promote dialogue between the regime and the political opposition, then symbolically headed by Nobel Peace Prize winner Aung San Suu Kyi.[57] Resolutions, except in rare circumstances, are not legally binding, however, and the ones issued in this case arguably had little to no effect on the human rights situation, which was consistently among the worst in the world during this time, according to the UN's own special rapporteurs.[58] Financial and trade sanctions had a greater, measurable impact. But there, too, the Western-led interventions did not dramatically change the military-led regime's conduct with regard to human rights. Instead, the sanctions prompted the successive regimes—The State Law and Order Council (1988–1997), followed by The State Peace and Development Council (1998–2011)—to develop alternate forms of income generation that effectively bypassed the sanctions, and the resulting profits arguably extended the military's direct rule.[59]

Fortunately, the overall human rights situation, "setting aside" the current Rohingya crisis and the armed conflicts involving NSAGs in Rakhine State, Kachin State, and northern Shan State, has improved somewhat in recent years. The once massive use of forced labor, a contemporary form of slavery, has largely disappeared. Child soldiers were identified and discharged. More than one thousand political prisoners were released. And a multilateral peace process began, first formalized in 2012, with the goal of ending the long-running armed conflicts in the country's border regions. The so-called peace dividend is genuinely felt in many former conflict areas, though new vulnerabilities (e.g., development-induced displacement) have replaced old ones (e.g., conflict-induced displacement). Western governments have removed the sanctions that had been in place for decades, in part because of these positive human rights developments. Nevertheless, the overall climate for constructive change has not significantly improved since the National League for Democracy (NLD) assumed power following the 2015 elections.[60]

Widespread hope existed that Aung San Suu Kyi, once in office, would bring in skilled technocrats, and substantive political and economic reforms would follow. In the years after she became the state councilor, the de facto head of state, such hopes proved to be misplaced. Suu Kyi was authoritarian in practice, and many activists as well as country experts find the NLD, which she heads, to be openly hostile to human rights documentation, lobbying, and advocacy. General Shwe Mann's Commission for the Assessment of Legal Affairs and Special Issues, also launched in 2015, further worsened the situation. Shwe Mann, previously the third-highest-ranking officer in the Tatmadaw, who was the Speaker of the Lower House of Parliament at the time, marginalized civil society organizations via the commission. "Government ministers said thanks for your input, your reports, but there was no result. Nothing happened," explained one Burmese political analyst, on condition of anonymity. "This led the grassroots to doubt [the organizations] because there was no change. They began to think that the civil society organizations were doing it for the money, but they are trying to work within a broken system."[61] In other areas, the climate markedly worsened, with freedom of expression being the prime example.[62] Political analysts and rights activists have put forward numerous explanations of why the "transition" failed to live up to what was promised. But the director of Thit Analytica, a nongovernmental think tank that promotes federalism, secularism, and civilian control as the means to strengthen democracy in Myanmar, summed up the explanation that I heard most frequently over the past five years: "The NLD lacks an ideology [and] they have no clear plan for the future."[63]

But even if the NLD-led government had had a realistic strategic plan for moving the country forward, the challenges it faced prior to the 2021 coup were daunting. Verisk Maplecroft, an internationally recognized risk analytics firm, categorized Myanmar as an "extreme risk" with regard to its political and economic climate.[64] Transparency International, an international NGO that publishes an annual corruption perception risk index, ranked Myanmar 132th out of 180 countries in 2018.[65] Also in 2018, the Natural Resource Governance Institute, an NGO that provides policy recommendations on this issue globally, rated Myanmar 83rd out of eighty-nine assessments for mining, and 77th out of eighty-nine assessments for oil and gas extraction.[66] In 2019 Freedom House, an independent watchdog NGO dedicated to the expansion of democracy globally, put Myanmar in the bottom third of one hundred countries surveyed with regard to political rights and civil liberties.[67]

Such rankings should not be taken at face value, however. Indicators are by necessity simplifications of complex realities, and difficult choices always need to be made about what to include and what to exclude from the process of quantification. Yet these choices and the calculative practices that experts, like the organizations cited earlier, use to generate data are poorly understood by most consumers of these rankings. Anthropologist Sally

Engle Merry, who studies the impacts of quantification and measurement on human rights research and policy, provides two relevant examples, both of which highlight the challenge of distinguishing facts found and facts produced across contexts. First, she explains, indicators create "false specificity"; that is, "they appear more accurate and precise than they are" because they do not explicitly acknowledge "the ambiguity of the categories, errors in counting, missing data, and lack of commensurability."[68] Second, Merry continues, indicators "camouflage the political considerations that shape the collection and presentation of data," by which she means the methodological choices behind who counts want, how it is counted, and how it is represented to others.[69] Despite these very real problems, which I revisit from different vantage points in later chapters, the Myanmar rankings are useful nonetheless. If nothing else, the rankings reveal broad agreement that much remains to be done in terms of strengthening good governance, itself a meta-indicator conventionally used to measure the extent to which public institutions conduct public affairs and manage public resources in publicly beneficial ways.

The Tatmadaw, however, remains the key obstacle to progress on good governance in the eyes of most analysts and activists, according to a leading member of the Women's League of Burma.[70] Several facts support her claim. The 2008 Constitution reserved 25 percent of the seats in Parliament for military members, with active duty or retired generals holding the most influential posts. The Constitution also granted the Tatmadaw direct control of the three key ministries concerned with border affairs, defense, and home affairs, including the National Defense and Security Council, the most powerful entity in the country. All of these entities operate with no civilian oversight, and all efforts to date to reform these pro-military structural arrangements have failed.[71] The Tatmadaw has access to significant financial resources as well. Since 2011, when the first nominally civilian government headed by former general Thein Sein assumed power, the Tatmadaw enjoyed an overall annual budget increase of more than 171 percent between fiscal years 2011/2012 and 2018/2019.[72] Military-owned enterprises generate substantial off-book revenue not subject to independent regulation, which is again highly problematic from a good governance perspective.[73]

Tatmadaw officials also continue to dominate discussions at the expense of the NSAGs regarding the peace process, which has significant implications for human rights protections in conflict-affected areas. The process began in 2015, during the last year of the Thein Sein government, and it has fundamentally failed to resolve the disagreements that have sustained the many armed conflicts, the longest of which lasted nearly seventy years.[74] In highly simplified form, these disagreements revolve around three main issues. First, what form should the government take: a strong central state with weak federalism or a weak central state with strong federalism? Second, what economic model is best suited for the country's near-term development: rapid, intensive resource extraction and the expansion of export processing zones, or smaller scale approaches that are more sustainable and equitable, but far slower? Third, what political process is best suited for managing responses to both questions: guided or representative democracy?[75]

Not surprisingly, the cease-fire agreements are still fragile in many places. The NSAGs want to obtain some substantive commitments on issues related to ethnic equality and self-determination as a precondition to a binding national peace agreement, whereas the Tatmadaw maintains that the NSAGs must completely disarm before it will engage is such discussions. As a result of this fundamental impasse, widespread concerns remain that it would take relatively little to undermine the "new" normal, which is neither resumed war nor a genuine peace, but something in between. One farmer in a conflict-affected zone in Karen State, who resides in a village that still uses land mines for self-protection, described this liminal state of affairs: "We don't worry every day about being attacked. We know there is a lull and that lines of communication have improved. The Karen National Liberation Army (KNLA) does not go into white [government-controlled] zones, and the Tatmadaw do not go into black [KNLA-controlled] ones. But things could change very quickly."[76] Should this occur, conflict-affected populations may once again see their hopes and dreams for a "genuine" peace destroyed.[77]

Such hopes and dreams are particularly salient to "the Karen," an ethnonym that subsumes a wide array of disparate subgroups.[78] The controversial 2014 census, the first one conducted in thirty years, found that approximately 7 percent of the total population of 51.4 million people self-identified as Karen, making them the third largest ethnic group in Myanmar. But this book is *not* about the Karen per se; it is, instead, about the state-sponsored violence Karen communities living in eastern Bago Region and northern Kayin State endured for decades and the concomitant efforts of fact finders to document it. An untold number of civilians died over the course of the armed struggle, which officially began in 1949 when the Karen National Union (KNU), the political wing of the Karen National Liberation Army (KNLA), went underground. Low-level conflict was a defining feature of the asymmetric conflict, but large-scale seasonal offensives increased markedly in the mid-1980s, when Tatmadaw units, as the human rights archives indicate, began targeting civilians on a widespread and systematic basis. The conflict dynamics, discussed at greater length in the next chapter, annually displaced hundreds of thousands of people throughout the southeastern region. The KNU signed a cease-fire agreement with the Tatmadaw in 2012. Internally displaced persons (IDPs) in Karen areas have since begun to rebuild their lives, albeit in highly circumscribed ways. But more than 92,000 registered refugees, 80 percent of whom are Karen, remain stranded in nine "temporary shelters" (i.e., camps) along the Thailand-Myanmar border. Such violence is not directed solely at Karen populations. The Tatmadaw targeted many other ethnic populations because of their real or imagined ties with the NSAGs that claimed, with varying degrees of honesty, to legitimately represent their peoples' interests. However, Tatmadaw operations in predominantly Karen areas of southeastern Myanmar are by far the best documented; hence my spatial focus on this part of the country.

According to government-delineated maps, this area covers Kayin (formerly Karen) State and the eastern part of Bago (formerly Pegu) Region. KNU-delineated maps include all of Kayin State, large portions of neighboring Kayah and Mon States, and significant parts of western Bago and Tanintharyi Region. The KNU historically referred to this entire area as Kawthoolei, a Karen term that can be translated in multiple ways. One is the "land burnt black," meaning that it must be fought for, which this NSAG did for nearly seven decades. I employ KNU-delineated administrative units throughout the book for geographic rather than political reasons, as the fact-finding organizations I feature in the case studies used these terms, as do their Karen informants. But my broader point here is that the competing boundary-making practices, which are distinct in some cases and overlap in others, are reflective of "the competing regimes of truth and legitimacy" that Mark Duffield, whom I quoted in the notes on terminology, termed a "battlespace."[79] These competing representational regimes have material effects, which can be identified by answering the following questions: "Who is to be protected, by whom, against what and whom, and at what price?"[80] Closely examining human rights archives as "subjects" in addition to "objects" of analysis reveals how the answers to these questions affect human rights "fact" production with regard to Myanmar.

MYANMAR IN ARCHIVAL FORM

Decades of human rights documentation have produced many different types of human rights archives on abuses in Myanmar. These archives can differ greatly in terms of the "rawness" of the materials they contain, the scope of temporal and spatial coverage, and restrictions on access by nonstaff. But broadly speaking, the archives I worked with can be divided into three main categories: organizational, report-based digital, and aggregate. Organizational archives typically include original prepublished report data in material form, such as survey responses, interview transcripts, hand-drawn maps, photographs, meeting minutes, funding requests, and so on. The materials often reside in file cabinets or boxes located in the back rooms of offices, the contents of which may or may not be cataloged in any systematic fashion. Preserving these records is important because they are the best examples of the least-processed elements of the "fact" production process—aside from documentary materials related to the actual formulation of the research design and the methodologies to be used prior to the start of fact-finding. Unfortunately, these records are vulnerable to loss due to seizure by immigration authorities or more quotidian processes like recycling as a result of space constraints, misplacement, and physical decay.[81] (One of the most important archives that I examined consisted of years of ink-smudged documents printed on flimsy fax paper.) Preserving and safeguarding these materials for future use for historical, if not also legal, purposes is urgent for these reasons.[82]

Other archival holdings are digitized and readily available on the Internet, most often in report form. The Online Burma/Myanmar Library has long served as a clearinghouse for such reports and related "grey" literature (research produced by organizations and published outside of traditional channels), though it was not possible for people inside Myanmar to access its contents prior to the 2012 by-elections, when the quasi-civilian government removed the ban on the site.[83] Created and supported by the Burma Peace Foundation, the website's administrators claim that it has categorized and annotated links to more than sixty thousand full-text documents on Myanmar, a considerable percentage of them on human rights–related issues.[84] The "facts" in these reports have undergone significant processing prior to publication; this forecloses some avenues of investigation but opens up others. In terms of the latter, a growing number of human rights reports came to include more detailed accounts of the research methodologies used and the international legal standards against which the findings were evaluated. The gradual standardization of reporting strategies across organizations over time thus offers insights into the emergence of human rights "print culture," which contributed to the homogenization of previously diverse NGO narratives on state-sponsored violence in Myanmar.

Still other archives are aggregate in nature. Such archives consist of multiple and often very different data sources, which makes tracking the "fact" production process very challenging because much of it inaccessibly resides in a "black box." During the late 1990s, for example, the ILO, a Nobel Peace Prize–winning UN agency, conducted a multisited investigation into widespread allegations that the Tatmadaw used forced labor on a massive scale. The ILO released its findings in 1998. The conclusions, the fact-finding report's authors noted, were based in part on the 274 documents that NGOs had submitted to them over a two-month period. The documents totaled nearly ten thousand pages of testimony and photographs, in addition to the contributors' analyses of them.[85] But as is the case with other UN-commissioned fact-finding reports, it is very difficult for non-UN staff to examine the original source material out of which the composite was constructed.[86]

The chapters in this book provide further details about how these three different types of archives (organizational, report-based, and aggregate) affect human rights "fact" production. Regardless of type, all of the archives examined share several important features that reinforce documentation archipelagoes, a problematic phenomenon that is not unique to Myanmar. Such archipelagoes are the result of multiple archives, each of which provides only a "fragmented or partial picture" of the human rights situation within the same area.[87] Three practices contribute to this outcome.

First, despite the considerable number of archives on human rights issues in Myanmar, researchers, activists, and policymakers continue to face a persistent challenge known as "information dispersal" across archipelagoes.[88] Cass Sunstein, a legal scholar, developed the concept of information dispersal to describe instances when groups making critical research and advocacy decisions fail to collect or incorporate directly relevant information that other individuals and groups are known to possess. Philip Alston and Colin Gillespie, who are legal scholars as well, note that information dispersal adversely affects organizations involved in human rights documentation, with the result being a "fragmented or partial picture that each of them presents in relation to a given situation."[89]

The overarching assumption behind eradicating the problem of dispersal is problematic, however, as it implies there is a minimum threshold for what would suffice as being "epistemologically sufficient." The who, what, and how of making such a determination is the more fundamental question. The assumption thus reflects a totalizing fantasy—namely, that it is possible to combine different archives into a single, unified one, if only there were sufficient organizational will, technical cooperation, and, of course, funding. Such a vision is utopian in nature because "no archive can be the depository history of society, of all that has happened," as explained by Achille Mbembe in his analysis of the power of archives and their limits. "Through archived documents, we are presented with pieces of time to be assembled, fragments of life placed in order, one after another, in an attempt to formulate a story that acquires its coherence through the ability to craft links between the beginning and the end."[90] The ability to craft such fragments into stories, which is what I do and undo throughout this book, is inextricably shaped by choices regarding archival creation, records management, and permitted use.[91] Again, such choices are inherently political because decisions must be made: what to include and to exclude from the archive, how to organize and administer its contents, and which procedures should govern access. Without these decisions, an archive simply cannot exist.

Second, nearly all of the NSAGs are organized along ethnic lines. Consequently, the NGOs that documented violations in conflict-affected areas typically reported on affected members of their own ethnic group, for reasons of language, geographic access, security support, and so on. Thus, ethnic Karen researchers collected information on affected Karen communities, Shan on Shan, Kachin on Kachin, and so on. Very little of the extant human rights documentation on Myanmar places cross-ethnic experiences within the same comparative frame, which creates not only gaps in the archival record but also significant variation among the collected materials in them in terms of methodological rigor, comprehensiveness, and credibility.

Third, structural factors further exacerbated information dispersal. NGOs based in Thailand that implemented programs across the border in Myanmar had no legal standing, and their staff faced considerable risks as a result (e.g., extortion, arrest, and deportation, as well as possible torture and death upon forcible return). The situation meant that the environment for cross-border NGOs was characterized by intense "organizational insecurity, competitive pressure, and fiscal uncertainty," which in turn promoted dysfunctional and opportunistic behavior.[92] Different approaches for carrying out human rights fact-finding also complicated these identity-based and organizational issues. Some fact-finding NGOs, often with the assistance of foreigners, developed extensive networks of well-trained field staff to report on human rights issues in conflict zones. But many did not, which again makes comparative analysis of "fact" production difficult and the creation of a singular human rights archive, such as the kind Sunstein seems to call for to reduce information dispersal, an impossibility.

Nevertheless, the Network for Human Rights Documentation-Burma, more commonly known as ND-Burma, formed in 2004, is trying to address this issue, albeit in a limited way. Its staff are creating a secure platform for sharing highly sensitive and unredacted human rights information in standardized and searchable ways across organizations. The network currently consists of thirteen organizations, and several more are affiliated with it. All carry out human rights documentation as part of their organizational mission and are politically independent, which is a requirement for membership. (The requirement, while understandable, excludes a number of important organizations, such as humanitarian ones, that conduct fact-finding activities as part of their own operations but have ties to NSAGs.) According to its director, the Data Management Team uses standardized reporting templates to enter the field data into a single, searchable database. The database facilitates the ability of ND-Burma to analyze patterns of violations over time and across space.[93] Benetech, a nonprofit technology firm, has provided Martus (Greek for "witness") software for this project, and a very modest amount of grant money covers the operating costs. The effort still faces a number of technical issues, struggling with the limited capacity of its staff and that of its member organizations, as well as an uncertain political climate, which limits its ability to explore what kinds of transitional justice initiatives are best suited for the situation.[94] Human rights data archipelagoes remain firmly in place as a consequence.

Significant silences, as I suggested earlier, further distort what it is possible to know about state-sponsored violence. The Tatmadaw produces its own conflict-related documentation, such as combat updates from field commanders to their superiors, more detailed situation reports, and meeting minutes.

But with few exceptions, nonmilitary personnel cannot review this documentation.[95] The resulting information asymmetry—the accounts of survivors and witnesses are vastly overrepresented by comparison—poses analytical challenges for understanding human rights "fact" production. Collectively, NGO and civil society organization (CSO) accounts of human rights violations provide the rich basis for a "history from below" based on statements made by ordinary people in the first person. Consequently, because of these accounts we know an immense amount about the strategies and tactics Tatmadaw units used, their variation across time and space, and their material effects (villages destroyed, crops burned, people displaced, etc.).

By contrast, we have extremely few accounts from perpetrators. These accounts are almost entirely limited to those rare cases in which Tatmadaw soldiers defected and shared details during interviews about state-sponsored violence and, in some cases, their direct role in it.[96] Due to this asymmetry, perpetrators do not "speak" for themselves. Instead, what we know of them comes to us in the form of reported speech, that is, what others claim they said and did. ("Here's a quote, we didn't say it, just happened to record it," as one human rights scholar-practitioner colloquially put it.)[97] Perpetrator "silence" in the human rights archives examined also complicates efforts to determine whether the *mens rea* requirement (i.e., proof of intent to commit the offense, combined with the knowledge of the broader context in which the offense occurs) has been met in the absence of other supporting documentation. Such documentation is critical for determining whether the perpetrator was acting on their own or under orders from a superior, who could also be held accountable for the human rights violations committed by the subordinate under their command.

Unfortunately, political conditions do not now (and may never) permit access to the former military regimes' records of its repression of human rights activists and the violence the Tatmadaw carried out against other ethnic minority populations, such as the Karen.[98] (The deeply problematic Records and Archives Law, promulgated in 2020, enables the Tatmadaw to block the release of any materials it declares would pose a threat to "national security." No appeal process exists, which all but guarantees that secrecy rather than transparency will remain the norm on sensitive issues.)[99] But even if access to such records were to become possible, and the disclosure of who collected and provided information regarding past abuses no longer posed a security risk to them, official amnesties present a significant obstacle. Section 445 of the 2008 Myanmar Constitution grants immunity to government officials, including military personnel, "who have committed any crime, as long as the crime was committed as a result of their official duties."[100] The 2016 Former Presidents Security Law also protects the heads of state from prosecution for "actions," a term that is not defined, committed while in office. And finally, the Myanmar Human Rights Commission, established in 2011 and which skeptics regard as being largely unable or unwilling to challenge the government on issues that fall under its mandate, has no power to investigate abuses that occurred prior to the institution's creation.[101] Given these impediments, the materials that non-state archives of state-sponsored violence contain are critical for truth-seeking, whether or not legal proceedings ever occur. Indeed, these non-state archives, which often "serve as important supplements, counters, or correction to the records held in official archives," may be the only ones ever available to us.[102]

CRIMES AGAINST HUMANITY AND THRESHOLDS OF PROOF

The question of who is fully human and thus entitled to particular rights and protections and who is not has a very long history. But "the capacity of humanity to govern so much of the contemporary political and ethical imaginary, and to have such demonstrable and significant effects on people's lives," is relatively recent, observe Ilana Feldman and Miriam Ticktin, two anthropologists whose research focuses on what they call "the government of threat and care."[103] Feldman and Ticktin pair these terms because they exist in continual tension with one another: for example, humanity, in its abject form, such as large-scale refugee flows, can be both a source of anxiety *and* the object of compassion.[104] (The Syrian civil war and the radically different reception people seeking refugee status received in different parts of Europe is a case in point.) "Crimes against humanity" occupies a somewhat similar paradoxical space. The concept "signifies that all humanity is the interested party and that humanity's interest may differ from the interests of the victims," explains legal scholar David Luban.[105] The tension exists because the crimes committed, while they directly affect the victims physically and psychologically, also injure all of humankind; hence they require a legal response that differs from that of the injured parties. This imperative is, in many respects, quite new as well.

Crimes against humanity, the key evidentiary threshold discussed through-out this book, is a twentieth-century invention. Some genealogies locate the emergence of the concept in 1915 when French, British, and Russian governments denounced the Turkish one for the "crimes against civilians and humanity" committed during the Armenian Genocide (1915–1923). But most legal scholars identify the Nuremberg Charter, issued in 1945, as the institutional starting point. The charter set forth the laws and procedures for the trials, and its authors listed crimes against humanity as one of the three categories eligible for prosecution. The UN General Assembly and the International Law Commission officially recognized the category fol-lowing the Nuremburg and Tokyo trials after World War II, but unlike for genocide and war crimes, no specialized convention on crimes against humanity yet exists.[106]

A number of subsequent ad hoc trials—the International Criminal Tri-bunals of the Former Yugoslavia and Rwanda, followed by the Special Court for Sierra Leone—contributed to the version of the definition of crimes against humanity codified in the 1998 Rome Statute. The Rome Statute established the International Criminal Court (ICC) as the first permanent body to prosecute individuals accused of having committed mass atrocity crimes.[107] Article 7, paragraph 1 of the Rome Statute enumerates eleven acts that, when "committed as part of a widespread or systematic attack against any civilian population, with knowledge of the attack," constitute crimes against humanity. This book concerns itself with the first three of the eleven acts (murder, cruel and inhumane treatment, and enslavement), but discusses them in reverse order. Chapter 2 examines forced labor, detailing how Tatmadaw practices fixed bodies in time and space. Chapter 3 details the military strategy of forced population transfers via the destruction of food stores, a tactic that displaced bodies en masse from contested areas, with the alternative being starvation.[108] Chapter 4 explores the Tatmadaw's willful killings and indiscriminate attacks on civilians, including the reputed "shoot-to-kill" policy, which it denies exists. Chapter 5 builds on this dis-cussion by analyzing the successive, but ultimately unsuccessful, efforts to convince the UN Security Council to establish a commission of inquiry (CoI) to investigate alleged international crimes in Myanmar—a move that could have resulted in a referral of the case to the ICC, raising the possibility of future prosecutions.[109] In all these chapters, the question of whether the gross violations of human rights documented were widespread or systematic in nature occupies a central place in my analysis of "fact" production, archival formations, and advocacy.

The terms *widespread* and *systematic* function as thresholds to determine whether a deliberate attack on a civilian population can qualify as a crime against humanity. Jurisprudence, which emerged out of the Former Yugoslavia and Rwanda tribunals, established that these thresholds are disjunctive rather than conjunctive in nature, meaning that one *or* the other of the threshold requirements had to be met, but not both of them. The qualifiers—widespread and systematic—thus serve as important tests, as not all abuses defined in the eleven proscribed acts in the Rome Statute constitute crimes against humanity in and of themselves.[110] "The term 'widespread' requires large-scale action involving a substantial number of victims, whereas the term 'systematic' requires a high degree of orchestration and methodical planning," according to legal scholar Darryl Robinson.[111] But the two thresholds function in different ways. The former threshold has a numerical element, yet it has never been quantified because "a single act committed by an individual perpetrator can constitute a crime against humanity if it occurs within the context of a broader campaign," as explained by Sean Murphy, the special rapporteur on crimes against humanity.[112] The "systematic" threshold has a qualitative element and refers to the policy requirement, meaning the acts must not be isolated. Instead, the acts must reflect patterns of conduct that indicate command-and-control relationships between superiors and their subordinates exist. The ICC defines such patterns in Article 7 as "pursuant to or in furtherance of a State or organizational policy to commit such attack [on any civilian population]." Determining whether such "command responsibility" exists, especially in the absence of official documentation, can limit the ability to prosecute higher-level officials.[113]

Obviously, then, both the widespread and the systematic thresholds are directly relevant to the question of "proof" and thus to the interface where "facts" fashioned and facts found meet. The four case studies in this book detail how different fact-finding bodies sought to determine whether the gross human rights violations they documented constituted crimes against humanity. In each case, the "archivists" (a human rights organization, a consortium of cross-border humanitarian agencies, an international law clinic, and a transnational NGO-led campaign) created archives with various instrumental goals in mind: to report on what happened, to obtain aid for those populations in urgent need, and/or to mobilize international support to hold those responsible to account. The issue of intent is thus at the center of the discussion in three ways: the intent of the perpetrators, the intent of the fact finders, and the intent of the author of this book. Why three? As anthropologist Sally Engle Merry pointed out with regard to quantitative indicators: who counts what, how it gets counted, and what gets disclosed is highly political and not just technical in nature. The same holds for human rights documentation at each stage of the "fact" production process and the forms of advocacy the process does and does not make possible, especially in the legal sphere. "The law" carries its own set of complications, however.[114]

Legal discourse has fully marginalized philosophical and ethical approaches to understanding and advancing human rights as a result of its codification and institutionalization within the UN system. On this point, Tony Evans, a scholar of global politics, writes: "Underpinning the hegemony of international law is an assumption that the protection of human rights can be guaranteed, provided international society musters sufficient ingenuity, creativity, and resourcefulness when drafting treaties and creating international human rights institutions."[115] "The purpose of this move, he continues, "is to resolve the contradictions between the cosmopolitan claims of human rights and the principles of sovereignty, non-intervention, and domestic jurisdiction, upon which the tradition of international law is built."[116] Evans's critique of technocratic approaches to reestablishing the rule of law through the exercise of yet further international law—the structural constraints of which limit its implementation rather than addressing the broader drivers of violence—is an important one. But a more fundamental paradox underlies this contradiction. Here, it is worth quoting at length an argument made by Christopher Tomlins, a legal scholar, and John Comaroff, an anthropologist. They ask whether it is possible to write a counter-history of "the Law" given the widespread and persistent faith in its "instrumental capacity, as a systematic repertoire of rational practices, to yield an ordered, equitable, just society."[117] Such a counter-history, they explain, would need to challenge the magical thinking—the belief that unrelated events are causally connected despite the absence of any plausible causal link between them—that permeates mainstream understandings of the origins and power of "the Law":

> What could be more enchanted than to believe that law has a life of its own: that it has the wherewithal to shape the very forces and relations that actually shape it, to create the world in its own image, to determine, for both good and ill,

rational solutions to irrational problems. These are all entirely magical ideas. Collectively, they indicate that it is in the very hyper-rationality of the law that is fetishization, its ultimate enchantment, lies.[118]

Their statement on magical thinking is a direct rebuke to Max Weber's famous argument that secularization and the formal rational logics and processes that have accompanied it (e.g., law) are a defining feature of modernity, which he famously characterized as being disenchanted. Weber aside, the theme of "the Law" as fetish pervades this entire book. As a matter of routine practice, the fact finders featured in it, like human rights, humanitarian, and refugee organizations everywhere, submitted appeal after appeal to the UN and other related bodies, such as the ICC, in the hope that the proper application of law, as a "form of pedagogy, a discipline, and a project of reform," would end rights violations.[119]

The conventional view is, of course, problematic, as philosopher Jacques Derrida has pointed out, because "there is no law without enforceability, and no applicability or enforceability of the law without force," a solution that often engenders further human rights abuses in the name of "doing good."[120] (His point echoes an earlier one made by Walter Benjamin, who argued that "the law" is grounded in violence, both in terms of its foundations and in its preservation.)[121] But it should be stressed that this book does not attempt to present a "counter-history" of the international human rights, humanitarian, and refugee laws invoked by the fact finders featured. Instead, my focus is squarely on "fact" production, followed by the use and abuse of these "facts" by various actors to achieve their respective instrumental goals. So, although I regularly draw attention to the ways in which fact finders write like lawyers, "the Law," as a form of "fact" production in its own right, will not receive extended discussion, as it would require a separate book to cover in satisfactory fashion. I do, however, strategically revisit the issue of magical thinking where the fetishization of international law presents human rights "facts" as unambiguous and self-evident when they are, in fact, anything but.

INTERVENTIONS

"What is the self-claimed rhetoric of authority for research undertaken in situations where the places and scenes of fieldwork are defined by regimes of intervention?" asks George Marcus, a keen analyst of the gradual fragmentation that the discipline of anthropology has undergone since the 1980s and its reinvention in new forms.[122] According to Marcus, anthropologists conducting research in settings of intervention have had three "identity poses" available to them: the consulting expert, the reporter, and the witness. (One could also add working in solidarity with, which comes with its own ethical complications.) I have assumed all of these poses at various points in my research and practitioner-based work on human rights violations in Myanmar since 2001.[123] I have spent a total of three years "in the field" in one form or another, during part of which, as a program manager, I supervised fact finders in southeastern Myanmar. Since then, I have coauthored seven major fact-finding reports and six policy briefs on human rights issues. I have published more than a dozen peer-reviewed academic articles and book chapters on topics ranging from forced labor and land mine contamination to internal displacement and extractive resource politics. I have also presented on more than two dozen occasions in a variety of forums (donor meetings, invited talks, NGO workshops, academic conferences, and so on). In the course of doing so, I have worked with people directly involved with policymaking (e.g., lawyers, diplomats, and the heads of major international organizations) and those people (e.g., staff of civil society organizations, humanitarian aid workers, and frontline human rights defenders) who witness a state of (often chronic) emergency on a regular basis.

I could claim an insider's perspective on human rights "fact" production for these reasons. But others might counterclaim that I am an outsider because neither am I a scholar of Myanmar in the traditional sense nor do I speak the relevant field languages. (My formal graduate training in anthropology and history instead focused on the Socialist Republic of Vietnam—specifically, how the government, over the course of seven decades, sought but frequently failed to make the countryside amenable to centralized rule through the use of different kinds of official documents.)[124] Thinking of positionality in terms of an insider/outsider binary misses the point, however, because this book is not an ethnography of Myanmar or any of its "ethnic nationalities," the term officially used. It is instead an investigation into the ways in which human rights "facts" regarding state-sponsored violence against Karen civilians in southeastern Myanmar were produced, archived, and mobilized by others at different spatial scales and in different politico-legal contexts. Consequently, the work that provides the basis for such investigation was always multilingual, multicultural, and collaborative in nature. As such, it involved people in multiple countries, many of whom infrequently, if ever, met in person, despite the key roles they played in producing, archiving, and mobilizing human rights "facts"/facts.

At first glance, my efforts to tease apart these processes would appear to differ little from the interpretive move that is characteristic of the discipline of cultural anthropology as a whole. Graham Jones, an anthropologist himself, argues that the discipline has always been centrally concerned with "dynamics of concealment and revelation," with the primary task of the ethnographer being to make known the "hidden meaning and order behind what people say and do."[125] To view my approach as being part of this tradition would be wrong, however. Instead, it is more akin to the one Annelise Riles, a legal anthropologist, pioneered. She focused ethnographic attention on the institutional "artifacts" that NGOs and advocacy networks generated (e.g., mission statements, organizational charts, and grant proposals) as part of their routine bureaucratic work. Placing the artifacts in the context of their actual use enabled her to highlight the extent to which the analytical practices these actors employed "mirrored" those of social scientists such as herself. She found that the classic distinction between emic (insider) and etic (outsider) points of view, also historically fundamental to anthropology as a discipline, no longer held as a result. The effect of this mirroring problematized "not so much my position in the field," Riles observed, "as the way the field is both within and without myself."[126] My account of human rights "fact" production wrestles with this same problem, especially as it extends beyond the making of "artifacts" to include their subsequent use and reuse in different contexts. I, like Riles, did not merely observe these knowledge practices; I participated in them, directly in some instances and indirectly in others. My efforts to challenge "the distance between data and method in the ethnographic imagination of information," as Riles put it, requires me to make my own analytical decisions explicit as well.[127] The tension between transparency and secrecy, which is inherent to human rights documentation and advocacy, complicates my ability to do so.

TRANSPARENCY AND SECRECY IN HUMAN RIGHTS WORK

"The file made me contemplate what it means to be suspected of spying and to what extent ethnography, the research practice of anthropologists, necessarily makes us a kind of spy."[128] This comparison of the two activities arose out of anthropologist Katherine Verdery's efforts to understand why and how Romanian security services had generated such a massive intelligence dossier on her. The files contained nearly three thousand pages of speculation about the "true" intent behind her ethnographic research during the final years of the Cold War, with competing theories fashioned out of a combination of ideological stereotypes, cultural miscomprehensions, and political paranoia. But Verdery's question about the relationship between ethnographic practice and spying is not limited to cultural anthropology. The comparison also applies to human rights documentation, the primary goal of which is to make public information that perpetrators want to be kept secret—especially the identity of alleged perpetrators. For this reason, fact-finding, at its core, is a mode of surveillance (a polite word for spying), regardless of whether it is conducted in real time as abuses occur or after the fact.

Not surprisingly, the practice of spying is often framed in terms of treachery. The Tatmadaw and its defenders are a case in point. Decades of chronic conflict have enabled most human rights fact finders to become intensely familiar with the contours of state-sponsored violence, and the contents of their reports reflect this ethnographic intimacy. As a result, Burmese critics of these fact finders often refer to them as "traitors" (*ThitSarPhauk*), accusing them of selling out the country by assisting foreign governments and organizations hostile to the Tatmadaw. (People accused of personally profiting from doing so are sometimes called *Dollar Sar*; that is, they "eat dollars," in the belief that they are paid in US currency for their "treachery.") These same critics also refer to human rights workers as "spies," particularly when their professional activities, like those of independent journalists, generate damning information that is shared with others at home and abroad. The choice of which term is used is not consistent, however.[129] But regardless of the term employed, they share a conceptual similarity, which is the act of "betrayal."

A betrayal of trust in the context of human rights documentation can take several forms. Avoiding betrayal, for instance, means recognizing that not everything that can be divulged should be divulged in the name of transparency. In other words, transparency is not always a virtue. Important details, generally regarded as essential to proving credibility, may inadvertently reveal what people involved in the collection and analysis of intelligence call sources and methods. To avoid unwanted and potentially dangerous disclosures, trustworthy human rights organizations implement data redaction policies to protect their informants from retaliation. Responsible

organizations also take steps to preserve the anonymity of their fact finders, who frequently lack official identity documents and thus must also avoid
immigration officials, police officers, and intelligence agents stationed along
the Thailand-Myanmar border, in addition to military patrols inside the
country. The imperative to redact also holds true for the reports published,
which rarely include the names of the authors, some of whom are foreigners
who work illegally on "tourist visas." (Except in rare circumstances, the Royal
Thai government did not grant formal permission to foreigners to engage
in Myanmar-related human rights work, which necessitated time-consuming
and, over time, expensive trips to neighboring countries, most often Malaysia
or Lao, every two to three months to obtain a new tourist visa.)

In the context of Myanmar, another important detail is routinely omitted
as well. Most of the cross-border organizations that engage in some form
of human rights documentation do not disclose information regarding the
abuses the NSAGs themselves have committed, which have ranged from
forced labor and extortion in the name of taxation to torture and extrajudicial
executions. This omission has two primary causes. The first silence is logistical. Many, but not all, of these organizations, including humanitarian ones,
are dependent on the NSAGs to provide them with a degree of assistance to
gain access to conflict-affected populations. The support ranges from military
intelligence on Tatmadaw troop movements to armed escorts. To report on
NSAG abuses would likely constrain or possibly end such assistance altogether. The second silence is political. Successive military governments were
keen to place NSAG abuses on a par with their own as part of their public
relations efforts. The tactic was (and remains today) designed to discredit
NSAGs' claims to be fighting on behalf of "their people" by charging them
with committing comparable violations, without refuting or disproving their
own criminal acts—a rhetorical maneuver known as "whataboutism." "The
[human rights] groups have gone back and forth [on the issue of NSAG vio-
lations], but there is no consensus. But everyone agrees that they must deal
with it," explained a program officer with the Open Society Institute, an
international philanthropic organization that supports organizations that
promote freedom, democracy, and human rights.[130] Progress in this area
remains extremely unlikely, however, given the current state of affairs, a topic
I return to in the epilogue.[131]

One final comment on the tension between trust and betrayal also needs
mentioning. "In order to know, I had to become an expert in demonstrating

that there were things, places, and people I did not want to know," explained Allen Feldman when describing his fieldwork experience researching sectarian violence in Northern Ireland.[132] Feldman's realization applies to me, though not in terms of personal safety. Aside from periodic trips into areas under the control of NSAGs where land mines and malaria posed genuine threats, the primary risk I ran was deportation and a multiyear ban on return, a practice known as being "PNGed," that is, declared persona non grata. However, key aspects of human rights documentation are and should remain public secrets, commonly defined as "that which is generally known, but cannot be articulated."[133] To honor personal promises, professional nondisclosure agreements, and the safety of others, there are things I chose not to know about cross-border human rights documentation, as well as other things I chose not to reveal here, such as details regarding weapons procurement, the redistribution of humanitarian aid to NSAGs, fee structures for bribes to police and immigration officials, information sharing between NGOS and Thai intelligence, procedures for obtaining unofficial passes to travel inside Thailand and abroad, the cost of black market identity documents, and smuggling networks, among many other things illicit and illegal.

Finally, three more omissions require further explanation. I do not discuss several topics, despite their importance, because they introduce excessive complexity, lack sufficient archival documentation, or require attention to issues not germane to the specific focus of this book. For example, the book concentrates on the forms of state-sponsored violence that have affected Karen civilians in southeastern Myanmar over the past four decades because they are the best documented, and I am deeply familiar with the details. But the book could just have easily been written about many other "ethnic nationalities" around the country that have endured the same forms of violence for generations and, in several cases, continue to do so today. The complexity of such a project would require several volumes to sufficiently convey and would be of interest only to a small number of experts. Also, the book does not examine the gendered effects of violence, particularly sexual violence by Tatmadaw units against women and girls, which has been a persistent feature of all the armed conflicts in Myanmar. References to rape regularly appear in human rights reports. But only a few NGOs—all of them women's groups—have published studies solely focused on rape as a weapon of war.[134] Consequently, a critical mass of documentation solely devoted to this problem does not yet exist. Finally, I do not explain how

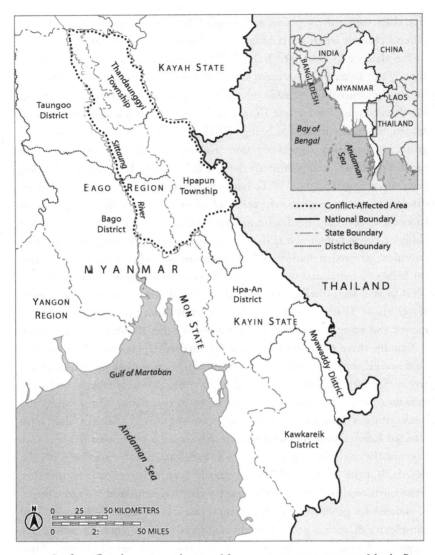

MAP 1. Conflict-affected zone in southeastern Myanmar, 2005–2008. SOURCE: Map by Ben Pease.

foreign actors, typically from the Global North, have repeatedly failed to recognize the self-protection strategies civilians use to cope with the militarization of everyday life and, for those in frontline areas, life "on the run." Thus, the central role external advocates play in defining the "problem" (i.e., what rights violations should be prioritized), and thus the "solution" (i.e., what forms of direct action are best suited to solve them), go largely unexamined here for reasons of space rather than lack of importance.[135] In short, all three of these issues warrant far more attention, and I deeply regret that I cannot give it to them in this book.

CHAPTER SUMMARIES

The chapters that follow focus on different types of crimes again humanity, the archives that arose from the fact-finding methods used to document them, and the advocacy strategies employed to publicize the "facts" produced as well as found. Despite important differences across the chapters, all of them intersect—to varying degrees—with the Northern Offensive (2005–2008), which is why I devote some attention to it here.

By most accounts the Northern Offensive began in November 2005, when Tatmadaw units under the Southern Regional Command attacked Hee Daw Kaw Village in Thandaung (also known as Thandaunggyi) Township. Soldiers burned down approximately thirty homes, emplaced mines, and fired mortars at the villagers, who had fled the patrols and were hiding in the surrounding forest.[136] But others pinpoint the start of the Northern Offensive to January–February 2006, when at least seven combat divisions began widespread operations in northern KNU-delineated Karen State.[137] The Northern Offensive, which concluded in late 2008, was the largest sustained offensive since the one the Tatmadaw carried out in the southern KNU-delineated districts of Hpa-an, Dooplaya, and Thaton during 1995 and 1997.

In total, troops from more than fifty battalions participated in the Northern Offensive, with attacks reoccurring on two- to four-week cycles. "A key distinguishing factor of the 2005-2008 offensive was the fact the attacks did not cease temporarily with the onset of rainy season," as was historically the case, explained one military expert who wanted to remain anonymous because of his ongoing work on sensitive security issues.[138] Typically, frontline battalions withdraw from their forward positions before the monsoon rains cut supply lines. When the dry season returns another cycle of preemptive search-and-destroy operations begins once roads and paths again become passable.[139] "This new tactic not only threatened the physical security of the villagers in internally displaced hiding sites," the same expert stated. "But [it] also prevented many villagers who had fled the initial stages of the offensive from returning to their villages to plant or tend paddy crops during the crucial monsoon agricultural period, as well as gather possessions, retrieve food stores or take shelter from the rains."[140] The attacks and subsequent roving patrols reportedly forced more than sixty thousand people into remote hiding places, a very significant number given the region's low population densities.[141] (Government-delineated Kayin [Karen] State, large parts of which were affected during the Northern Offensive, averages forty-seven people per square kilometer due to its mountainous terrain and the low carrying capacity of its soils.)[142] The result was dramatically increased rates of malnutrition and morbidity, in addition to the physical and psychological injuries the sustained violence caused.[143] By the end of the offensive, Tatmadaw units had reportedly constructed 103 new infantry and light infantry battalion bases and camps in the affected area, which further restricted the ability of civilians to reconstitute their livelihoods and to live without fear of future violence.[144]

The Northern Offensive was thus both singular and representative. It was singular in the sense that the violence was continuously sustained over a nearly three-year period, in sharp contrast to dry-season offensives, which were the norm. But the Northern Offensive was also representative in the sense that the human rights violations reportedly perpetrated during it were typical of those Tatmadaw units had committed against different "ethnic nationalities," in addition to Karen communities, for decades, as documented by dozens of fact-finding organizations and the United Nations. Both aspects of the violence—its singularity, which helps narrow the scope of discussion, and its representative nature, which highlights how the Northern Offensive expands the scope of discussion across Myanmar—are themes that run throughout this book as a whole.

Chapter 1 examines the assumptions that have shaped dominant narratives regarding "counterinsurgency" campaigns in Myanmar. The chapter puts colonial-era interpretations of such insurgencies into conversation with postcolonial ones to highlight the paradoxical effects of preemptive violence. The first period begins in the mid-nineteenth century and ends during the early decades of the twentieth. The second period begins in the mid-twentieth century and ends during the early decades of the twenty-first. Marked differences, besides time, separate the two periods. But they do share a common feature. "Pacification" campaigns, as the British referred to them, were a defining feature of both periods. In the case of the former, British-led forces, with mixed success, devoted significant resources to pacifying populations in much of what is now lowland Myanmar. In the case of the latter, the Tatmadaw similarly devoted a disproportionate share of the country's resources, again with mixed success, to pacifying what the British had not: nonmajority ethnic populations in the country's upland border regions. The strategies and tactics both armed actors used bear striking similarities that are worthy of note in their own right. But the larger purpose of the comparison is to lay the foundation for the analysis of the different genres of bodily violence featured in later chapters. The relationship between the different genres of preemptive violence and the approaches used to document the "facts" related to them produced distinct archival formations. The formations, in turn, created opportunities for specific forms of advocacy and foreclosed others, and these patterns have important implications for future transitional justice projects—a topic I return to in the conclusion.

Chapter 2 traces the emergence and transformation of an unintended archive into an intentional one. The transformation is the result of the decades-long fact-finding efforts of the Karen Human Rights Group (KHRG), a cross-border NGO. KHRG staff collected, analyzed, and re-presented documentation of the Tatmadaw's widespread and systematic use of forced labor across KNU-delineated Karen State. The core of the chapter compares and contrasts two types of "verbatim" evidence: thousands of written forced labor orders Tatmadaw units issued in brown (mixed-administration) areas, on the one hand, and oral testimonies of escaped convict porters who transported military supplies in black (alleged free-fire) areas during the Northern Offensive, on the other. In the case of the former, the "facts" in question are not dependent on victims' accounts of forced labor. Rather, the documentation rests upon the Tatmadaw soldiers, who "speak" via the written orders. The contents of these orders illustrate what I term "slow violence," the steady erosion of people's ability to sustain themselves in biological, as well as socioeconomic, terms. In the case of the latter, the "facts" were dependent on the escaped convict porters' oral accounts of forced labor, which I term "fast violence," as the practice carried with it the ever-present possibility of sudden death. (The comparison of the two modes of "speaking" draws much-needed attention to the possibilities and limits of "verbatim" as a social practice and as a factual artifact within human rights discourse.) In both cases, the slow and fast forms of violence left behind patterned traces that resulted in an archive, one that helped provide the evidentiary basis for the ILO's ultimately successful campaign to facilitate the eradication of forced labor in the face of significant government resistance.

Chapter 3 shifts the focus to the scorched earth tactics Tatmadaw units employed to forcibly relocate Karen civilians out of contested areas by destroying the ability of people to feed themselves. The chapter features the fact-finding efforts of two humanitarian organizations: the Karen Office for Relief and Development (KORD) and the Committee for Internally Displaced Karen People (CIDKP). Together, these two humanitarian organizations produced a massive intelligence archive documenting Tatmadaw military operations as part of their relief missions to assist IDPs in areas affected during the Northern Offensive. The IDP profiles, designed to calculate aid needs, thus doubled as human rights field reports, though that was not their intended purpose. Instead, the information was circulated internally to provide the evidentiary basis for the humanitarian "facts," namely, the scale of the emergency and the empirical validity of the request for food aid in the form of cash with which to purchase it. The raw data crucially informed the subsequent efforts of an international humanitarian consortium, of which KORD and CIDKP were a part, to numerically represent the crisis to international audiences, especially foreign donors and other human rights advocacy organizations. The interface where the two forms of documentation—one in unredacted but unpublished form, the other in redacted but published form—meet illustrates how "facts" about famine crimes—that is, the use of food as a weapon of war—emerged out of distinct quantitative logics employed to visually represent "authoritativeness" to different, and sometimes skeptical, publics.

Chapter 4 shifts the discussion to the epistemological and methodological challenges of working with victim/victim-witness/witness testimonies gathered from people who fled the Northern Offensive. The chapter features the documentation efforts of the International Human Rights Clinic (IHRC) at Harvard Law School. IHRC conducted a multiyear research project on alleged willful killings of and indiscriminate attacks on civilians, including the elderly and children, by Tatmadaw units during the offensive. The project, which generated well over one thousand pages of "quasi-affidavit" statements, produced a confidential archive that is currently unavailable for public review. However, portions of the archive, in heavily footnoted form, did circulate as part of a legal memo that asserted sufficient prima facie evidence existed, according to the authors, to charge three senior Tatmadaw generals for the international crimes that troops under their command committed. The similarities and differences between the first-person testimonies, both in their full and redacted forms, highlight the narrative ambiguities human rights fact finders have to wend their way through to differentiate probative "facts" (i.e., proof of evidence) from nonprobative ones. Particular attention is devoted to interview transcription practices, especially in terms of how they shape both narrative content (i.e., what is conveyed) and narrative discourse (i.e., how it is conveyed). The decisions made regarding how the testimonies can be "read" have important implications for transitional justice initiatives, particularly the creation of a criminal case file should a human rights body, such as the ICC, decide to prosecute at a future date the commanding officers who oversaw the Northern Offensive.

Chapter 5 highlights the long-running but ultimately unsuccessful efforts of a transnational NGO-led campaign to convince the UN Security Council to authorize a CoI into the international crimes Tatmadaw units reportedly committed during the years before, during, and after the Northern Offensive. The chapter explores the knowledge effects of citational practices, particularly the use and abuse of footnotes, to bolster human rights "truth" claims. Close attention to the similarities that exist across the reports in terms of their analytical framework, structural form, and rhetorical style highlights an important but often unremarked upon feature of human rights reports: their intertextuality. Texts can cite one another in a variety of ways to produce new meaning beyond what is contained in them separately. In this instance, the authors of the reports on the long-running human rights and humanitarian crisis in Myanmar utilized the practice of intertextuality in an attempt to bolster their authority, to refine recommendations, and to persuade others, including governments, to act upon them. The strategy, deliberate in some instances but not in others, produced a recursive archive, the credibility of which rested not only on the "facts" presented in a given report but on the stockpiling of "facts" produced in prior reports, including UN-authored ones. The stockpile provided what the advocates of the CoI believed to be a compelling argument: that the UN's own documentation demonstrated there was sufficient evidence for the Security Council to conclude the situation in Myanmar posed a "threat to peace and security," which the NGO-led campaign argued would justify international intervention.

I examine two key documentation practices, quotation and redaction, in the conclusion. I do so to illustrate how the addition and subtraction of "facts" has shaped Myanmar-specific human rights documentation, the archival formations arising from it, and the forms of advocacy both processes make possible. All of the "archivists" featured in the book—a human rights organization, two cross-border humanitarian agencies and their consortium partner, an international law clinic, and a transnational NGO-led campaign—used these two documentation practices to varying degrees. Attention to these practices points to a series of still largely unexamined epistemological, methodological, and ethical questions that human rights practitioners and scholars have yet to engage with in a sustained fashion: how "facts" are produced as well as found, and the implications of this for their respective "truth" claims.

I close with an epilogue, which includes a range of voices that underscore some of the key issues conflict-affected Karen communities continue to face. Their opinions, while specific to the situation in southeastern Myanmar, are not limited to their own communities. A durable peace, national reconciliation, accountability, and justice remain widely held aspirations, the realization of which still seems very unlikely at present. It is my hope that my efforts to highlight the possibilities and limits of the "facts" mobilized in the past toward these goals will inform future ones in a constructive fashion.

CHAPTER I

Pacifying Bodies

Histories of Preemptive Violence

The power to exclude is a fundamental aspect of the archive.
Inevitably, there are distortions, omissions, erasures,
and silences in the archive. Not every story is told.
—Rodney Carter

What would an ethnographic history of "counterinsurgency" in Myanmar look like? How should we categorize the complex and changing forms of state-sponsored violence that the Tatmadaw directed at civilians in order to maintain its privileged place in the national order of things? What units of analysis would be the most appropriate to use if the goal was to make interpretive sense of nearly seven decades of successive military operations in light of their diverse temporal rhythms, different spatial trajectories, varied tactics, and shifting targets? And perhaps most importantly, do the answers to these questions change significantly if we reverse the dominant narrative and conceive of the Tatmadaw as the "insurgent" and the NSAGs as the "counterinsurgents"?

I put forward my answers to these questions as they relate to human rights "fact" production, the archival formations that resulted from them, and the effects of both on advocacy in subsequent chapters. But I offer some initial thoughts here on the last question: What happens when we reframe the Tatmadaw as the insurgent, given that it has direct bearing on those later answers? Such a reframing, which opens up the space for revisionist histories of the armed conflicts in Myanmar, requires us to keep in mind what Jennifer Meehan observed as part of her efforts to develop an archival theory of evidence. Her work in this area directs attention to the often "uneasy relationship [that exists] between documentary practices, canons of representation, politics, and scholarship."[1] Put more directly, she argues, facts do not speak for themselves. Rather, the "facts" are, to a considerable extent, the product of these relationships, which are dynamic in nature. Consequently, facticity (i.e., the quality or condition of something being a fact) changes over time, though rarely in consonance with the shifting relationships themselves. The discussion that follows explores aspects of this uneasy relationship as it has shaped the dominant narrative regarding the history of counterinsurgency in postcolonial Myanmar. This effort requires the careful differentiation of the ultimate fact to be proved (*factum probandum*) from the evidentiary facts (*factum probans*) that prove it.[2] Casting the Tatmadaw as the insurgent, the ultimate fact here, thus requires a reassessment of the evidentiary "facts" normally mobilized to claim the opposite. Identifying some of what the epigraph describes as "distortions, omissions, erasures, and silences" in the archive on armed conflicts in Myanmar, at least as customarily told, provides the means to this end.

Reframing the Tatmadaw as the insurgent, a deliberate provocation on my part, is not intended to dismiss the security threat that its leaders believed the NSAGs posed to the country's sovereignty and territorial integrity. The threat was real at various points in time. However, the existential threat— if defined as the capacity of NSAGs in border areas to forcibly seize land under government control and retain, much less expand, their influence into the country's ethnic majority Burman heartland—was extremely limited. Instead, it was the Tatmadaw that, as the reports in the human rights meta-archive have documented over the course of decades, conducted one offensive after another to extend territorial control into border regions where it previously had none and over the minority non-Burman populations that resided in them. Nor is the reframing of the Tatmadaw as insurgent intended to minimize the serious human rights violations NSAGs committed against civilians, a significantly underdocumented problem that some local organizations are quietly beginning to address. Nevertheless, no credible evidence has emerged to prove that these abuses were either widespread or systematic, with the possible exception of the presence of child soldiers, which all of the armed groups, including the Tatmadaw, once routinely used. By contrast, the evidentiary record concerning the severity of Tatmadaw human rights violations is immense and, for the most part, persuasive.[3]

Given the stark differences between the Tatmadaw and the NSAGs in terms of who posed what kind of existential threat to whom and the scale of the violence carried out against civilians, one could justifiably ask what the Tatmadaw's "counterinsurgency operations" were meant to counter.[4] A closer look at the underlying logic of the Tatmadaw's operations, which to a surprising degree reproduced those of the British during the colonial past, makes it clear why this is the wrong question to ask. Instead, the question should concern the phenomenon of state terrorism, a topic that is almost completely absent in accounts of the Tatmadaw's strategy and tactics.

The critical turn in terrorism studies began in the mid-2000s, and it is now a stand-alone field of theory and practice in its own right. Proponents of critical terrorism studies (CTS) strive to deconstruct the foundational assumptions that inform orthodox understandings of the origins, dynamics, and solutions to "terrorism." The critiques of these foundational assumptions were wide-ranging. But a central one concerned the "ghost" that haunts mainstream approaches to combating terrorism. The ghost, according to Richard Jackson, one of the leading figures in CTS, is the state itself.[5] Due to the narrow focus on actors rather than actions, such approaches to national security have obscured the ways in which states routinely utilize terrorism against civilians to achieve their objectives, and often do so on a scale far greater than what non-state groups can reach.[6] The *state*, of course, is a problematic category on theoretical and empirical grounds.[7] So, too, is *terrorism*, a concept for which there is no consensus definition. But linking the two words together is nonetheless a useful reminder that, broadly speaking, state terrorism also is premediated; targets a wider audience than the immediate victims, who are often selected at random; violently transgresses social norms; and seeks to change political behavior with a particular goal in mind.[8] This broad, action-oriented definition invites us to consider the central role terror has played in state-making in Myanmar historically. When terror, as a critical aspect of this process, is taken into account, it will become clear why it is useful to regard the Tatmadaw, which was the functional equivalent of the state for decades (ca. 1962–2011), as the insurgent.[9]

The chapter revisits the dominant narratives concerning the Tatmadaw's counterinsurgency practices, known as the "Four Cuts," and one of their main targets, the KNU/KNLA. My larger purpose is to lay the historical foundations for my subsequent discussion of human rights "fact" production in southeastern Myanmar. With that in mind, the next section presents my overarching argument regarding the logic of preemption and the insurgency-producing practices it engendered in Myanmar. My summary of these practices reveals an interesting but largely unremarked upon continuity. The forms of preemptive violence the Tatmadaw utilized from the country's independence in 1948 onward did not develop in a linear fashion. Quite the contrary; it was more of an iterative process, one in which the hard lessons British-led forces learned in the colonial era were not always quickly incorporated into the postcolonial period. Instead, the Tatmadaw repeated many of the same strategic and tactical mistakes. Among other things, these mistakes underscore the extent to which the lines on official maps of the country's border regions remained cartographic fictions for more than 150 years. In fact, Tatmadaw efforts to convert all of the country's "non-state spaces," political scientist James Scott's term for "locations where, owing largely to geographical obstacles, the state has particular difficulty in establishing and maintaining its authority," is only just approaching completion.[10] But completion does not mean cessation. Preemptive violence is an intensely coercive project politically, economically, and culturally, which is why meaningful progress toward the establishment of a sustainable peace within these once non-state spaces remains elusive.

PREEMPTION

Preemption has become the dominant logic behind the exercise of large-scale coercive force today, displacing strategies of prevention and deterrence in the process, according to social theorist Brian Massumi. Prevention, he explains, "assumes an ability to assess threats empirically and to identify their causes."[11] The logic of prevention is thus premised upon the assumption that it is possible for us to know and to manage risk, such as the likelihood of a terrorist incident, through data collection and analysis followed by the timely dissemination of actionable intelligence. The logic of deterrence is similar in this respect, but extends the logic to its extreme. For deterrence to work, Massumi argues, it must paradoxically become the very threat that it is designed to prevent from occurring, such as mutually assured destruction through nuclear warfare.

Preemption, by contrast, differs from prevention and deterrence on an ontological as well as epistemological level. Preemption, Massumi writes, "starts where prevention ends." It is focused on "immanent threats," and

requires "immediate action," often at the expense of normal operating procedures and standardized codes of conduct. ("Enhanced interrogation," which is
widely regarded as torture by another name, is one such example.)[12] Furthermore, practices of preemption, though always implemented in the present,
are nevertheless oriented toward a *potential* future threat: one that can never
fully be known or overcome because "it tends to proliferate unpredictably,"
often due to unintended consequences.[13] Therefore, the logic of preemption
necessitates continual offensive action because, Massumi asserts, "the most
effective way to fight an unspecified threat is to actively contribute to producing it."[14] (In Myanmar, critics of the Tatmadaw sometimes refer to such
prevarication as "talking peace, waging war.") For Massumi, the open-ended
war on terror, which relies heavily on the exercise of state terror against civilians, typifies the logic of preemption as it is practiced today. His argument
is not limited to the present, however. A close look at pacification campaigns
in postcolonial Myanmar indicates that this same logic, whereby preemptive
efforts to suppress a security threat helped produce it, was also operative.

The uncritical use of the term *counterinsurgency* in the context of Myanmar, to return to my opening provocation, is thus problematic for several
reasons, particularly if we utilize Massumi's arguments regarding the logic
of preemption when connected to the concept of state terrorism. *Counterinsurgency* predisposes us "to see like a state," that is, to adopt a state-centric
perspective.[15] Such a perspective is important, of course, if we wish to understand how successive military regimes that held power directly and indirectly
for more than four decades conceptualized internal and external threats to
the country and, by extension, their continued rule. Tatmadaw billboards,
once posted around the country, offer some insight. One well-known and
much photographed billboard describes the "People's Desires" as follows:

> Oppose those relying on external elements, acting as stooges, holding negative
> views.
> Oppose those trying to jeopardize stability of the State and progress of the
> nation.
> Oppose foreign nations interfering in internal affairs of the State.
> Crush all internal and external destructive elements as the common enemy.

It is important to note that these elements have not remained constant
over time, but the framework behind their conceptualization has. The
Tatmadaw has long claimed that the armed forces are the sole institution

capable of defending what it calls the Three Main National Causes: the "non-disintegration of the Union, the non-disintegration of national solidarity, and the perpetuation of sovereignty."[16] Such claims are disingenuous, however. Decades of political repression, economic mismanagement, and chronic underinvestment, particularly in health and education, meant that no other independently functioning institutions existed outside of the armed forces until quite recently.

So, what accounts for the continued dominance of state-centric narratives that frame the conflicts in Myanmar as a narrative in which the Tatmadaw is engaged in defensively military action against a range of "insurgent" groups? Orin Starn, in his well-known critique of "Andeanism," describes how cultural anthropologists were so preoccupied with ethnographic minutiae and theory-building that they "missed the revolution," that is, the brutal rise of the Shining Path (Sendero Luminoso), a Maoist-inspired insurgency, in Peru during the 1980s.[17] But whereas Starn faulted cultural anthropologists for their political myopia, the opposite is the case in the context of Myanmar. We have been slow to recognize the realities of what is actually being "countered," by whom, and to what ends in Myanmar because the category of insurgency preemptively directs our attention to the domain of elite military politics.[18] This tendency explains the long-standing preoccupation among scholars, policymakers, and journalists with the strategic ramifications of Tatmadaw promotions, purges, factional splits, and so on, as well as with those affecting the leadership of the leading NSAGs. Attention to these matters remains important, as they open up the opaque decision-making processes of and patron-client relationships within the Tatmadaw, though typically only after the fact. But three important issues get downplayed or lost altogether in the attempt to "read Burmese tea leaves," a pastime that closely resembles Cold War era efforts to understand Soviet politics and policies from afar (aka Kremlinology).

First, the label "counterinsurgency" locates a vast and highly diverse array of violent conflicts under the same generic heading, organized resistance against the state, a conclusion that also fails to note that some NSAGs have engaged in long-running conflicts with other NSAGs, for example, the KNU/KNLA with the Democratic Karen Benevolent Army (DKBA). But when these conflicts are examined closely, it quickly becomes apparent that very few of them can be solely defined as ethnonationalist struggles that sought to gain greater regional autonomy or, in a few cases, independence from the state.[19] This is not to deny the legitimacy of principled opposition to the successive military regimes and the nominally civilian government. But it is frequently unclear whether NSAG leaders genuinely represented the aspirations of the ethnic populations they claimed to lead and/or whether that is the case today. Some Karen communities, for example, have come to view the KNU/KNLA "as just another group making demands," despite the provision of some services, such as health and education, according to Kim Jolliffe, a researcher who specializes in security, humanitarian affairs, and postconflict development in Myanmar. "Even where they [previously] supported the KNU's broad cause," he explains, "the desire for a single and consistent authority that would allow people to live in relative stability [has become] the primary desire for many Karen civilians in these areas."[20] Similarly, the Karen who live outside of KNU-delineated Karen State, who constitute the clear majority in terms of total population, are preoccupied with their own livelihood challenges.[21] "Karen in the city and the [Irrawaddy River] Delta don't grasp the conditions for people in the conflict zones," Nan Khin Aye Oo of the Karen Peace Support Initiative told me. "They are far away from politics," she said, and "this fact limits the ability of Karen political parties to understand the vastly different needs of their co-ethnics."[22]

Second, the focus on politico-military disagreements, a key cause of state-centric narratives, has often directed attention away from the complicated ways different armed groups, including the Tatmadaw, extract the labor, food, money, and other resources (e.g., timber, jade, gems, and drugs) they need to assert their de facto control in particular places.[23] "Mixed administrative areas," as they are commonly known, are one result. In these areas, two or more armed groups oversee local affairs; consequently, different personal networks compete and collude with one another to expand their regulatory authority and to accumulate wealth by working both through and around formal government and NSAG institutions.[24] Rent collection, such as extralegal taxes, and natural resource concessions, including cases in which armed groups on different sides of the conflict participate in informal time-share agreements, are two of the most common of these practices. Greater attention to how and why what I refer to as "actually existing governance" occurs enables us to move beyond the analytical dead ends that arise when we try to determine where "the state" or, for that matter, the Tatmadaw, begins and ends both theoretically and empirically. We should focus instead on how de facto forms of authority are asserted at specific moments and locales. Doing so provides insights into not only patterns of competition and collusion but also the challenges human rights fact-finding organizations encounter today—especially with regard to crafting effective advocacy strategies in the face of these on-the-ground complexities in (post-) conflict areas.[25]

Third, the reform process has prompted a discursive and financial shift from counterinsurgency to development in the southeastern part of the country. The language of development has become increasingly dominant as foreign direct investment continues to pour into the country, surging from US$2.6 billion in 2013 to US$4.3 billion in 2017, and forecasted upward again to US$5.8 billion for the fiscal year 2019–2020.[26] Not surprisingly, market-driven proposals for neoliberal forms of development are now the norm.[27] According to a consultant with the Myanmar Peace Support Initiative, a Norwegian-led effort to support the cease-fires through the provision of aid and technical support, the shift has effectively reframed the primary driver of armed conflicts historically as being chronic underdevelopment rather than decades-old political, economic, and cultural grievances that remain unresolved.[28] Saw Greh Moo, a research analyst for the Salween Institute, which provides assistance to community-based organizations that wish to help shape policies affecting their own lives, especially in Karen areas, calls this shift in discourse and practice a "development offensive."[29]

The new dominant narrative, that development will permanently end armed conflict, has material effects at the grassroots level, in addition to ideological ones. The narrative has strongly influenced donors, who continue to steadily reduce funding for the refugee camps and, equally importantly, away from the CSOs that provide cross-border assistance to conflict-affected populations. The majority of the donor funding now goes to government bodies and donor partners operating wholly "inside" the country, which is rapidly undermining the ability of the cross-border CSOs and their community-based organization (CBO) partners to provide services, especially health and education, to the conflict-affected populations that they have served for decades.[30] The director of the Burma Relief Centre, a cross-border humanitarian organization, described this increase in support through government service providers as an "aid offensive." "It is very hypocritical of donors to say that we support the peace process but do so in a way that strengthens only the government and weakens the ethnic groups," she explained to me. "The ethnic movement is in great danger," she stressed.[31] Her fear, which other cross-border international and local humanitarian workers have also voiced to me, is that the so-called development and aid offensives will accomplish what decades of preemptive Tatmadaw terrorism did not: an end to the possibility for these communities to meaningfully participate in and make informed decisions about what form their own futures should take. The next two sections explain how this situation has come about, through a genealogical retelling of some of what has been, to varying degrees, "distorted, omitted, erased, and silenced" in the dominant history of (counter-) insurgency in colonial and postcolonial Myanmar.

NARRATING PREEMPTION

Perfunctory histories of counterinsurgency do sometimes appear in major human rights reports to provide background for non-country specialists. Reports that fall into this category typically begin with some brief comments on colonial conquest, which I elaborate on in greater detail here, as elements of past practices inform those of the present. These histories begin with the birth of a colony through preemptive violence. Over the course of three "wars," British-led troops—most of whom were actually north Indian—"conquered" various territories that now constitute the national boundaries of Myanmar: first Tenasserim and Arakan (1824–1826), then Pegu and Martaban (1852–1853), and finally, the remaining "frontier" areas (1885–1886). Conquest, these reports typically fail to note, did not result in meaningful control, and a lengthy "pacification" campaign, as the British called it, followed.[32] The campaign lasted approximately five years (1886–1890), though armed conflict targeting British interests continued for nearly two decades in some areas, especially the Kachin Hills in the far north. Pacification did not, however, resolve disagreements over who should govern which parts of the country and manage their resources, including human labor, and in what manner. A range of contemporaneous sources (memoirs, government correspondence, and newspaper accounts), in combination with later scholarly research, indicates instead that the pacification efforts exacerbated the problems.[33]

British policies, which relied on direct rule in some places (Ministerial Burma, also known as Burma Proper) and indirect rule in others (Excluded Areas, which also included Unadministered Areas) replaced local forms of hierarchically ordered power in the case of the former but did not meaningfully alter governance structures in the case of the latter. British attempts to pacify the countryside thus did not fully replace one form of order with another, according to historian Michael Aung-Thwin. Rather, British insurgency-producing practices, especially scorched earth tactics and the indiscriminate killing of civilians, created what he terms "order without meaning." The precolonial kingdom, headed by King Thibaw Min, was largely hegemonic in the area under its control, according to Aung-Thwin. Its dominance, he explains, was based on tributary relationships and broadly shared Buddhist religious beliefs that interwove material and symbolic power into a meaningful whole. By contrast, the colonial state was never hegemonic. Instead, Aung-Thwin points out, the colonial state's dominance rested on the principle of coercion rather than consent and consequently lacked any such unifying wholeness in the eyes of the "conquered."[34] While I broadly agree, I argue further, contra Aung-Thwin, that no single "order with meaning" existed at the time of conquest within the territory that would become Myanmar, if one's gaze extends beyond the royal kingdom to include the many other forms of governance then in existence. As a result, contemporary conflicts regarding the pros and cons of a centralized versus federal state structure cannot be reduced, as NGO-authored reports often claim, to British policies of divide and rule.

Strikingly, the postcolonial iteration of the "state as insurgent" did not differ substantially from its colonial predecessor. Evidence to support this point, here stated as a fact, which some might critique as a disputable claim, comes from a variety of primary and secondary sources. The evidentiary sources range from military historians with limited access to the archival records of the armed forces to individual experts with decades of firsthand experience documenting preemptive Tatmadaw violence in the border regions. The abbreviated account that follows is an example of what anthropologist Michel-Rolph Trouillot calls, in his discussion of power and the production of history, the moment of "fact retrieval," the point at which the author selects some source materials but not others to craft a desired narrative.[35] The "facts," that is, the specific materials retrieved from a combination of official documents and interview statements selected by me, allow for a historical account of the state as insurgent that was not self-evident at the time. Without fuller access to Tatmadaw archival materials, however, it is difficult to avoid writing a Whiggish history, one that presents the past as an inevitable progression toward the present, which I have sought to avoid here.

My narrative, which reflects this challenge, has its roots in a paradox. On the one hand, contingency, more so than certainty, shaped the Tatmadaw's "invention" of a postcolonial strategy for destroying real and imagined security threats through a set of increasingly codified insurgency-producing practices. But on the other hand, this same preemptive strategy, when examined more closely, appears to be less of an "invention" than a reinvention of the pacification practices colonial British forces used a century earlier.

In 1886, Grattan Geary, the editor of the *Bombay Gazette*, summarized these practices. He wrote that it "was in too many cases accepted as an axiom that all that was necessary was to shoot out of hand whoever was found under circumstances of suspicion, and thereby to establish terror, which would produce the immediate submission of the population." "The idea," he continued, "fades that the population, which has to be brought into subjection by terror, has any claim whatever to be regarded as possessing human rights. The one virtue is to inspire fear, anything not calculated to produce that effect is regarded as evidence of weakness, which will interfere with the effect to be produced," a conclusion that presages Massumi's argument regarding preemptive violence.[36] The striking similarities between the past and the present, which I do not assert are causal in nature, underscore the pressing need for human rights organizations to more fully take history into account as part of their conflict analysis and reporting. That they generally do not reflects a number of factors: lack of sufficient expertise, time pressures, and the absence of desire on the part of policymakers and diplomats to read lengthy discussions of background information, among many other others. Yet such nuanced contextual information is often crucial to understanding how past decisions shape particular forms of state-sponsored violence in the present, which in turn is critical to understanding why long-sedimented assumptions and the routinized actions taken based on them are so difficult to change. The next section presents a case in point.

NARRATING (COUNTER-) INSURGENCY

Not surprisingly, after World War II military strategists continued to think of solutions to security threats in narrowly military terms. Myanmar's armed forces demonstrated this truism when British-led troops launched the first large-scale wave of preemptive violence against civilians in lower and central Myanmar in 1947 as part of Operation Flush. (Lieutenant-Colonel

Ne Win who, fifteen years later, seized power in a coup, led the operation.) Hugh Tinker, who reviewed the extensive British intelligence reports produced during this turbulent period, notes that their authors overwhelmingly described the outbreaks of rural unrest in terms of *dacoity*, a catchall term then used to describe banditry in particular and criminal activity more generally. (Tatmadaw documents and state-managed media outlets similarly referred to NSAGs, such as the KNU/KNLA, for decades as "bandits" and "terrorists" rather than "insurgents.") The word choice is significant, as it revealed that the authors' understanding of the primary cause behind the disturbances had not changed substantially from those held during the nineteenth-century pacification campaigns.[37] The possibility that at least some of the unrest was political in intent rather than criminal in nature remained largely unthinkable from the British perspective despite contemporaneous nationalist movements openly challenging Britain's rule in some urban areas. Tinker notes that at least some of the official reports split the difference, using the combined phrase "*dacoit* dictatorship" to conceptually link banditry with the widening "Communist underground."[38]

Subsequent clearance operations, carried out by the Tatmadaw after independence in 1948, broadened in scope to target nonmajority ethnic populations, in addition to this vaguely defined "Communist underground." Karen communities living in the Irrawaddy River Delta and adjoining lowland areas were among those targeted, allegedly because they widely supported separatist movements, most notably the KNU.[39] The tactics used during these early operations—indiscriminate attacks, extrajudicial executions, and the destruction of the villages in which Karens lived, if they were suspected of aiding separatist groups—the precise ones used by the British, were counterproductive, said long-since retired colonel Chit Myaing. During an interview with military historian Mary Callahan, the colonel admitted, "We didn't believe those killed [in these operations] were really insurgents. These were just men, women, *pongyis* [monks] and children."[40] The relevant SITREPS (situation reports) that battalion commanders were required to submit to their superiors at the time may or may not make similar admissions. (Unfortunately, the SITREPS are not currently available for review.) But Chit Myaing's role as a commander during later clearance operations in southern and central Myanmar, and thereafter, in the Wa and Kachin States in the north, suggests that his confession may in fact represent what occurred across all of the conflict-affected areas at the time.

During the early 1950s, as the NSAGs proliferated and gained strength in several of the country's border regions, especially the armed wing of the Communist Party of Burma (CPB) in northeast Myanmar, Tatmadaw strategists began to consider how best to respond. Their ability to do so was complicated by competing pressures. First, growing tensions between military leaders and political elites fostered parallel forms of governance that, broadly speaking, pitted the interests of one against those of the other. (The 1962 military coup, led by now general Ne Win, eventually resolved the issue.) Second, the Tatmadaw's regional commanders were able to maintain a great deal of operational independence following World War II. A diverse array of unofficial alliances between them and other NSAGs regarding who was to control what areas and how the resources extracted would be redistributed was one result of this independence.[41] The conflicting trends—centralization in the case of the former and decentralization in the case of the latter—not surprisingly meant that the Tatmadaw lacked a unified approach to national security.

The absence of a coherent doctrine became abundantly clear in light of the threat the Tatmadaw's leaders believed the Kuomintang (Chinese Nationalist troops) posed to the sovereignty and territorial integrity of the country. Fear of a potential invasion from the north prompted the Tatmadaw to launch a large-scale preemptive attack, known as the Naga Naing (Victorious Dragon) Operation, targeting the Kuomintang in 1953. According to another leading military historian, Maung Aung Myoe, the operation was, in his interpretation of the underlying archival source material, "badly executed under unfavorable terrain and a lack of resources," resulting in "a complete and humiliating defeat for the Tatmadaw."[42] The Tatmadaw, long underfunded and undermanned, underwent massive expansion as well as reorganization because of this failure, he explains, citing an array of budget and recruitment figures. It was in the context of this process that the Four Cuts counterinsurgency strategy was purportedly invented, a claim that is, in fact, problematic.

Academics, journalists, and activists routinely quote the phrase "Drain the sea to kill the fish" to convey, in pithy form, the ultimate goal behind the Four Cuts strategy. "Draining the sea" entailed the use of preemptive violence, which ranged in scope from everyday patrols to multi–combat division offensives, in order to deny NSAGs access to four forms of support: food, money, intelligence, and recruits. The source of this widely cited aphorism is not known. (Its wording reverses the wording of the advice Mao

Zedong made famous in his 1937 call for asymmetric warfare, paraphrased here as, "The guerilla must swim in the people as the fish swims in the sea.") But unlike counterinsurgency efforts in conflict settings elsewhere around the world, the Tatmadaw's Four Cuts tactics made no pretense of attempting to win the "hearts and minds" of civilians. The preemptive violence, if judged by the outcomes documented in hundreds of human rights reports, including those from UN bodies as well as its special rapporteurs, sought instead to alienate civilians from the postcolonial, ethno-majority-led, Burman nation-building project entirely.

One foreign expert, who possesses insider knowledge of the Tatmadaw's command structure and field operations, explained during a deposition with international human rights lawyers what the Four Cuts sequentially entailed. The first phase was the military assault itself. The purpose of the assault, he stated, was to depopulate the targeted area, with pincer movements frequently used to drive civilians in desired directions, either toward areas already firmly under military control or deeper into remote ones. The second phase, the expert continued, entailed the destruction of livelihood infrastructure, such as property (homes, tools, and cooking implements) and, most importantly, food stores (rice granaries and cash crops). Third, troops captured and interrogated civilians, frequently using torture, to obtain information on NSAGs. The emplacement of land mines—throughout the former village, in surrounding fields, and along heavily traveled forest paths to prevent safe return—constituted the final phase.[43] In practice, however, as a significant body of human rights documentation again makes clear, troops did not always follow this four-step sequence. Eyewitness testimonies collected by fact finders over the course of decades indicate that some of the phases could be done concurrently, whereas others might not happen at all. Regardless of the number and sequencing of the phases, the Four Cuts had devastating effects on civilians, details of which appear in the coming chapters.

But the origins of the Four Cuts are far more complicated than is typically portrayed in human rights reports, the authors of which typically devote only a few sentences in highly schematic and often ahistorical form to the Tatmadaw's strategy and its associated tactics. The reasons for this report shorthand are, of course, understandable. But the gloss obscures the ways in which multiple factors shaped and reshaped the Four Cuts and did so in a nonlinear manner that makes ending its continued use against civilians in some parts of the country extremely difficult.

Military historian Maung Aung Myoe locates the precise origin of the Four Cuts strategy in the form of a 124-page report that Colonel Kyin Win submitted to the Tatmadaw annual conference in 1958. (The date, a full decade after the KNU began its armed struggle, raises the question of what strategy the Tatmadaw used against the NSAG prior to this point.) But Maung Aung Myoe fails to note something of crucial importance in his claim regarding the strategy's creation: namely, "conceptualizing an originary source is not the same thing as positing a singular point of origin," as archivist Jennifer Meehan has pointed out in her discussion of what counts as archival evidence.[44] Her insight, which I appropriate for use in this context, reminds us that the proposed Four Cuts strategy did not emerge sui generis in 1958. Rather, the strategy had historical antecedents, such as the ones British forces employed during the colonial period "to pacify" what became Myanmar, and/or was influenced by contemporaneous cases, such as the Malay Emergency (1948–1960), in which British forces again used much the same strategy and tactics to combat a Communist insurgency there. Still other possibilities exist.[45] The key point here is that more needs to be done to identify the (pre-) histories of the Tatmadaw's Four Cuts to understand the role preemptive violence has played in the (re-) production of state terror over time.

According to Maung Aung Myoe, Colonel Kyin Win detailed the shortcomings of the Tatmadaw's traditional approach to combat, called for the adoption of one based on unconventional (i.e., guerrilla) warfare, and recommended that future operations have a political component to garner popular support.[46] The General Staff Office (GSO) provided a more detailed assessment in a report of its own prepared for the annual conference in 1959. The colonel's report, Maung Aung Myoe explains, identified intelligence gathering (for both offensive and defensive purposes) as being the most serious weakness.[47] (The Tatmadaw, in other words, lacked sufficient information to plan, conduct, and sustain its forward operations in a factually informed manner.) However, the GSO, for as yet unknown reasons, did not circulate a draft of the principles that training centers should use to strengthen capacity in this area until after General Ne Win seized power in March 1962.[48]

Again, for unknown reasons, another full year passed before the GSO asked the Tatmadaw's regional commanders to provide feedback on the draft principles. According to Maung Aung Myoe, the regional commanders collectively provided a list of twelve obstacles that hampered their operational effectiveness. The absence of a coherent national doctrine and concomitant strategy, as well as the growing involvement of field battalion officers in local administrative affairs, which was a direct consequence of the regime's decision to militarize the state bureaucracy, importantly were among those obstacles. But the most significant problem identified in the list, as related by Maung Aung Myoe, was poor coordination across the regional commands. The coordination problem limited the ability of field battalions "to conduct long-range penetration with a tactic of continuous search and destroy," the report stated.[49] And without this ability, it would remain impossible for the Tatmadaw to consolidate any future territorial gains in contested areas, which was one of the armed forces' primary objectives.

The Tatmadaw's internally self-admitted limitations with regard to coordination may help explain General Ne Win's decision to initiate peace talks with the CPB, the KNU, and several other NSAGs in April 1963. The talks continued for six months but collapsed in mid-November, reportedly due to the conditions that Ne Win sought to impose upon these groups, which included severe restrictions on their ability to raise funds, strengthen organizational capacity, and move outside designated areas.[50] (The same restrictions remain contentious today, as the Tatmadaw requires NSAGs to adhere to them as part of the National Ceasefire Agreement, but does not do so itself.) Due to the collapse of the talks, internal attention shifted to the more abstract subject of military doctrine, which became the focus of considerable debate during 1964. Archived military documents indicate that the debate centered on the perceived need to create a nationwide network of militias to help defend the country from invasion by unnamed "enemies." The KMT troops were possibly the only such force, but earlier offensives, conducted with the assistance of the Chinese army, had by this point driven almost all of the soldiers into scattered locations in northern Thailand and northern Lao.

The "People's War" approach, derived from models then in use in several European socialist countries (e.g., Yugoslavia, Czechoslovakia, and East Germany), became official doctrine in the following year. The goal of a People's War was to stretch out the supply lines of an invading force by allowing deep penetration into one's own territory and then disrupt their ability to resupply their forward operations through guerrilla-style attacks. But the newly adopted doctrine still lacked a clear plan for "either strategic denial or a counter-offensive capability against [such] foreign invasion," concludes Maung Aung Myoe.[51] (Or, to put it more bluntly, it was a plan without a plan.) Despite the glaring absence of both elements, the emphasis remained on the nationwide development of the Tatmadaw's capacity to mobilize newly created local militias to deter such a foreign invasion and to engage in guerrilla warfare if it did occur. Little actual effort was made to make the infrastructure for a People's War a reality, however.[52] (The militias were, as remains the case today, poorly trained and without proper weapons to make them of any combat use.)[53] Instead, for the next several years the Tatmadaw focused its attention inwardly on strengthening its own planning, administrative, and operational capacities.[54]

During this period some Four Cuts operations, not yet linked with the People's War doctrine, continued to target areas under the influence or control of the CPB in the north and the KNU in the southeast. The situation changed significantly during 1967–1968 when the Tatmadaw formed three light infantry divisions (LIDs) to operate under the Office of the Chief of Staff in the capital rather than under the regional commanders as would otherwise have been the case. LIDs, unlike the regional commands, were not constrained by patron-client relationships and thus "had few qualms about local sensibilities," as military historian Martin Smith puts it.[55] (Smith does not specify what he means by this phrasing, but it is easy to imagine what human rights violations the euphemism refers to when Colonel Chit Myaing's confession to Mary Callahan is recalled.) LID-88, once formed, conducted a rapid series of preemptive military operations against scattered CPB forces still active in the Arakan Mountains, Irrawaddy Delta, and Pegu Mountains.[56] Within a relatively short amount of time, the battalions under the command of LID-88 drove the CPB out of the targeted areas entirely.[57] These territorial gains across the bottom geographic third of the country convinced the Tatmadaw leadership to expand the use of the Four Cuts nationwide, but to first prioritize the central plains, which were not yet fully under the control of the armed forces. (Further military successes reportedly followed, but a detailed archival accounting of what did and did not actually happen is not yet possible.) Consequently, the leadership decided at its 1968 annual conference to broaden the People's War doctrine, despite its serious operational limitations, to include the simultaneous use of the Four Cuts to achieve such territorial control, suggesting (perhaps) that Tatmadaw strategists saw the two as being on an equal footing.[58]

The Tatmadaw's often remarked upon color classification scheme, which sometimes appears in cursory form in human rights reports as well, reportedly emerged at this time, in the late 1960s. (Who was responsible for its creation is not presently known, however.) Areas under strong government control were now coded "white" on maps, whereas those in areas where the government presence was not yet consolidated, and NSAGs were able to contest the military's control to a degree, were categorized as "brown." By contrast, "black" areas were under the firm control of NSAGs, and the Tatmadaw's presence in them was generally limited to patrols by troops stationed at frontline camps and their satellite outposts, except during dry season offensives, when multiple battalions carried out their operations. Civilians in conflict-affected areas, as reported in many fact-finding reports, frequently did not need Tatmadaw maps to know which areas where brown and which were black. The boundaries demarcating where one area ended spatially and another began were often quite clear, according to Karen civilian, in addition to KNLA, sources. Natural geographic features, such as rivers, and manmade ones, such as roads, frequently performed this delineating function. But in many cases the dynamics of asymmetric conflict meant that brown areas often bled into black ones and vice versa over time, though the former expanded dramatically at the expense of the latter beginning in the 1990s. The result was significant fragmentation of previously contiguous NSAG territory, which had a significant impact on human rights fact-finding practices and the ability of humanitarian groups to provide emergency food aid and medical assistance, two trends discussed in later chapters.

The type and severity of the human rights violations that occurred in differently color-coded areas varies when the fact-finding reports are read in conjunction with one another with this spatial component in mind. Forced labor, for example, was documented as being extremely widespread in brown areas due to the frequency of everyday interactions between military personnel and civilians, while indiscriminate attacks on the latter, including an alleged "shoot-on-sight" policy, were reportedly common in black areas due to the aforementioned tactics utilized by Tatmadaw units.[59] The color code scheme, as a result of the patterned forms of preemptive violence within such areas, thus reflected "differentiated forms of military conduct," according to one expert (name redacted) on Tatmadaw tactics.[60] By this the expert meant that official policies existed to guide the rules of engagement in brown and black areas, which if factually true, could open up Tatmadaw commanders to criminal charges for grave breaches of humanitarian and human rights law for the abuses committed by their subordinates. For many years the Tatmadaw leadership has denied the existence of a color-coded system and, by implication, of differentiated rules of engagement, despite the fact that mention of the scheme occasionally appeared in speeches during the 1980s and 1990s.[61] Public references to the Four Cuts disappeared at some point after that; however, operational details regarding the strategy periodically appeared in confidential Ministry of Defense documents as recently as 2008, according to this same expert.[62] Further references to the Four Cuts may or may not be included in more recent documents not yet reviewed by non-Tatmadaw personnel. But even if such references to the Four Cuts did completely disappear in such documents, the strategy and its associated tactics have not gone away for those for those who continue to experience its violent implementation today in conflict-affected areas of Rakhine, Kachin, and Shan States.[63]

NARRATING "THE KAREN" AND THE KNU

Colonial and postcolonial state formation through preemptive violence contributes to identity formations that might not otherwise come into being. The emergence of "the Karen," the third largest nonmajority population in Myanmar, is an example of such a conflict-induced ethnogenesis, one in which the Four Cuts played a crucially important but not defining role. A considerable body of literature exists on "the Karen," the KNU, and its armed conflict, once the world's longest. The contours of the dominant narrative have considerable evidentiary support from a wide range of historical and contemporary sources. But reframing selected aspects of this narrative here provides important historical context for understanding the impacts of preemptive forms of violence against "Karen" bodies featured in subsequent chapters.

Historically oriented accounts, which very rarely appear in NGO reports, usually begin with the gradual and multistranded emergence of "the Karen" as an ethnoracial and, later, politico-military project.[64] Nineteenth-century Christian missionaries, where such accounts often begin, helped fashion a singular history of "the Karen" out of various heterogeneous groups. But this story is only partly factual. For example, "the Karen" continue today to speak approximately a dozen different and not always mutually intelligible dialects, have quite distinct local histories, maintain varied cultural traditions, and practice diverse livelihood strategies.[65] (As a result, Karen communities in the former capital, Yangon, and the Irrawaddy Delta today have very limited understanding of the lives, needs, and aspirations of Karen in conflict-affected areas.) Nevertheless, the missionaries did provide the conceptual basis for later nationalist claims to self-determination. These claims took various forms during the colonial period, as educated Christianized elites, primarily Baptists and Seventh Day Adventists, articulated their successive visions of what such a project would entail.[66] The Karen National Association, which later became the Karen National Union (KNU), proposed a highly inclusive vision. The association aimed to represent all Karen regardless of their differences, religion among them.[67] (Approximately 80 percent of all Karen are Buddhists.) Yet these Christianized elites dominated the organization, something that would continue under the KNU and, later, in the refugee camps in Thailand, which raises a difficult question.[68] When the KNU claims to speak for Karen, whom, in fact, is it actually speaking for?

These ethnonationalist visions began to take more focused form following World War II. Many Karen elites, even today, maintain that the British failed to honor their promise to grant them greater self-determination, if not an independent state, in exchange for helping them to defeat the Japanese during the war. (Burmans initially allied themselves with the Japanese in the hopes of later obtaining independence from the British.) The rising power of Burmans, headed by General Aung San, Nobel Peace Prize winner Aung San Suu Kyi's father, compounded this sense of betrayal and contributed to fears that a postcolonial Myanmar would result in the political, economic, and cultural subordination of the Karen.

Negotiations regarding the "ethnic question," as it was then called, failed to resolve the issue, and in March 1948, shortly after Myanmar's independence, the CPB launched an armed rebellion. Several separatist groups, such as the Karen National Defense Organization (KNDO) and the Karen Peace Guerillas, followed suit. In June 1949, the KNU declared that it too would begin an armed struggle, which Saw Ba U Gyi, who became the organization's prime minister, said would be based on four principles: "1. Surrender is out of the question, 2. Recognition of the Karen State must be completed, 3. We shall retain our arms, and 4. We shall determine our destiny."[69] In April 1949, the KNU declared Karen State as independent, and it formed its own government in June. Four years later, the KNU's governing body went one step further, announcing that it intended to seek UN recognition for a Kawthoolei Free State. At the time, the KNU claimed to have approximately twenty-four thousand men under its command and several thousand more volunteers, though these numbers, routinely presented as statistical facts, have never been independently verified.[70]

Tatmadaw efforts to gain control of territories under the control of the KNU, an organization it depicted as an "illegal 'bandit' [i.e., *dacoit*] organization," accelerated during the 1960s and 1970s, as evidenced by increased waves of forced migration.[71] Oral histories indicate that successive Tatmadaw military offensives utilizing the Four Cuts forced substantial numbers of Karen communities living in the cities of Yangon and Insein, the neighboring Irrawaddy Delta, and the western part of the Bago Region east into the mountains toward the border with Thailand. The waves of displacement over these decades contributed to the further reconfiguration of Karen identities in these mountainous areas, as lowland and upland Karen populations, which were different from one another in terms of language, culture, and religious beliefs, mixed at the same time that the KNU leadership asserted that it represented a homogenous and politically unified ethnic nation.[72]

But not all divisions changed. Much of the Karen elite had been educated in Christian missionary schools in urban areas and lowland towns, while most of the rank-and-file KNLA troops were recruited from upland areas and were largely Buddhist. This division of labor and the disparities it contributed to over time—namely, differential access to health care, education, and wealth-generating opportunities via the taxation of illicit cross-border trade—led to a devastating split in 1994. That year, a group of KNU soldiers, citing discrimination, defected and formed a new NSAG, the Democratic Karen Buddhist Army (DKBA), now known as the Democratic Karen Benevolent Army. The following year, the DKBA guided Tatmadaw troops via secret routes into Manerplaw, the KNU's main headquarters, which fell following a concerted attack.

Dry-season Tatmadaw offensives over the next two years resulted in further losses of territory and permanent KNLA bases, fragmenting previously contiguous black areas in the process. The scale of these offensives was such that more than 500,000 people were reportedly displaced in 1997 after the Tatmadaw "attacked all of eastern Burma from Shan State in the north to Mon State in the south."[73]

David Eubank, the founder of the Free Burma Rangers (FBR), a well-regarded, faith-based, cross-border humanitarian organization, provided this figure during a deposition with international human rights lawyers.

FIGURE 2. Civilians forced to porter supplies to frontline Tatmadaw camps. SOURCE: Photo by Karen Human Rights Group.

The stated figure should be treated with some skepticism, however. The first official IDP survey in these conflict-affected areas did not occur until 2002, and it had significant methodological shortcomings. But the number cited, which is in fact a guesstimate, should not be dismissed out of hand, either. Subsequent, expert-designed surveys conducted annually for more than a decade documented levels of conflict-induced displacement largely consistent with the figure Eubank claimed.

Regardless of the number's facticity, the KNLA demonstrably lost its ability to function as a conventional fighting force as a consequence of the 1997 offensive.[74] Large areas of the seven districts that the KNU/KNLA had previously controlled to varying degrees became subject to what military historian Mary Callahan terms both an "occupation" and "ongoing but, de-territorialized war," meaning that there were no fixed lines of control.[75] Deterritorialization always contributes to a new, non-place-based reterritorialization, however. In this instance, this reterritorialization resulted in the creation of what one KNU administrator called a "mobile ministry" approach, whereby its representatives would meet community members in secret outside of their villages to share information, discuss new policies, and so on.[76] Such meetings enabled KNU-affiliated and nonaffiliated organizations to identify the specific needs of displaced populations and to collect testimonies regarding human rights violations, which they then reported to external audiences over the next several decades of chronic humanitarian emergency reproduced through state terror. But the reterritorialization also weakened the KNU/KNLA, as numerous commanders gradually abandoned the armed struggle because they were tired of the conflict and/or sought private economic gain through resource extraction in partnership with Tatmadaw battalions and armed forces–affiliated business enterprises—a localized and effective divide-and-rule strategy organized around the principle of wealth creation rather than one based on violent pacification.

Despite significant territorial losses during the 1990s and 2000s, the KNU continued to have significant influence over local affairs in southeastern Myanmar, operating as a "de facto federation" in which each of the seven districts "enjoy[ed] significant autonomy in local governance and financial management, but are united through various legislative and executive bodies," explained one researcher.[77] Approximately 100,000 people still live in (black) areas that the KNU firmly controls. On KNU maps, these areas include southern Taw Oo District, Mu Traw District, and eastern Kler Lwe Htoo District.[78] Another 250,000–350,000 people reside in mixed-authority (brown) areas, such as Hpa-an, Dooplaya, and southern Doo Tha Htoo Districts, again, as delineated on KNU maps, where government control is much stronger and other armed groups, such as the DKBA and Border Guard Forces, are also present, according to a recent survey.[79] The legacies of the conflict remain omnipresent, however. Two years after the 2012 cease-fire, one credible IDP survey reported that more than 109,000 people were still displaced throughout the southeastern region, some 68,500 of them in IDP "hiding areas" in government-delineated Kayin (Karen) State and eastern Bago Region, still uncertain whether or not the cease-fire would hold.[80] Ongoing skirmishes between the KNU, the DKBA, and the Tatmadaw mean this question remains an open one today.

The militarization of everyday life and the forms of violence connected with it (e.g., armed threats to safety and security, including periodic fighting, which contributes to further displacement) is the key reason for these concerningly high estimated IDP figures, though other factors (e.g., land mine contamination and lack of land tenure documents) have also limited the ability of IDPs to resettle and rebuild their lives.[81] Another recent survey, conducted by the respected humanitarian organization Thai-Burma Border Consortium (TBBC) in conjunction with its cross-border partners, supports this point. Its researchers found that 72 percent of all the village tracts in the country's southeast host at least one fixed military camp. The survey further revealed that Tatmadaw troops and the Border Guard Forces, according to local sources, have garrisons in 49 percent of the region's tracts, while NSAGs maintain camps in 51 percent of them.[82] And 28 percent of the village tracts have camps from both sides deployed within them.[83] The survey, which included GPS coordinates of the camps, indicated that the 2012 cease-fire agreement did not contribute to the demilitarization of these former conflict-affected areas. Instead, all of the armed actors sought to "harden" their existing positions (replacing bamboo and wooden structures with cement, for example) and construct new ones, transforming the presence of soldiers in everyday village affairs from sporadic and limited to permanent and widespread in the cease-fire zones. The now formalized "military normal," to borrow a concept from anthropologist Catherine Lutz, has shaped and will continue to profoundly shape the possibilities of civilian life moving forward, a topic discussed in the epilogue.[84]

CONCLUSION

The Tatmadaw's insurgency-producing practices, organized around the preemptive exercise of state terror, resulted in what postcolonial scholar Ranajit Guha's calls "domination without hegemony," that is, governance through violent coercion rather than consent.[85] In this regard, the strategies and tactics Tatmadaw battalions used in upland areas had much in common with those the British-led forces employed during their "pacification" campaigns in lowland areas. The violence mobilized against civilians had the same end goal in mind: to project militarized-state power into geographic areas where it previously had no presence and then use resource extraction to fund its rule. Sociologist Charles Tilly's famous dictum—"war made the state, and the state made war"—thus appears particularly apt when these colonial and postcolonial "pacification" campaigns are viewed side by side.[86] Of course, the dynamics of this actual process were far more complicated, as was Tilly's explanation of what he meant by coercive state formation. But the broader point, which military historian Mary Callahan similarly demonstrates in her research on war and militarized state-building in Myanmar (1826–1962), remains valid.[87] The two processes were inextricably intertwined, which is why it is useful to consider how the dominant narrative concerning armed conflicts in Myanmar changes when the Tatmadaw is conceptualized as the "insurgent."

My own narrative, while not without its own "distortions, omissions, erasures, and silences," to return once again to the epigraph, nonetheless suggests that much can be gained when the facticity of the received "facts" is subjected to renewed scrutiny. Massumi's analysis of preemptive violence is instructive for these reasons. Massumi argues that the logic of preemption necessitates continual offensive action because "the most effective way to fight an unspecified threat is to actively contribute to producing it."[88] The Tatmadaw was no different, judging by the meta-archive on human rights violations in Myanmar. Because of such preemptive action, the Tatmadaw's military operations continually reproduced what the successive regimes sought to prevent: armed opposition to centralized military rule.

Strikingly, the Tatmadaw's insurgency-producing practices did not result in high civilian body counts. Nevertheless, the sheer number of chronic, low-intensity conflicts nationwide and the decades-long duration of many of them likely meant that the cumulative totals were still sizable. Martin Smith, the leading expert on the history of postcolonial armed conflicts in Myanmar, places the nationwide figure at approximately 10,000 conflict-related deaths per year over the course of four decades (1950s–1980s). Unfortunately, Smith does not explain how he arrived at this estimate (roughly 400,000 people killed in total), which he states in published form is "probably fairly accurate."[89] The number 10,000 per year has since become the unofficial official one (i.e., an accepted "fact") despite the absence of further corroborating documentation. By contrast, no one has offered any estimate regarding the number of conflict-related deaths since the end of the 1980s, which is when they are likely to have increased markedly. The largest offensives, particularly in southeastern Myanmar, began in the late 1990s, and they continued for nearly two decades in many places, especially in KNU-delineated Karen State. However, the scale of displacement during these years, which heavily targeted civilians in brown and black areas, offers a potentially useful proxy for the magnitude of the preemptive violence, though the number of conflict-related deaths during these decades will never be known.

A proxy is a figure that can be used to represent the value of something in calculative terms. Here, credible proxy data take two main forms, both discussed at length in a later chapter. First, the aforementioned TBBC and its cross-border humanitarian partners mapped the destruction, forced relocation, or abandonment of villages in southeastern Myanmar between 1996 and 2011. The total, they reported, was in excess of thirty-seven hundred villages.[90] Researchers compiled the 1996–2001 data using archival information provided by local officials, humanitarian organizations, and human rights groups. Figures from 2002 onward were the product of annual IDP surveys, the methodological sophistication of which developed rapidly over subsequent years with the assistance of technical experts. Second, while it is impossible to independently verify the figure of thirty-seven hundred plus villages, the IDP surveys carried out every year between 2002 and 2012 do provide an indication of the scale of forced migration. The total number of IDPs in southeastern Myanmar fluctuated during this period, according to TBBC and its partners, which their funders, including bilateral government agencies, found sufficiently credible to continue providing them with considerable financial support. But on average, the surveys estimated that the southeastern region was "home" to between 400,000 and 500,000 IDPs every year over the course of this ten-year period, a figure that lends support to David Eubank's earlier "guesstimate."[91]

Having personally reviewed a substantial amount of the underlying documentation of both data sets, I am confident that the reported figures are, within an acceptable margin of error, evidence-based. That said, it is important to bear in mind "what the objects in question are being counted *for*," as sociologists Aryn Martin and Michael Lynch stress in their discussion of the politics of this enumerative practice.[92] Proxy indicators, such as these regarding IDPs, are indirect measures used to approximate or represent a phenomenon in the absence of direct measures. In other words, proxy indicators only come into being when someone deliberately creates a comparison that someone else might not otherwise make, which is what I have done here, producing human rights "facts" about cumulative death tolls in the process. But the comparison still leaves open the question "evidence of what?" In philosopher Jeremy Bentham's view, evidentiary facts, such as the posited relationship between the number of internally displaced IDPs and the number of civilian casualties, "serve to produce . . . a *persuasion* concerning the existence of such and such other facts."[93] Restated more directly, evidence relies not only on the existence of provable facts, but on the degree to which an audience finds them to be convincing.

Genealogies, like proxy indicators, are by definition selective in nature, and they often require difficult choices concerning which lines of descent are foregrounded and which are not. ("The power to exclude" is not only "a fundamental aspect of the archive," as the epigraph stated; it is also true for genealogies.)[94] These choices are frequently limited by the unevenness of and asymmetries within the archive, an issue discussed at some length in this book's introduction, particularly in light of the paucity of Tatmadaw-produced conflict documentation. The asymmetry was also an issue here with regard to my reframing the state as the insurgent rather than, as is normally the case, the counterinsurgent.

My goal in doing so was to write, while at the same time to the degree possible unwrite, two key conflict phenomena that run through this book—namely, the Four Cuts and the KNU/KNLA struggle—to highlight how uneven source densities produce identifiable silences in the archival record. Historical silences, as Michel Rolph-Trouillot explains, take different forms depending on the moment examined, which he differentiates in terms of "fact creation (the making of sources); fact assembly (the making of archives); fact retrieval (the making of narratives), and retroactive significance (the making of history in the final instance)."[95] Each of these silences (other moments beyond the four Trouillot identified may also exist) affects what questions are thinkable. The relative thinkability and unthinkability of such questions both shape and are shaped by the "uneasy relationships" that Meehan identifies between "facts" and the contexts that frame them as such. The next chapter, which analyzes one NGO's efforts to document the Tatmadaw's massive use of forced labor, a contemporary form of slavery according to the ILO, continues the task of making sense of silences as they shape "fact" production. The chapter does so through an examination of an unusual archive that reportedly enabled Tatmadaw soldiers "to speak for themselves" in verbatim form.

CHAPTER 2

Enslaving Bodies

Verbatim in Replicated Form

We then should ask, what kind of social, technological/technical, and ideological processes are necessary to turn a particular text, whether spoken or written, into a credible or otherwise weighty copy of another text? Why and in which kinds of social and political contexts are such claims mobilized and for what purposes?

—Miyako Inoue

The Latin phrase *verbatim ac literatim* dates back to the late fifteenth century, and it literally means "word for word, and letter for letter." The phrase, since shortened to "verbatim," now connotes "exactly as written." Linguists Richard Bauman and Charles Briggs developed the concept of "the image of intertexual fidelity" to convey, in similarly shorthand fashion, the conventional assumption that "texts created through transcription, translation, and editing should bear a direct and intrinsic connection to their sources, such that the former are extensions or synecdoches of the latter."[1] But the nature of this connection, even where the copy is an exact reproduction of the original, is far more complicated that it first appears. Miyako Inoue, another linguist, stresses the need to engage with this complexity when she writes, "It is imperative for us to call into question the epistemological stability of verbatim both as a social practice and as an artefact, and to disclose the historical, technological, and sociopolitical conditions that both demand and make plausible such fidelity."[2]

I include these direct (i.e., verbatim) quotes to foreground two issues that I discuss at length in this chapter concerning the documentation of forced labor, which is a crime against humanity under international law.

First, *image*, in the context that Bauman and Briggs employed it, refers to a general impression. But "image" also signifies the representation of an external form. I utilize *image* in both senses of the word to illustrate the visual components of verbatim, as they relate to human rights "fact" production in the archive to be examined. Second, as Inoue observes, verbatim is both a process and a reification of it. When these dual aspects of verbatim are kept in mind, it becomes possible to "reverse engineer," if only to a modest degree, how the illusion of epistemological stability is brought into being and perpetuated in a manner that partially hides but never fully erases the conditions of its creation.[3]

Verbatim, it should be noted, takes several common forms: speech to speech (e.g., oral transmission), speech to text (e.g., dictation), and text to text (e.g., document duplication).[4] Regardless of form, Greg Urban notes, replication is "an attempt at reproduction, at relocating the original instance of discourse to a new context—carrying over something from the earlier to later ones."[5] This carrying over must not only be logical in nature for A* to be an accurate replication of A, but ethical as well in the sense of fidelity to the original. The ethics of replication are critical to human rights "truth" claims for this reason, which is why the "epistemological stability" of verbatim, both real and imagined, is so important to understand where the dynamics of "fact" production are concerned.

I feature two different types of verbatim in this chapter. Both entail chains of replication. The first chain consists of handwritten Tatmadaw documents translated into typed verbatim English copies, which were then visually relocated into thematic reports for use as part of a multiyear advocacy campaign against the widespread and systematic use of forced labor in conflict-affected areas in KNU-delineated Karen State. The second chain involves the replication of speech to speech to text in translation, the contents of which were then relocated in excerpted verbatim form in reports, once again for advocacy purposes. Despite the significant differences between the chains—the first concerns the documentation of "slow violence" in brown areas and the second of "fast violence" in black ones— both evince an important similarity. Specifically, each step in the replication process involved strategic choices, and these choices, while rarely made explicit to the publics that read and acted upon the advocacy reports, crucially shaped not just what, but how, we know about forced labor in southeastern Myanmar.

An overview of the ILO's efforts to eradicate forced labor in Myanmar follows, as its 1998 CoI report serves as the temporal point of departure for the chapter as a whole. Attention then shifts to the KHRG, a prominent cross-border NGO. KHRG's fact-finding work convincingly demonstrated how much more the regime needed to do in order to end the practice, which the military regime eventually banned, in conflict-affected areas of KNU-delineated Karen State. On one level, the chains of replication featured convey the empirical effects of forced labor on the people's bodies in brown and black areas. On another level, the same chains illustrate how the apparent "epistemological stability" of these effects is achieved through verbatim sleight of hand.

A COUNTRY IN CHAINS

The Southeast Asian Information Network (SAIN), a short-lived NGO, published a striking, full-color poster in support of an international effort to convince foreign tourists to boycott the military regime's "Year of Tourism," which it had scheduled for 1996. (The regime's goal was to attract a half million visitors by year's end, a number substantially higher than had been the norm since the Tatmadaw had killed thousands of people in 1988 when its troops crushed pro-democracy demonstrations nationwide.) SAIN alleged that the regime was using forced labor on a massive scale to build and "to beautify" the infrastructure needed to handle the hoped-for influx, which would bring in much-needed foreign exchange. The title of the poster, "A Country in Chains," included a large photograph that provided visual "evidence" to support the claim. The image depicted several men wearing heavy leg-irons as they used hand tools to repair an access road leading to a religious site. Western advocacy organizations then distributed the poster widely as part of the anti-tourism advocacy campaign. The photograph was right for the wrong reasons, however. It was later discovered that the men were not civilians, but convicts who, under then existing domestic law, could be made to perform compulsory labor.[6] SAIN never acknowledged the mistake, if indeed it was one. Nevertheless, the poster helped draw wider international attention to this practice, which human rights organizations had begun documenting several years prior.

Further credible evidence in statistical form of the widespread and systematic use of forced labor came from an unexpected source. Back in 1989, after the brutal crackdown ended the civilian challenge to military rule in August of the previous year, the regime authorized a series of large-scale construction projects (especially roads, railways, and dams) nationwide. According to the Ministry of National Planning and Economic Development's annual reports, the projects relied heavily on "people's contributions," which upon closer investigation proved to be a euphemism for forced rather than voluntary labor. Richard Horsey, the former ILO liaison officer, references the ministry's line-item data in his personal account of the UN organization's efforts, in which he played a leading role, to convince the regime "to eradicate forced labor in all its forms." (The ambitious goal, quoted here in verbatim form, was of the ILO's own making.)

Economists working in the US embassy, Horsey writes, calculated the market value of the "contributions," which they stated had increased in real terms twenty-five-fold between fiscal years 1989/1990 and 1995/1996, the eve of the start of the "Year of Tourism." The total "contribution," the economists concluded, without explaining the methodology used, was equivalent to 7 percent of Myanmar's reported GDP, that is, approximately one-quarter of the government's annual expenditures.[7] Official statistics in Myanmar are not known for being accurate or complete. (For example, revenues from two Tatmadaw-owned conglomerates, Myama Economic Holdings Limited and Myanmar Economic Corporation, which are widely believed to be very substantial, are kept "off book" so there is no external and independent oversight over expenditures.) But to focus on the question of whether or not the ministry's reported figures are valid misses a key point. Namely, the ministry's official statistics constituted an ideological rather than an auditable "fact," one that framed the steady increase in "contributions" over this five-year period as a genuine reflection of the people's desire to voluntarily donate their labor to (re-) build the nation.

Horsey, after citing the economists' analysis of the ministry's figures, proffers a statistic of his own. By his estimation, "perhaps [as many as] one million people were being forced to work on infrastructure projects on any given day."[8] Horsey's estimate, which appeared in his 2011 account of the ILO's efforts to convince the regime to end the use of forced labor, is not without some empirical support. In 1997, the governing body of the ILO, which had pushed the regime to address the use of forced labor by civil servants and military personnel for decades, finally decided that a full-scale CoI was warranted. (CoIs are investigative bodies that produce fact-finding reports for specific audiences, but they can also function as a "preliminary mechanism of legal adjudication.")[9] The CoI consisted of three phases: the collection of evidentiary material, primarily published NGO reports; followed by hearings in Geneva with fourteen eyewitnesses; and then a fact-finding visit to the region, but not Myanmar itself, during which they interviewed several hundred more individuals.

The military regime rejected the ILO's request to visit the country on the grounds that "such a visit would not contribute much towards resolving the case" and "would interfere in the internal affairs of [the] country," an objection it would reiterate on a regular basis for many more years.[10] The refusal forced the CoI to interview eyewitnesses in nearby countries (India, Bangladesh, and Thailand), an outcome that Horsey states was actually advantageous because it avoided a host of problems that would have ensued had the regime granted the CoI access to the country—most importantly, informant protection.[11] But the denial of access also meant that the CoI's conclusions did not produce new knowledge about the dynamics of forced labor in Myanmar so much as provide UN-level confirmation of what other fact-finding organizations had been reporting since the early 1990s.[12]

The CoI released its report in July 1998. Its authors concluded that overwhelming evidence existed of the regime's massive use of forced labor nationwide, with the most serious violations occurring in connection with Tatmadaw operations in conflict-affected areas. "A State which supports, instigates, accepts or tolerates forced labor on its territory commits a wrongful act and engages its responsibility for the violation of a preemptory norm in international law," the report's authors wrote, and "if committed in a widespread or systematic manner, is a crime against humanity."[13] The CoI presented three recommendations based upon its central finding. First, bring the colonial-era domestic laws that permit forced labor into conformity with international law. Second, ban the future use of forced labor in all circumstances. And third, enforce section 374 of the Penal Code when the ban is violated, as "the power to impose compulsory labor will not cease to be taken for granted unless those used to exercising it are actually brought to face criminal responsibility."[14] The ILO then announced that it would suspend all cooperation with the regime, except for that designed to implement the three recommendations. The ILO's recommended solution, in other words, reduced a socioculturally complex and deeply institutionalized practice to a technocratic problem: international alignment through legal reforms and the subsequent implementation of a ban through punitive criminal action by a regime that relied heavily on forced labor for military as well as economic purposes. Not surprisingly, reforms on paper proved to be much easier than reforms on the ground.

Complex, high-stakes negotiations ensued, eventually resulting in the regime's decision to institute a partial ban in 2000. A supplementary order that completely banned the use of forced labor under all circumstances unexpectedly followed in 2001.[15] (The supplementary order nullified two secret military directives that had previously legitimized forced labor on development projects provided that payments were made and the "misery and sufferings" associated with what the regime diplomatically termed "undesirable incidents" were reduced.)[16] The regime's sudden decision to fully criminalize forced labor after years of fierce resistance to international pressure was met with considerable skepticism, especially by human rights organizations and trade unions. (Following the ban, village heads increasingly found themselves "summoned to meetings" where they received orders verbally, which left no written record of the demands, for example.)[17] Nevertheless, the ILO quickly renewed talks with the relevant government ministries in the hopes that the ban signaled a more cooperative stance, at least among some factions within the regime.

Further negotiations and minor concessions on the regime's part over the next several years led to incremental progress. The year 2007 marked a key milestone with the long-awaited introduction of a formal complaint mechanism, which was designed to enable "genuine victims" of forced labor, with the assistance of the ILO liaison officer, "an opportunity to seek redress and/or remedies from the government authorities in full confidence that no retaliatory action will be taken against them."[18] The complaint mechanism very slowly began to challenge impunity in regime-controlled white areas through an extremely limited number of successful cases (penalties were almost entirely administrative rather than criminal in nature). It did nothing, however, to substantively reduce the use of forced labor in brown and black areas in the years that followed.

THE KAREN HUMAN RIGHTS GROUP

Here is an origin story in abbreviated form. In 1991, Tatmadaw troops shelled a Karen village in Myanmar where Kevin Malseed was illegally working as a volunteer teacher. He fled to Thailand in the aftermath of the attack with the surviving villagers, but soon returned to Myanmar, where he traveled to KNU/KNLA headquarters in Manerplaw. Once there, he encountered hundreds of other people who had similarly abandoned their homes due to preemptive Tatmadaw violence. Despite his efforts to publicize their experiences, foreign journalists "were only interested in the people with the guns," Malseed lamented during one interview."[19] Frustrated by the situation, Malseed began to collect their stories himself, which he documented using an old manual typewriter and carbon paper. Within a few short months, Malseed had hastily assembled an international mailing list and begun to publish the testimonies in report form under his pen name, Kevin Heppner. By year's end, Malseed had recruited several other local volunteers to assist him, and in 1992, they formally named their new organization the Karen Human Rights Group (KHRG).

KHRG quickly rose to become the premier fact-finding organization in southeastern Myanmar. (It received two Nobel Peace Prize nominations in recognition of its work, in 2000 and 2001.) Politically independent from the start, KHRG nonetheless took a strong political stance in its mission statement: "We aim to increase villagers' capability and opportunity to claim their human rights, and ensure that their voices, priorities, and perspectives influence decision-makers. We encourage other local and international groups and institutions to support villagers' self-protection strategies."[20] KHRG's villager-centric approach stands in marked contrast to the dominant model, which was (and remains today) heavily extractive in nature: fact finders collect testimonies from villagers and analysts transform the information into reports, which activists then use for advocacy purposes. Human rights organizations obtained funding, built professional reputations, and sometimes enjoyed comfortable lifestyles in the process, but the people whose traumatic experiences made all of that possible rarely received anything directly in return.

KHRG formally launched its "village agency program" in 2005 to address this problem. The program, which later became KHRG's central mission, sought to strengthen the strategies villagers used to "evade and resist" abuses, then share them with villagers elsewhere. (Approximately two thousand people per year participate in these programs, which also train them to become volunteer human rights monitors.)[21] Other rights-based organizations, KHRG staff assert, must take these strategies into account when designing interventions, such as humanitarian assistance programs and international advocacy campaigns, in order to make them relevant, effective, and sustainable at the local level.[22] Malseed did precisely that in 2007 when, following a concerted capacity-building effort to enable a leadership transition, he stepped down as director, at which point KHRG became a fully Karen-managed organization.

KHRG, which has been in operation for over twenty-five years, has generated numerous thematic archives documenting various human rights violations. Forced labor was the original one. KHRG's very first report, published in 1993, focused specifically on this issue. Dozens of short situation reports followed over the next five years. Typically, the situation reports concerned either major infrastructure projects (e.g., the reconstruction of the 177-kilometer Ye-Tavoy Railroad in Mon State, which reportedly required the forced labor of hundreds of thousands of people to complete) or specific conflict-affected areas (e.g., Toungoo District in Karen State, where the 1997 Tatmadaw offensive against the KNU/KNLA reportedly involved the involuntary recruitment of thousands of civilians to porter military supplies.) KHRG, like other fact-finding organizations at the time, such as EarthRights International and the Federation of Trade Unions of Burma, submitted a growing number of fact-finding reports to the ILO, the contents of which contributed to the evidentiary foundations of the UN agency's 1998 CoI findings. But the KHRG forced labor reports, published between 2000 and 2013, produced a unique archival formation built on two different but related chains of replication that presented their contents as if they were "verbatim reproduction[s] of prior discourse."[23]

KHRG released its first major "orders" report in May 2000 to mark the one-year anniversary of the regime's initial partial ban on the use of forced labor. The report's main conclusion was that the scale of the problem in brown areas across KNU-delineated Karen State had remained fundamentally unchanged. The core of the report consisted of three hundred verbatim translations of handwritten Tatmadaw orders that KHRG fact finders had collected from village leaders, whose job it was to decide which people had to go and to provide the type of labor the troops had demanded.[24] KHRG's thematically organized forced labor archive quickly began to take shape as further orders reports, employing the same verbatim presentation format, followed. KHRG released the next report in October 2000; it contained 250 more written orders.[25] The NGO published a third (453 orders

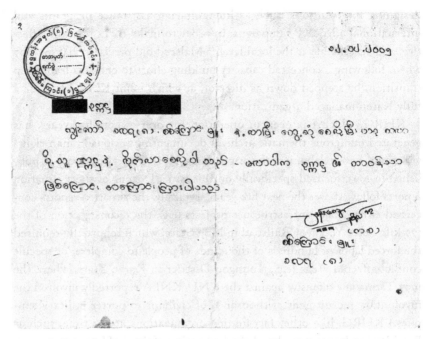

FIGURE 3. Tatmadaw forced labor order. SOURCE: Karen Human Rights Group.

reproduced out of a total of 1,500 acquired) in 2002 and a fourth in 2003 (783 orders reproduced out of the more than 1,000 secured).[26] KHRG subsequently issued several more shorter reports, again using the same verbatim format, in 2007 (145 orders), 2011 (207 orders), and 2013 (25 orders).[27] All told, the thematic archive replicated, in visual form and narrative content, more than two thousand orders out of the almost three thousand KHRG had obtained over this period, during which the organization produced numerous reports on other human rights issues.

KHRG also released three additional "oral" forced labor reports, one of them coauthored with Human Rights Watch. These reports analyzed testimonies KHRG fact finders had collected from prison convicts whom Tatmadaw battalions had forced to porter rations and military supplies in frontline black areas during the Northern Offensive (2005–2006) and the final one against the KNU/KNLA (2010–2011).[28] The total number of convict porters forcibly pressed into service will never be fully known, but several different fact-finding NGOs placed the figure, which they conceded during conversations with me was a "best guess" estimate, at between two thousand and three thousand people per offensive. All told, KHRG fact finders interviewed 142 convict porters who had fled to the Myanmar-Thailand border zone to safety. The number of testimonies, which appear in excerpted form in the body of the three reports, is understandably small given the rarity of successful escape and rescue. Nonetheless, the oral testimonies, like the written orders, are valuable on several levels. Empirically, the testimonies, elicited through semistructured interviews, evinced a high degree of consistency across both offensives, which occurred a half decade apart, suggesting that official policies in written form existed to standardize procedures across institutions. The similarities KHRG identified revealed a curious paradox, however. The mobilization of convict porters was organized and rational, while the Tatmadaw's use of them once in black areas was disorganized and irrational. Conceptually, the chains of replication at issue here originate with the reported speech of soldiers, who "speak" for themselves in a manner that is quite different from the written orders. The chapter's conclusion presents the significance of this difference with regard to the epistemological politics of verbatim and human rights documentation.

SLOW VIOLENCE

A combination of archival records and official histories of the armed forces provides a numerical sense of the Tatmadaw's metastasizing over time. In 1949, it possessed 10 battalions. By 1988, the number had grown to 422, likely only on paper. (Tatmadaw battalions, which at full strength contain 500 men under arms, are notoriously undermanned due to its inability to recruit sufficient numbers of people without the use of considerable coercion and to stem their subsequent desertion.) The size of the Tatmadaw similarly shows unprecedented growth, again on paper. It reportedly more than doubled in size, from 180,000 people in 1988 to over 400,000 in 1998, even though the country faced no credible external threats. While a portion of this claimed total can be attributed to the further bureaucratization of the armed forces, the Tatmadaw significantly expanded its organizational capacity to conduct forward operations as well. (By 2000, its capacity, in organizational terms, had allegedly increased to twelve regional commands, fourteen military operations commands, three regional control commands, and ten light infantry divisions, with numerous combat infantry battalions under them.[29] Military logistics badly lagged behind, however. Again, according to the Tatmadaw's own records, the ratio of combat infantry battalions to support units was 2:1 during this period, when the target rate was actually 1:3.[30] The ratio, when translated into actual conditions in the field, meant the Tatmadaw struggled to supply its troops, in brown areas but especially in black areas, where roads were either limited or nonexistent.

The War Office issued a policy in 1997 to address this pressing problem, the same year that the ILO was conducting its CoI into the regime's use of forced labor. But the War Office did so in a manner that encouraged more rather than less violence against civilians. Instead of taking concrete steps to correct the problematic ratio, the new policy now required the Tatmadaw's regional commanders "to meet their basic logistical needs locally, rather than rely on the central supply system," as military historian Andrew Selth explains.[31] Tatmadaw units stationed in brown areas quickly capitalized on the policy shift by increasing their demands not only for forced labor but also for food, money, and other materials from people living in proximity to their bases and camps.[32] Large-scale preemptive violence, primarily directed at civilians, gradually converted more and more previously KNU/KNLA-controlled black areas into brown ones over the next two decades. The ability of Tatmadaw units to consume the scarce resources of people previously not subject to its soldiers' constant demands thus followed in tandem.

KHRG's thematic forced labor "orders" reports, published between 2000 and 2013, presented handwritten Tatmadaw documentation of the material effects of the policy shift from the demand side. (By contrast the testimonies, featured in the next section, provide details of how convict porters experienced the policy on the supply side.) Importantly, the reports were not designed to be exhaustive, KHRG fact finders wrote. Instead, they purposefully chose to reproduce "typical" orders so as to highlight what they saw as the normal range of demands that soldiers continually issued on a day-after-day basis. The concept of "typical," while not explicitly defined by KHRG, did take identifiable form in two ways: through the chronological presentation of the orders, which provided a longitudinal perspective, and through the thematic presentation of the orders, which organized them by the "contribution" demanded. Categories included, but were not limited to, everyday soldiers' needs (e.g., delivering messages, cleaning, and cooking), routine security operations (e.g., carrying food and ammunition to camps and acting as sentries), transportation (e.g., "lending" boats, bullock carts, and motorbikes), infrastructure (e.g., building roads, bridges, and fences), and food (e.g., providing their own rice, fruit, and cash crops to soldiers for consumption or sale to others).[33] All of these types of forced labor originated with a written order.

The majority of the orders that KHRG fact finders obtained from village heads in brown areas were handwritten in blue or black ink, though red was periodically employed if the need was presented as being particularly urgent. Typed or carbon-copied orders, if sent to multiple villages, were sometimes used, as were more rarely cyclo-styled forms. Village leaders, after receiving an order, had to arrange for people to provide the labor, food, and/or fees within the time frame given. The failure to successfully do so placed the village leader at risk of interrogation, torture, and/or arrest. (Over time, this pressure prompted many villages to rotate who served as leader to spread the risk beyond one person. In some cases, this strategy included the appointment of elderly women in the hopes that they would be less likely to suffer violent retaliation.) A threat, often included as part of the order itself, normally took indirect form: "come without fail," "you are informed," and "if you fail it will be your responsibility." Direct threats, although relatively rare in written orders, were extremely alarming when specified: "If you fail to come [we] will take harsh action"; "If [you] fail, the elder will be tied up with rope"; "If [you] fail, [we] will send a bullet"; and "If you fail, we will send a bomb [i.e., a mortar or artillery shell]."[34] In other instances, no words were used. A small piece of charcoal enclosed with an order, for example, meant that troops intended to burn the village unless the demands were met.[35]

Regardless of whether or not a threat was embedded in the text, all orders shared the same formal bureaucratic features: an official stamp in the upper left-hand corner, details regarding the issuing authority, the date, and blank space on the bottom right for the officer's signature. The instructions appeared in the middle of the document, sometimes preceded by a subject heading. Instructions were not always clear, however, as some orders only stated the number of people that had to report to the Tatmadaw base or camp without specifying what they were needed for. The orders also frequently included the amount of food (e.g., rice, fruit, poultry, and livestock) to be "donated" to the troops and/or the "fees" the villagers had to pay—the purported "cost" of performing the forced labor itself among them.

Forced Labor Order

Stamp:	Date	Time
# xxx Infantry Battalion	13	1200
Shooting Support Platoon		

Chairperson

xxxx (xxxx)

Sir:

- [You] need to pay the Battalion donation money for 4/2000.
- Also remaining to pay [i.e., provide], 12 ducks and 15 chickens for the *Sa Ka Ka* [military operations command].
- The *loh ah pay* [forced laborers] must be in my camp [i.e., they must come now].
- [We] also have to discuss and coordinate other things.

Respectfully,
Your soldier,
[S.d.] xxxx
xxxxx Deputy Warrant Officer

xxxx

IB xxx
Xxxx [town][36]

Due to these common features, which I have reproduced from the report in verbatim form here, the orders exhibited a surprising degree of uniformity, both in terms of visual layout and the written content. The uniformity is notable given that hundreds of different unit commanders stationed throughout KNU-delineated Karen State, an area the size of Belgium, likely authored tens of thousands of orders following the regime's ban on forced labor.[37] (My "guestimate" is based on the sample number of orders KHRG's monitors gathered along with those that other fact-finding organizations reported they collected during these years.) KHRG has long maintained that the formal consistency of the orders over time and space provided indisputable material evidence of the Tatmadaw's routinization of forced labor in brown areas. But this consistency is indicative of something else as well: the existence of a shared conceptual understanding among Tatmadaw officers of what an "official" forced labor order should look like in terms of form and content. Interestingly, the standardized "template," possibly the result of officer training prior to deployment, was not limited to those officers. The

Democratic Karen Buddhist Army and the Karen Peace Army, two NSAGs that often served as proxies for the Tatmadaw, also replicated these features in their respective forced labor orders.[38]

The emulation of an administrative form by the NSAGs, while interesting, is difficult to assess in terms of its broader significance because the Tatmadaw's own orders served no clear bureaucratic end. Officers did not submit copies to their superiors to be filed away for official preservation in military archives. Instead, it was entirely up to the village leader to decide whether to retain or to dispose of the order once received, which is what makes KHRG's documentation efforts so historically important. KHRG's fact finders, with the assistance of the village leaders, collected what Tatmadaw officers clearly regarded as ephemera. The eventual result was a rare archival formation, one in which the officers, through their written orders, "spoke" for themselves, a genre of verbatim that is otherwise almost completely nonexistent in the voluminous documentation on human rights violations in Myanmar. The verbatim representation of their speech in textual form was far from straightforward, however.

KHRG's report writers, as part of their concerted effort to replicate the style and tone of each order, translated the Burmese text as directly as possible into English. But as is the case with all translation, this goal was impossible to fully achieve. The sentence structure (subject-object-verb) of the orders had to be reorganized throughout and care taken with the "helper" words (e.g., particles and prepositions), which are not present in English but are often essential to accurately conveying the nature of the relationships between specific words. These relationships were not always clear because the sentences in the orders were long and convoluted, and the personal subject and object pronouns were missing in the Burmese as well.[39] Furthermore, many Tatmadaw field officers were semiliterate, and the poor grammar necessitated heavier editorial interventions on KHRG's part for the purposes of intelligibility.

The reports, which KHRG acknowledged at the outset as having been edited in these ways, contained no visible traces of these changes in the text itself, beyond strings of letters (e.g., xxx) that indicate places where identifying information was redacted for the protection of the fact finders' sources. Translators' notes do leave recognizable traces, however. Indeed, a very significant percentage of the orders could not be fully understood without them, a fact that challenges the earlier claim that these documents constitute instances in which Tatmadaw officers "spoke" directly for themselves in written form.

Translators' notes, for example, unsettle the epistemological stability of verbatim in several ways by illustrating its constructed nature. First, the notes can provide the reason(s) behind the interpretive decision to translate a cultural concept from the original to the target language in a particular way. This type of note is fundamentally concerned with problems of fidelity to the original. But the need for such a note usually indicates that the semantic relationship between words is one of correspondence rather than equivalency. As a case in point, the military regime claimed for decades that "voluntary contributed labor" (*loh ah pay*) was synonymous with the Buddhist concept of "giving" (*dana*), an act done by a person of their own free will and out of the goodness of their own heart without an expectation of any immediate reward. The extensive documentation of forced labor in Myanmar proved this culturalist claim to equivalency to be false. Yet the phrase *loh ah pay* continued to appear in the written orders as if it were a secular form of *dana*. KHRG decided for this reason not to translate the Burmese phrase as "voluntary contributed labor," even though it is literally correct, to indicate that the terms were not commensurate in any way.

Second, translators' notes often add crucial contextual information, without which the significance of a word or a phrase would remain unknown to the reader. "Emergency servants" (ad hoc porters), "we will go to the village" (a threat indicating that the village may be burned or relocated if the forced labor is not performed), "ringworm" (pejorative name for the KNU/ KNLA), "messenger fees" (bribes to avoid forced labor), and "books be closed" (destroy the written order upon receipt) are a few common examples. Both types of notes produced meaning internal to the text—in this instance, the "hidden" significance of Tatmadaw terminology—that was not apparent in the "to the extent possible" verbatim English translation of the original Burmese. But translators' notes importantly produce meaning in a manner that is external to the text as well; their steady accumulation generates the appearance of ethnographic expertise with regard to the intricacies of forced labor in brown areas, which was critical to the construction of KHRG's credibility with international organizations, such as the ILO.

Orders in which the demands give the impression of being straightforward rarely receive translators' notes, however. The absence of such a note can be problematic. For example, KHRG's forced labor reports are organized in categorical terms, which means that each order is "filed" chronologically in terms of the genre it predominantly falls into (e.g., camp construction). When viewed from this perspective, each order functions as another evidentiary fact in that designated file, what an archivist would term a *fonds*.[40] The point of the separate "files" is to convince the reader that the Tatmadaw continued to use forced labor in functionally diverse ways on a widespread and systematic basis after the regime had officially banned the practice. But reading the "files" separately, something that the structure of the report encourages, unintentionally obscures the manifold ways in which one type of forced labor can beget other types of forced labor that are separately "filed" under different headings. When these cross-genre connections are taken into account, an individual order ceases to be an example of a discrete, stand-alone event (i.e., a specific act performed on a specific date). Instead, the order must be viewed as part of a sequence of physical and material exploitation that links different types of forced labor together over time.

Forced Labor Order

To: Date: 14-11-2002
Chairperson
Xxxx village

1. Send the *set tha* [messengers] to the [Army camp] on time.
2. [We are] not satisfied with the road [work] we ordered.
3. [You] must clear [the bushes] for fifty feet from the left/right sides of the road.
4. [You] must clear the branches of the bamboo and bushes that are hanging over the road.
5. The Chairperson yourself must supervise and carry it out.
6. Come to report to the camp when it is likely to be finished.
7. If the things listed above aren't completed [properly], they must be done again.
8. The previous *set tha* were already released on 11-11-02, you are informed.

Signature 14-11
Camp Commander
Xxxx Camp[41]

The ordinariness of this order, a task that routinely appeared in the "file" labeled "general forced labor," belies its broader cyclical import, whereby one task generates future tasks, further seizing the labor-time and labor-power of villagers in the process. For example, few roads in brown areas in south-eastern Myanmar are sealed, so soldiers force villagers to repair damaged sections of them each year using hand tools after the monsoon rains end, a task "filed" under "construction." The rains, in turn, contribute to the rapid growth of brush and vegetation alongside the road, which soldiers then require villagers to clear to the width of a dozen or more meters along both sides. The point of doing so is to make it much harder for NSAGs, like the KNLA, to ambush Tatmadaw conveys, plant land mines, and help people (e.g., IDPs, human rights fact finders, and humanitarian aid teams) cross the road surreptitiously. Villagers are often forced to build huts for this reason every couple of hundred meters along the road, staff them on a rotating twenty-four- or forty-eight-hour shift basis, and report on any of the aforementioned activities under threat of severe penalties, a task "filed" under "sentry duty."[42]

Slow violence, as the preceding interconnected, processual example makes clear, was "attritional" and "dispersed," meaning that it affected a wide range of villagers, including those who did not have to perform forced labor for one reason or another.[43] The continual seizure of people's labor, as well as their scarce material resources, thus produced extreme precarity over time. Slow violence was indirect in this sense, as it did not kill people out-right. However, the routinized system ensured that villagers could not easily obtain sufficient food to avoid chronic hunger and malnutrition, fulfill their ritual obligations, earn supplemental income, or devote energy to meaning-ful interactions with family and friends. In short, civilians regularly subject to forced labor found it nearly impossible to reproduce their daily lives.[44] "We [were] not free to work for ourselves," as one Karen farmer bluntly put it.[45] By contrast, portering, the most deeply feared form of forced labor, could be lethal due to fast violence. Fast violence in black areas was foresee-able, but impossible to predict, which required KHRG, in these reports as interpreted by me, to use different chains of replication to represent it.

FAST VIOLENCE

Richard Horsey, the ILO liaison officer during the UN agency's multiyear pressure campaign, claimed that the use of "military operations servants" (i.e., porters) to carry supplies and food rations in active conflict zones declined between 1989 and 1997. He attributed the decline to the nearly two dozen cease-fire agreements the Tatmadaw reached with NSAGs nation-wide over this period.[46] The regime later conceded to using civilians as por-ters to support military operations, a factual admission that appeared in the ILO's 1998 CoI report. But a spokesperson for the regime emphasized that "these porters were never required to accompany the troops in the actual scene of battle, nor exposed to danger . . . [and that] all these allegations about the [mis]treatment of porters by the armed forces are untrue. They mainly emanate from outside sources with ulterior political sources."[47] Again, Horsey's conjecture, which is based on a correlation of his own mak-ing, is likely correct. It is impossible, however, to assess the degree to which a decline occurred in quantitative terms due to the cease-fire agreements, as cross-border humanitarian organizations did not carry out the first major survey of IDPs, who would have been the best source for such information, until 2002.[48]

Regardless, the cease-fire agreements enabled the Tatmadaw to concen-trate its military operations in a progressively smaller number of black areas. The upland areas of KNU-delineated Karen State were key among these. Given the rugged terrain, low population densities, and an almost nonex-istent road system, convict porters became logistically central to the three large-scale offensives that occurred in these areas after the complete ban on forced labor (2003–2004, 2005–2008, and 2009–2011).[49] Convict porters, unlike civilians in black areas, who fled whenever soldiers approached, could be cheaply transported en masse by truck from prisons located around the country to forward staging areas, provided with heavy loads (thirty kilograms on average), and then forced to accompany military columns for weeks at a time—conclusions all based on common patterns that appeared in the escaped porters' separate testimonies.[50] Convict porters, again unlike local populations, were also unfamiliar with the region and could not speak Karen, two factors that made successful escapes even more difficult, the result being an exponentially smaller sample size than the written orders archive.

KHRG published three reports, one of them in collaboration with Human Rights Watch, on the Tatmadaw's use of convict porters in KNU-delineated Karen State during the 2005–2008 and 2009–2011 offensives.[51] The nearly fifty battalions that participated in the Northern Offensive uti-lized between three and five thousand convict porters according to KHRG estimates, which were based on extrapolations of escaped porter testimo-nies, head counts made by villagers in the affected areas, as well as figures compiled by other fact-finding groups, such as the Free Burma Rangers.[52] (The range does not take into account the possibility of double counting or the use of the same porters over time, however.) The 2009–2011 offensive represented a continuation of unfinished business. Tatmadaw battalions once again launched large-scale operations to extend control into the black areas that it had failed to turn into brown ones during the Northern Offensive. Tatmadaw battalions used approximately seventeen hundred convict porters to support this offensive, with the (guess-) estimate based again on these same assorted sources, as a systematic survey was not possible.[53] Based on semistructured interviews with nearly 150 escapees, the testimonies, which appear in excerpted form in the body of the report, detail strikingly similar stories of arrest, conviction, prison life, transport to conflict areas, types of human rights abuses witnessed as well as experienced, tales of escape, and the life options available afterward. When taken together, the KHRG reports provide a process-oriented account of convict porters as a specific category of dehumanized and readily disposable life.

Like the written orders reports, the interview excerpts were "filed" into separate moments that, when read together, formed a composite biography of the "typical" convict porter, a point made by me rather than explicitly by KHRG. The chains of replication in these three reports importantly differ from the chains that structured those of the written orders, however. In the case of the testimonies, Tatmadaw soldiers "spoke" through indirect speech, that is, via what the convict porters stated they said. "I climbed a mountain carrying twelve mortar shells and the soldiers threatened to kill me the whole time." "They said that if we ran away, they would shoot us." "The SPDC soldiers ordered porters to sweep the NCOs' [noncommissioned officers] and soldiers' sleeping places for land mines along the way."[54] Such reported speech, which appears again and again in the convict porters' accounts of their experiences during the two offensives documented, point to a complication connected with what I term verbatim-once-removed. Specifically, the epistemological stability of the stated facts hinges upon the report reader's belief that the porters' hearsay accounts are sufficiently "faithful reproduction[s] or reenactment[s]" of the soldiers' words when no record exists against which to verify whether this was indeed the case.[55]

In its final convict porter report, KHRG explicitly made the argument for why the reader should regard the hearsay evidence, normally not admissible in a court of law, as credible. The argument had five elements, which are reducible to two where the question of factual validity is concerned. First, KHRG researchers stated that they did not use a standard questionnaire. Thus, the cross-testimony similarities that emerged unprompted out of the interviews were not due to a predetermined set of questions, the NGO's researchers explained. KHRG attributed the similarities to the fact that the abuses documented were "not the product of isolated acts, but the actions of multiple individuals . . . operating independently of one another and in geographically distinct areas."[56] In other words, the reported acts, which routinely included beatings, torture, and extrajudicial executions, were widespread and systematic, an important criterion for KHRG's crimes against humanity and war crimes allegations. Second, the content of the testimonies as a whole was strikingly consistent with those KHRG and other human rights groups had gathered from escaped convict porters as far back as the early 1990s. According to KHRG, these two verifiable facts formed what can be called a human rights synecdoche, one in which the shared biography of the generic convict porter, despite being based on a small sample size, faithfully represented the experiences of individual convict porters as a whole. While the synecdoche appears straightforward at first glance, it becomes less so when more carefully examined. Land mines, a form of fast violence dreaded by soldiers and convict porters alike, are a case in point.

Land mines possess what Jane Bennett calls "thing-power." Man-made items, she argues, have the uncanny ability "to exceed their status as objects and to manifest traces of independence or aliveness."[57] Land mines no longer appear inert from this perspective; instead, they become nonhuman agents ("actants" in the language of science and technology studies) that can produce measurable effects in the world. These effects are not limited to the "dangerously vibrant matter" that land mines contain, namely blasting gelatin.[58] Land mines, although buried in the ground, actively contribute to the (re-) territorialization of who governs, how, and with what military, humanitarian, political, and economic goals in mind. The processes connected with (re-) territorialization during and after armed conflict reflect a paradox, however. None of the armed groups kept maps detailing where they had planted land mines. So although soldiers and civilians alike knew that land mines "existed" in black and brown areas, they generally did not know precisely where until the land mines ceased to exist, that is, exploded. Prior to this point, "sleeping soldiers," as land mines are sometimes called, only constituted potential threats. Land mines were thus an absent presence in the landscape; they were not there and there at the same time, which generated immense anxiety.[59] So much so that in 2007 a large-scale survey of one thousand households across southeastern Myanmar, including KNU-delineated Karen State, where the Northern Offensive was then taking place, found that 58 percent of IDPs in black areas identified land mines and military patrols as the biggest security threats they faced, while 43 percent of people in brown areas named forced portering and land mine sweeping as their primary fears.[60]

Tatmadaw units most commonly utilized either a copy of the US-made M-14 antipersonnel mines or the domestically produced MM-2, both of which have minimal metal content and can easily fit into the palm of one's hand. According to one military expert, "they placed them in areas used either partly or wholly by civilians," the intended purpose of which was to prevent displaced civilians from returning to their former villages in the hopes of salvaging any food and personal belongings that might have survived the preemptive clearance operations.[61] NSAGs, such as the KNLA, also relied heavily on land mines, primarily improvised explosive devices, but also claymores, as force multipliers during ambushes because they were "outmanned" and "outgunned" relative to the Tatmadaw.[62] The KNLA additionally planted land mines to slow Tatmadaw assaults to enable civilians to flee the area and to create temporary perimeters for humanitarian organizations to provide assistance to IDPs afterward. Land mine contamination is a problem in every township in KNU-delineated Karen State as a result, and it represents a significant obstacle to the many tens of thousands of refugees and IDPs who want to return "home" to rebuild their lives in postconflict areas.[63]

To reduce the risks they faced, Tatmadaw units often forced convict porters in black areas to walk in the front of the column as human minesweepers, according to the interviewees.[64] (The practice, also known as "atrocity demining," violates the principle of distinction between civilians and combatants and is both a crime against humanity and a war crime.)[65] KHRG report writers provided "proof" of this practice through what Ron Dudai, in his analysis of human rights reports, calls "stockpiling," which he defines as the steady accumulation of examples to construct a "truth" claim. Here, stockpiling is a form of indirect replication of oral statements through repetition rather than the verbatim reproduction of text that characterized the written order reports.[66] First-order stockpiling in the porter reports takes narrative form, and it relied upon a series of thematically linked quotes excerpted from the full testimonies to generate "objectivity" out of "subjectivity," as the following example indicates.

> Convict porter A: "They knew they were supposed to go in the front. But they ordered us to go first. They followed behind us. In their mind, if the mine explodes, the mine will hit us first. It won't hit them. They ordered us to go first with this objective."[67]

> Convict porter B: "The soldiers said, 'many of our soldiers are hit by mines. We will keep the porters at the front. If they don't go, we will shoot them in the back. We will shoot them if they don't go to front. We will order them to clear up the mines.' We were afraid of this, so we two discussed it and escaped."[68]

> Convict porter C: "Sometimes we had to sweep landmines with a kind of tool that has prongs. It is like a pitchfork. We used it to scrape the ground and found landmines. We did not know anything about landmines, but we had to scrape the ground and find landmines. We were very lucky that we were not killed by the landmines."[69]

> Convict porter D: "A corporal wanted to move forward, and he didn't dare step off the path, but he ordered the young guy [another convict porter] to move aside. After the young guy stepped on the mine, both of his legs were blown off."[70]

Credibility thus becomes a product of repetition, in this case: A + B + C + D . . . = "Fact." The result is a stand-alone minesweeping "file" outwardly amenable to comparative analysis across other reports.

By contrast, second-order stockpiling translated narrative accounts into two-dimensional forms such as tables, charts, and graphs, which represent lived experience in quantifiable terms. Fact finders do so to convert descriptive inferences into explanatory ones so as to identify correlations and, in some cases, to assert causality to support allegations of criminal responsibility. But a degree of quantitative indeterminacy always remains, and it raises questions here about the empirical status of the convict porter "facts" presented. For example, KHRG researchers utilized open-ended questions for the report "From Prison to Front Line: Analysis of Convict Porter Testimony 2009–2011" to enable the men to tell their own stories with a minimum of interviewer direction. But all methodological decisions have consequences. Or to put it another way, "numbers are only human."[71] This case was no different. Researchers explicitly asked only ten of the fifty-nine convict porters interviewed in this report about land mine–related incidents. However, a total of twenty-two provided information on injuries and deaths, meaning that twelve of the total number offered information voluntarily without a prompt. None of the remaining thirty-seven convict porters mentioned land mine incidents, a silence that raises questions about what KHRG described as the broader "data limitations and inferential challenges" of the qualitative survey.[72] For instance, the authors of the report used this uncertainty, the result of questions not posed, to suggest that incidents such as casualties and atrocity demining could be more widespread than the reported numbers indicate. But the opposite could also be true, and this uncertainty over the difference between the countable facts (known knowns) and the uncountable "facts" (known unknowns) highlights that who counts what and how it gets counted are not only technical questions, but political ones as well.[73]

The ILO's High-Level Team again visited the country in February 2011, as the Tatmadaw's final large-scale offensive in KNU-delineated Karen State was still taking place. During the visit, the ILO team members raised the topic of the Tatmadaw's ongoing use of convict porters in conflict zones. The High-Level Team, in its post-visit report, stated in a very understated way that the practice was "unacceptable" and should be promptly "discontinued."[74] A representative of the Corrections Department responded in equally diplomatic terms. He replied that the "review of the 1894 Jail Manual, which regulates the use of prison labor, was seventy-five percent complete and on completion would be submitted to the Parliament for adoption. He [further] indicated that the amendment would be in line with international standards and, as such, would meet ILO concerns."[75] The response, which again emphasized the law as the solution to a problem not reducible to it, is consistent with the strategy successive military regimes had long used with the ILO: issue a pledge that once the relevant laws and policies are amended, the prohibited practice(s) will automatically cease, and all subsequent violations will be investigated and punished—which in practice was very slowly implemented (if at all).

Not surprisingly, investigations regarding the use of convict porters did not take place, and perpetrators never faced consequences for their actions. But the number of reported cases of the military forcing people (civilians as well as convicts) to porter supplies did drop rapidly following the 2012 ceasefire with the KNU/KNLA, according to KHRG and other fact-finding organizations. The practice "is mostly finished, but not entirely," the ILO liaison officer who succeeded Richard Horsey told me in 2014. "It makes sense," he explained, "in places where there are ceasefires, the need for forced labor is not there. That is not the case where there are no ceasefires, such as

Kachin State, northern Shan State, and northern Rakhine State. Simply, human rights abuses go with conflict."[76]

CONCLUSION

Many archivists, particularly those who work with electronic records, explains Terry Cook, recognize that "reality is often logical and functional, not physical."[77] When this distinction is taken into account, the traditional archival preoccupation with *respect des fonds* loses its fundamental importance. The principle holds that ordering groups of records by creatorship generates authenticity because doing so demonstrates a direct relationship between the records within a "file" as they accumulate over time and in specific contexts. *Respect des fonds* is not possible in the case of KHRG's archive, however. Neither the written orders nor the oral commands had one single identifiable creator. Instead, there were thousands. But when viewed together, the forced labor reports constitute an organic "conceptual whole" due to the logical and functional similarities that existed across the sources; hence my decision to treat them as a single archive rather than a series of separate collections.[78]

Logical and functional similarities are not legally sufficient, however. The written orders, although reproduced to the extent possible in verbatim form, were incomplete in terms of evidence. The documents clearly revealed proof of perpetrator intent: the numbers and types of people required, items demanded, timelines imposed, and punishments forewarned. But the orders did not reveal—except by inference—the cumulative *effects* of forced labor. To understand these effects, the thematic "files" (*fonds* in archival terms), I argue, must be read in conjunction with victim testimonies reproduced in other KHRG reports to grasp the quotidian dynamics of forced labor as a mode of militarized governance in brown areas. In other words, the reader needs to put both types of reports into conversation with one another to understand how the two parts form a whole. By contrast, the convict porter reports relied exclusively on victim testimonies. The oral "files" thus lack the official written documentation that would help confirm the veracity of the hearsay statements (verbatim-once-removed) the convict porters provided to KHRG. Again, sufficient consistencies in the testimonies exist to support KHRG's claims that the practice reflected official policy rather than a conspiracy involving a limited number of civilian and military officials who participated in the convict porter "supply chain." But the overarching legal question of whether or not the criminal liability of the perpetrators of the alleged abuses and killings that the convict porters reported can be extended to include the soldiers' superiors remains less clear.[79]

The differential use of forced labor in brown and black areas also highlights the difference between slow violence and fast violence. Everyday forms of forced labor in brown areas, as illustrated by the content of the written orders, were slow because they gradually eroded the ability of ordinary people to exercise agency.[80] "The abuse [forced labor] lacks the sensational ring of rape, torture, and mass killings yet the implications on the lives of tens of millions of people across Myanmar are nonetheless atrocious," KHRG researchers explained.[81] The practice does so because it "undermines the livelihoods of whole communities, leading to complete collapses of village economies; creates large-scale displacement and refugee flows; and functions to support the structures of military power," to quote one KHRG report.[82] By contrast, portering in black areas, which constitutes a complete rather than temporary seizure of labor-time, produced fast violence. Carrying immensely heavy loads over rugged terrain for hours on end with little rest, food, or water could irrevocably damage one's health in only a matter of days, and summary execution frequently awaited convict porters who were no longer able to carry the supplies due to either exhaustion or injury. Becoming a casualty as a result of a KNLA ambush was a real possibility as well. But it was the presence of land mines that was arguably the most terrifying to soldiers and porters alike, as permanent injury or death was always only one misstep away.

The "epistemological stability" of KHRG's facts regarding forced labor in southeastern Myanmar remains an open question, however. To return to the epigraph that appears at the start of the chapter, we might begin by asking "What kinds of social, technological/technical, and ideological processes are necessary to turn a particular text, whether spoken or written, into a credible or otherwise weighty copy of another text?"[83] I have emphasized verbatim, both as a process and as a reification of it, as one answer to this question. Verbatim is never truly verbatim, however. Further meaning is always added and/or subtracted because verbatim is, in fact, a form of translation.

Traditionally, Ben Van Wyke writes, "ethical translators, in their quest to be faithful, have been expected to respect the hierarchy that places them under the authority of the author and to remain invisible, repressing any authorial desire that may produce visible signs of their interventions in the texts of others."[84] Human rights report writers, generally speaking, also aspire to maintain invisibility where data presentation is concerned, as the validity of their "truth" claims is judged on the degree to which the performance of methodological rigor, analytical objectivity, and evidence-driven conclusions are convincing. (The recommendations section is the obvious exception, for the simple reason that advocacy requires two highly visible interventions: first, the translation of the data into key findings; and second, the translation of these findings into the concrete actions different actors are urged to take to prevent further violations.) But the chains of replication that shape the "facts" in all of KHRG's written and oral forced labor reports illustrate why the verbatim presentation of the data in stockpiled form is not a simple act of ethical translation. The reorganization of the field data into thematically distinct "files," an editorial decision intended to convey continuities and similarities in the organization and use of forced labor across time and space, is one visible sign of an intervention. The translators' notes in the orders reports offer an even more obvious example of intervention. Designed to provide necessary interpretive context, the notes not only clarified elements of what the orders signified; they also generated additional "factual" meaning beyond it—specifically, proof of KHRG's ethnographic expertise, which was critical to the construction of the NGO's credibility with its target audiences, the ILO among them. As both interventions demonstrate, fidelity to the original, long the cornerstone of ethical translation, is not sufficient on its own. Human rights "data," in other words, cannot "speak" for themselves. They must always be re-presented and thus "spoken" for, a discussion I continue in the next chapter on famine crimes.

Starving Bodies

Visual Economies of Enumeration

Authoritative
1. Arising or originating from a figure of authority.
2. Highly accurate or definitive; treated or worthy of treatment as a scholarly authority.
3. Having a commanding style.

Synonyms
+ Definitive, precise, proper.
+ Of record.

—Wiktionary

Precisely where modern humanitarianism's core principles of neutrality, impartiality, and independence give way to something that becomes the opposite is not always clear or agreed upon. Médecins Sans Frontières (MSF; Doctors Without Borders), which was awarded a Nobel Prize in 1999, is the most commonly cited example of a humanitarian organization that often works in this grey zone. The Paris-based NGO insists on "bearing witness" (*témoignage*) to suffering on the grounds that the "principles of impartiality and neutrality are not synonymous with silence," a position it proudly states on its website. MSF came under significant criticism for its principled stance on this issue, which is sharply at odds with the official silence many humanitarian organizations, most notably the International Committee of the Red Cross, maintain to better ensure continued access to IDPs in politically hostile environments.

The problem is not unique to MSF, which eventually tempered its position on "bearing witness," which was arguably advocacy by another name.[1] All humanitarian organizations, if they are honest with themselves, struggle with the question of when the "apolitical" shades into the "political" and what, if anything, should be done when this occurs. The humanitarian organizations featured in this chapter did not engage in MSF-style advocacy as part of their cross-border aid delivery to IDPs in conflict-affected areas across southeastern Myanmar. However, the forms of documentation produced, which culminated in jointly researched annual IDP reports, did include recommendations that became more specific over time as well as increasingly couched in the language of international human rights and humanitarian law. These recommendations, the inclusion of which are now a regular part of the IDP report genre in general, are themselves an example of the a/political bind in which humanitarian organizations must operate. On the one hand, the delivery of humanitarian aid in politically hostile environments requires a degree of adherence to the principle of neutrality to maintain access to IDPs. But on the other hand, the denial of access may prompt organizations to transgress this same principle—cross-border aid without government permission violates the international legal principle of state sovereignty, for example—in the broader name of humanity. The dilemma then becomes how to determine whose lives are to be "saved" and whose lives are to be "risked" by respecting and/or violating international law and humanitarian principles.[2]

I presented a paper that touched upon this issue at a conference on Myanmar in Singapore in 2006, as cross-border aid in the country's conflict-affected areas required both determinations. Trevor Wilson, the former Australian ambassador to that country, was in the audience. Wilson spoke with me afterward about the practices cross-border humanitarian organizations used to enumerate IDPs in southeastern Myanmar and to calculate their relief needs. Wilson phrased his questions in a diplomatic but nevertheless skeptical tone. He questioned the rigor of the methods these organizations used to determine both numbers. Wilson further questioned the credibility of the groups' statistics, pointing out that cross-border humanitarian groups commonly had to rely on NSAGs for intelligence on Tatmadaw troop movements and, not infrequently, for armed escorts to gain face-to-face access to IDPs in active conflict areas. (NSAG soldiers would typically establish a

security perimeter for the duration of the aid distribution in such situations.)
Such practices, he pointed out, were deeply problematic from the perspective
of humanitarianism's core values. Inflated IDP numbers, Wilson continued,
also provided a way for these organizations to potentially obtain additional
funding beyond what was actually needed.

Wilson's first question was a methodological one. The second question
was a political one. Answers to both questions require engagement with a
point that Bridget Conley stresses when writing about human rights narratives more generally. "The ability to produce numbers," she emphasizes,
"is not the same as the ability to produce *authoritative* numbers."[3] Conley's
point is an important one, but there is another underlying issue that requires
consideration in tandem with it. With that in mind, I repurpose a question from Amit Pinchevski, who studies media representations of trauma.
"Who possesses," he asks, "the authority to archive as well as the authority
to determine what is archivable and classify it accordingly?"[4] Relations of
power, in other words, cannot be separated from claims to authority or
challenges to it. In this chapter, I take up these closely related concerns
through an examination of the calculative practices that shape the contours
of what does and does not count as authoritative "facts" with regard to IDPs
in southeastern Myanmar.

To be authoritative means to be trusted as a consequence of being reliably accurate or honest. However, being accurate and honest, with regard to
displaced persons, is a moving target in conflict-affected areas. Some people
remain in fixed locations in remote areas for lengthy periods of time, sometimes years (e.g., Ei Htu Hta IDP Camp). Other people experience multiple
displacements over the course of a year due to reoccurring military patrols.
Two to three times per annum is not unusual in black areas, for example.[5]
(As one Karen IDP painfully put it, "My life was always running, running,
running, running.")[6] Still other people, temporarily displaced but no longer
internally so, cross the border and disappear into Thailand's refugee camps
or informal economy. The differing degrees of mobility thus pose challenges
for good-faith enumerators. Do IDPs who remain in place for extended
periods of time still qualify as IDPs, and if so, when do they cease to be
displaced? Should IDPs who experience multiple displacements within a
twelve-month period be counted more than once? And to what extent can
survey data be assumed to accurately apply to other IDP populations that
researchers cannot directly ask? There are no widely agreed upon answers

to these questions, which are ontological and epistemological, in addition to methodological, in nature.

The concept of "textual economies," as defined by Bruce Curtis, a historian of science and technology, provides one means to understand the seeming fungibility of facts and "facts," which has a bearing on determinations of authoritativeness of quantitative representations of IDPs to different audiences. According to Curtis, textual economies link "the ways in which the presentation of information and the creation of knowledge result from ordered relations among devices such as images, tables, charts, graphs, or photographs, [with] descriptive or explanatory text."[7] To understand these linkages, and the way they shape what it requires to be seen as "authoritative," I focus on the role numbers play in fixing and unfixing meaning within these ordered relations. The articulated, private-public archive featured, the contents of which claim to document the Tatmadaw's widespread and systematic seizure and destruction of food supplies as a weapon of war against civilians, consists of two parts. The first part, based on confidential field reports prepared by two Karen cross-border organizations, is made up of number-dominated reconstructions: military operations summaries, lists of material losses, and tabulated IDP head counts. The second part, a decade of annually published IDP reports prepared by the organizations' international consortium partner, not only incorporates elements of these statistical reconstructions, it also elaborates extensively upon them with visual ones, adding layers of meaning in the process. The two parts of the articulated archive, when put into conversation with one another, highlight how different enumerative processes both contribute to and undermine "authoritative" knowledge about IDPs in KNU-delineated Karen State.

FAMINE CRIMES

International law criminalizes some types of government action that "creates or abets famine."[8] Such "faminogenic" action, as legal scholar David Marcus refers to it, can take a range of forms beyond official incompetence, corruption, and/or indifference. The most serious form, he argues, involves clear intent (*mens rea*) that, if "provable" in a court of law, may qualify as a mass atrocity crime under the Rome Statute, provided several other conditions are also met.[9] When a government "deliberately use[s] hunger as a tool of extermination," that is intent, "first-degree faminogenic action exists," he explains. By contrast, in a difference of degree, a government that implements policies that either give rise to or perpetuate starvation and "recklessly" continues to do so without regard to the human costs, is guilty of faminogenic action in the "second-degree."[10] Marcus's proposed framework is helpful conceptually. The concept of "famine crimes" is not formally codified in international law at present, however, and thus remains a proposal, though one not without some supporting precedent. Several human rights instruments guarantee a right to minimal food security. Article 25 of the Universal Declaration of Human Rights is one example. Article 11 of the International Covenant on Economic, Social, and Cultural Rights is another. But these and other documents do not define this right in precise and commensurate ways, which has left numerous issues unaddressed.

Another legal scholar, Daniel Butler, has called for a specific famine crimes amendment to the Rome Statute. Such an amendment, he argues, will address what human rights and humanitarian groups often refer to as an "accountability gap," business management speak for the disparity between what aid and rights advocates want international actors to do and what they are actually doing.[11] (In 2018, Switzerland proposed such an amendment on the "inclusion of starvation as a war crime in non-international armed conflicts into the Rome Statute," a move prompted by the weaponization of food, particularly in Syria and Yemen. Action on this issue remains stalled, however.)[12] International humanitarian law, especially the Geneva Conventions, thus remains today the primary reference point on this issue. The Conventions call on State parties to take meaningful steps to ensure that "persons or groups either not or no longer taking part in hostilities are not denied food or access to it," an International Committee of the Red Cross expert explains, but without noting that these documents have no enforcement provisions.[13] Importantly here, this protection principle embedded within the relevant conventions encompasses not only civilians themselves. The principle also extends to all of their "objects, which are not military objectives, [but also] include foodstuffs, agricultural areas for the production of foodstuffs, crops, livestock, drinking water installations and supplies and irrigation works."[14]

The documentation related to alleged famine crimes in Myanmar, presented later in this chapter and as found in the meta-archive on rights issues in Myanmar, makes it clear that the Tatmadaw was not intent upon the biological extermination of a group through "first-degree" faminogenic action (i.e., genocide). Instead, the widespread and systematic theft and destruction of the civilian food "objects" was "second-degree" in nature, using Marcus's definition. As explained, the strategic objective of the Four Cuts was to ensure that the IDPs were no longer able to provide any food support to NSAGs and, over time, force their leadership into cease-fire agreements with the Tatmadaw. Consequently, the Tatmadaw's tactical efforts focused on ways to starve nonmajority ethnic populations in conflict-affected areas, not to death, but to that the point that they were forced into either areas under Tatmadaw control or Thailand.

The famine crimes, which reportedly became more widespread and systematic starting in the early 1990s, prompted the creation of numerous cross-border humanitarian organizations, almost all of them exclusively structured along ethnic lines, to provide emergency assistance to the hundreds of thousands of IDPs believed to be displaced due to armed conflict in southeastern Myanmar. By late 2004 there was broad agreement that food insecurity in these areas had become severe—a conclusion that was based on several cross-border surveys carried out by researchers with medical training. One survey of 227 households in black areas claimed to have found that 19 percent of the IDPs had been able to eat two full meals per day for only three months during the previous twelve—meaning that they subsisted on one meal per day for a full nine months. Another 34 percent, in somewhat less dire circumstances, stated that they only consumed two full meals per day between four to seven months over the same twelve-month period.[15] Yet another large-scale health survey, also conducted in 2004, indicated that the overall health status of IDPs in black areas was consistent with those reported in war-torn Sierra Leone and the Democratic Republic of Congo.[16] In other words, if these statistics are in fact representative of IDPs in black areas across southeastern Myanmar at the time, the Karen civilians most affected by the Northern Offensive, which began at the end of the following year, were the least equipped to sustain themselves in the face of the second-degree famine crimes to come. The remainder of this chapter examines how two enumerative practices reconstructed alleged famine crimes in KNU-delineated Karen State and the representational effects of these practices on NGO claims to "authoritativeness."

RECONSTRUCTIONS

Two Tatmadaw offensives led to the establishment of the Karen organizations that would make the articulated (i.e., private-public) IDP archive possible. The 1992 offensive, which began in January and ended in May, stretched from Hpapun District in the north down to Pa'an District in the south. (The crescent-shaped attack targeted KNU/KNLA headquarters in Manerplaw, a military objective Tatmadaw units would not successfully seize until February 1995, with the help of DKBA troops who had previously defected from the KNLA.) The offensive, according to one chronology of the preemptive violence, displaced an estimated seventy thousand Karen, many thousands of whom crossed the border and entered the refugee camps in Thailand, where the head counts were more precise.[17] In 1993 the Karen Organization for Relief and Development (KORD), an independent humanitarian group, formed to provide relief to these IDPs, which it continues to do to this day. Another dry season offensive, larger than the one in 1992, occurred in 1997 after KNU/KNLA "hard-liners" rejected a Tatmadaw cease-fire proposal, the terms of which they deemed to be unsatisfactory. Military operations, according to this same chronology, reportedly involved more than ten thousand Tatmadaw troops, resulted in the destruction of nearly two hundred villages, displaced an estimated forty-six thousand people, and prompted sixteen thousand more, primarily women and children, to cross the border into Thailand seeking refuge in the camps.[18] The KNU established the Committee for Internally Displaced Karen People (CIDKP), its relief arm, the following year.[19] Like KORD, CIDKP continues to provide assistance to IDPs, as well as to support small-scale development initiatives.

Regardless of the accuracy of these reported figures, which later IDP surveys suggest are not outside the norm, the general pattern of violence was the same. Tatmadaw units timed their preemptive operations to interrupt key moments in the agricultural cycle, which made cross-border organizations, such as KORD and CIDKP, all the more essential to the survival of IDPs. Farmers normally planted upland fields between May and June and harvested their crops between October and November. Routine search-and-destroy patrols, like the larger dry season offensives, targeted food supplies during these two critical periods, seizing what they could consume and destroying what they could not, including emergency food caches in the surrounding forest. (Karen households located in conflict-affected zones typically maintained two to three such stockpiles in various locations.)[20] The stockpiles, if they went undiscovered, enabled IDPs in hiding areas to survive on a thin rice porridge mixed with bamboo shoots, yams, and roots for weeks, sometimes even months at a time. The primary task of KORD and CIDKP was thus to locate IDPs in hiding areas and then provide emergency relief to the extent their organizational resources permitted.

Following the 1997 offensive, when the Tatmadaw gained control of a number of strategic border areas, it had become apparent that the number of IDPs was many times greater than the approximately 100,000 refugees at the time living in the camps in Thailand. The TBBC, the primary service provider to the refugee camps, took steps to collect more authoritative data on the situation in 1998.[21] TBBC's initial desktop study, which relied on differing data sources provided to its researchers from various human rights and humanitarian organizations, estimated that there were perhaps as many as 700,000 IDPs in southeastern Myanmar. But "the information TBBC was collecting was fragmented and coming from sources which others might consider to be biased or self-interested," notes Jack Dunford, the former executive director of the organization.[22] The TBBC leadership group decided to address this concern head-on by working in concerted fashion with a select few cross-border humanitarian organizations, KORD and CIDKP among them. The still largely ad hoc nature of IDP data collection changed significantly in 2002, when TBBC launched the first-ever coordinated effort to verify the scale and severity of conflict-induced displacement across the entire southeastern region.

As part of this effort, TBBC created the first emergency rations assistance (ERA) template in 2003, which it later revised in 2006. The template formalized the reporting structure for the field data the cross-border teams needed to collect at three different moments in the aid delivery cycle: the ERA request, an ERA distribution summary, and, sometimes, an ERA impact assessment, which did not become common until 2008. The ERA documents always included local maps, initially hand-drawn and later computer-generated, which detailed the location of affected villages and often other logistical information, such as the travel routes taken by the aid teams. Less frequently, the ERA materials contained supporting information, such as letters of recommendation from local administrative and/or military officials, thumbprint-signed registries of the IDPs who received cash aid, photographs of the aid distribution, and so on. As a result, the length of the three ERA documents when added together varied depending on the degree of detail. Some cross-border partners, especially Karen ones, provided extensive documentation; others not. But most of the *fonds* totaled between twenty and thirty pages each.

The templates' functional purpose was to simplify situational complexity and standardize the information TBBC required to determine at a distance (i.e., its offices in Thailand) whether or not to approve the ERA requests from its cross-border partners. The templates, in other words, generated a specific bureaucratic process.[23] Approval, despite the claims of some critics, was not a foregone conclusion, however, even during the Northern Offensive. In all cases, TBBC's decision to approve an ERA request rested upon the cross-border partner's ability to persuade, using a combination of quantitative and qualitative reconstructed after-the-fact "facts," to convince the consortium of the nature of the losses and the resulting scale of IDP need. As a consequence, the most common cause of a TBBC rejection was insufficiently authoritative documentation, which was the case with the following request, submitted during the middle of the Northern Offensive:

> TBBC Comments:
> + Recommend rejection. List is based on losses CIDKP compiled between November-December 2007 [and are now out of date], but they are not sufficient for ERA.
> + Unclear how the information was collected or whether it was verified.
> + Unclear whether the people killed, wounded, or arrested come from the villagers targeted for ERA. Only 1 of the other 7 incidents included in the request occurred in the villages assessed.
> + The ERA request targets that same village tract as KORD 2008-09, though the villages are different. CIDKP and KORD should coordinate better to produce 1 good request rather than 2 weak one[s].
> + There is no mention as to whether the villages have received ERA in the past.[24]

The material aid, if approved, took cash form due to the rugged terrain, distances traveled, and security risks the relief teams faced due to roving Tatmadaw patrols. The portability of cash—tied up in large bundles, wrapped in waterproof tarps, and then carried by volunteer porters directly to the IDPs—also meant that the relief teams could provide several thousand IDPs at a time with sufficient funds for each of them to purchase a three-month supply of paddy (unhusked) rice at local prices. Not surprisingly, many of TBBC's donors were understandably skeptical of the plan to distribute cash directly to IDPs and concerned about the ancillary involvement of NSAGs, whose soldiers often acted as guides and provided a degree of security for the aid teams. But as one British aid agency official later put it, "Cross-border aid may not be considered a neutral form of assistance and it is highly dangerous. However, it is the only way to reach IDPs in several of Burma's conflict-affected states, and we believe that it can provide a cost-efficient and flexible way of delivering emergency relief where no other options exist."[25]

The ERA requests, although "image poor" in terms of visuals, did not rely solely on textual narratives. Numbers, which visually depicted meaning in a different manner, featured prominently. "The invocation of mathematical processes and language in texts that may have nothing to do directly with mathematics" are "gestural" in nature, according to historian Mary Poovey, by which she means that they often instead served metaphorical or rhetorical purposes.[26] The same argument also applies to the gestural nature of the numbers that appear in the ERA reports: day-by-day "diaries" on the Tatmadaw's military operations, food-related losses, IDP demographics, funds requested, and so on. These numbers, while not connected to other visual elements (e.g., diagrams, images, charts, or graphs, which dominate TBBC's annual IDP survey reports, discussed later), nonetheless produced an aesthetic of their own. In this case, the aesthetic consisted of arithmetic rather than visual representations of state violence in its material and embodied forms.

During the Northern Offensive, KORD and CIDKP humanitarian missions generated more than sixty ERA *fonds*, all of which were stored in hard-copy form in file cabinets in TBBC's northern Thailand office. The following verbatim ERA request, edited by me for purposes of clarity and length, highlights the impacts of military operations on the inhabitants of three villages over a two-week period. It also serves as an example of these representational aesthetics in arithmetic form:

KORD-2008-12
Emergency Rations Assessment Request Summary
14 July 2008

Demographics:
1,302 people (254 households) from 3 villages (That Kot To Baw, Tha Dah Der, and Tay Mu Der) in the northern part of Hpapun Township, Karen State.

KNU [administrative designations]: Tay Mu Der Village Tract, Lu Thaw Township, Hpapun District.

Affected villages south of Kyaukgyi—Saw Hta Road, near the KNLA's 5th Brigade Headquarters [east of the Yunzalin River and northwest of the Kho Lo Klo River].

Rationale:
+ 4 June 2008 LIB-240 and LIB-567, from Southern Command headquarters, fired mortars and guns into settlements and laid land mines in and around the 3 affected villages. Tay Mu Der Village was the primary focus according to the report.

+ Total losses reported: 50 houses destroyed, 70 hillside farms damaged, 90 paddy barns (with an estimated 6,380 baskets of paddy) damaged, and 1.4 million kyat abandoned when villagers fled.[27]
+ 10 June SPDC and KNLA firefight occurred.

Funds Requested:
Exchange rate: 100 Burmese kyat = 3.20 Thai baht.

1,302 people X 12,000 kyat/tin X 3 months = 46,872,000 kyat (1,499,90 baht) + monitoring costs (15,070 baht) = 1,516,000 baht total.

TBBC Comments:
+ Good human rights details and needs assessment.
+ ERA last provided to these villages in KORD-2006-07 (August 2006).
+ Due to the proximity to KNLA Brigade headquarters, KORD will need to be very careful to ensure that the IDPs are the recipients of the aid and that soldiers are not associated with the public meeting or distribution.
+ The conflict impact assessment needs to be stronger.

ERA Request
Assessment Team:
Saw [Name redacted] (District KORD staff), Saw [Name redacted] (District KORD field staff), and Naw [Name redacted] (Lu Thaw Township KORD field staff). Saw [Name redacted] coordinated the effort with the Tay Mu Der Village Tract headman.

Situation Analysis:
People are shot on sight as the area is regarded as the black area by the SPDC and also known as a free-fire zone. Whenever the SPDC come in, people have to run away to escape from torture or killing.[28]

During the 1997 Scorched Earth campaigns, road construction (Kyaukgyi—Saw Hta) bisected many of their cultivation sites, which [forced] villagers to move farther south, reducing the amount of arable land available.

During 2002–2003 cease-fire talks between the SPDC and the KNU gave the villagers greater "confidence" to cultivate plots near the road.

During the 2006 [Northern] offensive, people fled again.

Topography:
Remote highland area. People are largely dependent on shifting paddy cultivation [swidden]. Some people have access to lowland irrigated fields and/or work as traders. Betel nut and leaf gardens provide some people with cash income.

Recent Causes of Vulnerability:
3 June LIB-240 and LIB-567 (under Southern Command) departed Maw Tha Soe and entered the area near Thay Mu Der Village. Troops fired mortars

and guns into the area, and villagers left, unable to carry anything with them. Many family members were separated from one another. Heavy rain and possible SPDC patrols made it impossible to light small fires to stay warm.

4 June These battalions entered the village and killed/ate many animals (pigs, chickens, ducks, and goats). The troops also destroyed everything they found in the houses (pots, plates, spoons, baskets, and dumped paddy/rice on the ground.) They also destroyed the walls/roofs of all the homes, and then laid landmines. The troops then traveled to the "work sites" used by That Kot To Baw, Tha Dah Der, and Tay Mu Der Villagers. Troops found and destroyed food caches, destroyed the barns and huts, etc., as well as the infrastructure for irrigated fields. The rain destroyed the paddy/rice the troops dumped on the ground.

10 June SPDC troops engaged in a firefight with KNLA soldiers at 6:00 a.m. at a place called Thoo Ko Khee, halfway between Tay Mu Der and Tha Dah Der Villages. SPDC troops continued to fire mortars and guns into the surrounding area after the engagement ended.

11 June The battalions divided themselves into two groups. LIB-567 carried out patrols in Tay Mu Der and Tha Dah Der work sites, while LIB-240 moved to That Koy Yo Baw. The troops did not follow the paths, but bushwhacked, destroying seedlings and fences en route, as well as all the plots, and paddy/rice found while traveling there and back, laying land mines along the way [duration 1 week].

14 June Both battalions returned to outpost in Maw Tha Soe.

17 June Local KNLA soldiers cleared some of the land mines, enabling some IDPs to return to some of their hiding huts/barns [to retrieve food]. Operations coincided with weeding hillside plots and irrigating lowland ones. Saw [Name redacted], a Tha Day Der villager, said, "I don't know what to do, all my food supplies and plants were destroyed. It is really difficult for me. If I keep staying here, me and my children will go to hungry for more than next two months. Therefore, if I go to the refugee camp, it may be the best." Another person, Saw [Name redacted], a Yae Mu Plaw Villager who fled and stayed in That Kot To Baw Village, said, "When living in our own village, the SPDC came and destroyed our places and food, again here the SPDC came and destroyed, we are only have to face with poverty, so if we suicide ourselves [it] will be the best."

Total documented losses: 1,400,500 kyat; 1,283 baskets of pounded rice; 14 viss of tobacco; 103 pots; 100 chickens; 98 shirts; 98 machetes; 1,080 baskets of paddy; 90 weeding machetes; 3 gallons of pesticide; 15 single hand saws; 81 plough hoes; 30 flasks; 9 wide plastic sheets; 49 paddy threading mats; 90 plough handles; 90 ducks; 51 goats; 90 paddy barns (with 6,381 baskets of paddy); 9 wall clocks; 39 hoes; 72 pigs; 11 viss of chili; 91 weaving bags; 10 6 volt batteries; 35 basins; 113 spoons; 5 fishing nets; 108 women's longyis; 11 tins of cooking oil; 145 blankets; 9 viss of sugar; 72 viss of salt; 39 touch lights; 101 men's longyis; 59 sickles; 4 dozen notebooks; 15 textbooks; 10 packets of chalk; and 7 dozen ballpoint pens lost/destroyed. 9 buffaloes stepped on land mines, roofs

TABLE I VILLAGES AND IDPS AFFECTED BY TATMADAW VIOLENCE
(LU THAW TOWNSHIP, MU TRAW DISTRICT)

Number	Village Tract	Village	Number of Households	Number of Females > 5 Years	Number of Males > 5 Years	Number of Females < 5 Years	Number of Males < 5 Years	Total
1	Tay Mu Der	Tay Mu Der	64	216	206	84	60	566
2	Tay Mu Der	Tha Dah Der	61	185	211	77	50	523
3	Tay Mu Der	That Kot To Baw	25	73	75	22	43	213
			150	474	492	183	153	1,302

removed/destroyed on 93 paddy huts and 50 homes. Troops and animals destroyed 300 baskets of paddy seed from 70 hillside fields and 79 pieces of seedling in 450 baskets of paddy seed.[29]

Other:
Other villagers, especially from Yeh Mu Plaw Village Tract have relied upon food from the affected area [when their food security is threatened] for years. SPDC patrols no longer make this possible and have reduced the amount of arable land available for cultivation.

IDP Current Living Conditions:
IDPs are returning to their former villages, but do not dare to travel to their hiding huts, fearing land mines. They did, however, find some barns intact and with paddy still in them, enough for an estimated 2-month supply maximum. Some people have been able to borrow rice from contacts in Hpapun Town when local KNLA authorities are able to provide some protection for meeting outside of it.

They are weeding crops that escaped destruction and cultivating seedlings in some irrigated lands.

They are trying to reconstruct their homes in the rain. The area is very cool, blankets destroyed, and cough/cold/fever are widespread.

Relief Plan:
Team will consist of an estimated 13 members, including KORD staff, security men [KNLA soldiers], and porters. ERA distribution will take place near Tha Dah Der Village, where IDPs from 3 affected ones can meet. The trip will take approximately 25 days to complete.[30]

The actual aid distribution, carried out in August, involved seventeen people connected with KORD, five KNLA soldiers, and five villagers who voluntarily agreed to serve as porters. According to the ERA distribution summary, the route taken did not require the team to cross any roads, which Tatmadaw units closely guard and are littered with land mines on both sides, or to pass by any frontline areas. As a result, no security issues delayed travel, which took twenty-four days to complete round trip. The aid distribution process unfolded according to plan as well, the KORD distribution manager reported. The KORD staff gathered information on the current situation, created the IDP profile, and obtained a thumbprint "signature" from everyone after they received their cash disbursement, a copy of which was included with the summary.[31] Fortunately, the villagers did not experience any further abuses following their initial displacement, according to KORD, which was not always the case for IDPs in areas Tatmadaw units targeted during the Northern Offensive. However, the report noted, three Tatmadaw outposts were now located only a two-hour walk from the area where the IDPs were currently hiding. They lacked an early warning system, such as village lookouts or (much more rarely) walkie-talkies with which to communicate with KNLA patrols, the ERA monitor explained. In the absence of such a system, he continued, the IDPs could not bring anything with them, but especially food, whenever patrols approached.[32]

What are we to make of the cascade of numbers in the ERA request? To begin with, the numbers are "gestural" in the sense that they rhetorically serve to demonstrate the KORD team's commitment to having exhaustively documented the losses by personally interviewing the village leaders and the heads of the IDP households. To a significant degree, the credibility of the assessment from TBBC's perspective depends on the performance of such commitment. But KORD's gestural claim, while not to suggest it is without empirical basis, rests upon a series of "factual" reconstructions of the field data that are not made explicit in the text of the request. For example, people living in black areas normally flee whenever Tatmadaw troops approach their villages. This was the case here. The mortars and gunfire, according to the IDPs themselves, forced them to quickly abandon their homes without time to gather personal belongings or food, which begs a processual question. How did the KORD team compile such an extensive list of property losses? Did members of all the 254 displaced households return to their villages after the troops moved on to calculate their losses, then share the compiled data with the KORD ERA team, which arrived one month after the attacks occurred? Or did the IDPs generate a list of their losses using a survey format that KORD provided them for the purposes of the ERA assessment? In both cases, the numbers are reconstructions of what materially existed prior to the attacks but can no longer be found except through its absence. But the impetus for the calculations and the methods used to reconstruct the property losses are not the same—the former was self-initiated, while the latter was requested—and these differences have implications for how we determine the extent to which the numbers, when read uncritically as quantifiable empirical facts, were produced.

The cascading numbers regarding the scale of the agricultural losses similarly reinforces the statistical realism of the ERA request. Subsistence farmers are acutely aware of the amount of rice they have stockpiled, which explains the specificity of the amounts lost, precisely measured in baskets and tins (two standardized measurements of volume), that the ERA assessment team obtained from them. For this reason, KORD's request, like all other ERA requests in TBBC's very sizable IDP archive, includes the estimated size of the projected harvest *had troops not destroyed the farmers' ability to produce one.* These "under normal conditions" estimates present themselves as high-probability facts to the reader because the expected yields are based on local historical patterns, as reported by the IDPs themselves. However, this statistical "gesture" is somewhat misleading, too, in that the harvest estimates are actually unfulfilled conditionalities. That is, had the attacks not occurred, then the field(s) would have yielded X amount. But the attacks did happen, which means that the normal harvest could never have become reality, as the requisite causal relationship was absent. The point here is not to dismiss such gestures, as the forecasts (setting aside crop damage due to drought, floods, and wild animals) do serve as reasonable proxies for calculating the impact of the famine crimes on food security over time. But neither should the forecasts be accepted as simple facts.

Finally, all ERA requests begin with specific details on the Tatmadaw operations that caused the villagers to abandon their homes. IDPs in black areas generally do not have the ability to gather military intelligence; they are too busy trying to evade troops, who commonly fire mortars and automatic weapons into their suspected hiding areas. Cross-border ERA assessment teams are not able to observe what happened in real time either because they did not normally arrive in the affected areas until thirty to sixty days after the attack(s), based on the dates listed on the requests' cover letters. The delay begs another question. What was the source of military intelligence, which is critical to the approval of an ERA request? The answer in

KNU-delineated Karen State was almost always the KNLA, which possessed the technical capacity and human resources to document Tatmadaw operations. (Radio intercepts enabled them to identify not only the battalions involved, but quite often the names and ranks of their commanders.)[33] The KNLA being the source of these numbers would raise uncomfortable questions about the cross-border organization's adherence to the humanitarian principles of neutrality and independence, however, which is why the ERA requests represent military intelligence as their own, even though the origin of the information is an open secret to those familiar with the fact-finding process.

RECONSTRUCTIVE ELABORATIONS

All of the ERA *fonds*, like the preceding KORD excerpt, narrate famine crimes in a manner that makes the numbers they contain appear to "speak for themselves." But the numbers, despite appearances, are not fixed in value. They are instead provisional. Martha Lampland, a sociologist who studies rationalization as a social process, developed the concept of "provisional numbers" to draw attention to the varied ways numbers function as conceptual placeholders. Provisional numbers, she explains, are not "stable entities that carry the same meaning no matter what their context . . . [although they] parade as stable and fixed indicators."[34] Rather, provisional numbers are numbers of the moment; they are "temporary" and "impermanent," a liminal ontological status that raises further questions about their authoritativeness.[35] I raise this issue not with the goal of proving or disproving the facticity of the reconstructed numbers in the ERA *fonds*, which TBBC's annual IDP reports elaborate upon. I direct attention to it instead as a reminder of the need to attend to the ways in which provisional numbers are produced and the "gestural" function they serve in different contexts.

IDP head counts, for example, have a short statistical lifespan, as displaced persons do not remain "in place" after the ERA teams enumerate them. Some IDPs return to their villages, if they have not been totally destroyed and contaminated with land mines, when the soldiers withdraw. (In IDP hiding areas, this cycle of displacement and provisional return commonly happens multiple times each year.) Alternatively, IDPs might migrate to nearby villages and towns. Still other IDPs head toward areas more firmly under NSAG control or to the Thai border, either to enter the refugee camps or to join the vast number of people from Myanmar working in that country's underground economy. IDPs who spend time in Tatmadaw-controlled relocation centers may choose any of these options. IDP head counts by KORD and CIDKP are thus snapshots in time. As a result, the cumulative numbers, although fixed on the pages of the ERA *fonds* as tabulated "facts," are always unfixed off them.

TBBC's annual IDP reports, which draw heavily upon the tabulated "facts" presented in the ERA *fonds*, but in unacknowledged ways, provide a good example. Classification systems, science and technology scholar Bruce Curtis observes, tend to acquire their "own momentum, expanding the breadth and increasing the depth and density of its coverage as subdivisions and correlations [are] introduced" over time.[36] The annual IDP reports evince the same pattern. The initially statistically crude details on IDP demographics (age and sex) that appeared in the first reports quickly evolved into much more fine-grained breakdowns across brown and black areas, where conditions often varied considerably. An explosion of visual representation, such as graphs, charts, and tables, in addition to photographs, was one consequence of this momentum.

For this reason, the annual IDP reports are best viewed through an arithmetic lens, both in the word's literal sense (the manipulation of numbers) as well as in its entomological one (the "art of counting"). TBBC's cross-border partners carried out large-scale IDP surveys in the field, typically more than one thousand households per annum, every year beginning in 2003. With the help of experts, the surveys became increasingly methodologically sophisticated over time, and the adoption of multicluster sampling techniques enabled the teams to quantify the manifold challenges different categories of IDPs faced in brown and black areas across southeastern Myanmar. (The drivers of displacement are diverse, IDPs responses to them vary, and their support needs, as well as protection requirements, may differ dramatically; hence the categorical focus.) The surveys, unlike the ERA *fonds*, sought to identify patterned similarities and differences across time and space, which meant erasing individual experiences of displacement and replacing them with broader categories, such as "threats to safety," "demographic stressors," "coping strategies," and "food security." Regardless of the thematic focus of the reports, which varied from year to year and thus made comparisons challenging, all of them elaborated upon their textual content with extensive visual representations of statistics.

Visuals can convey an immense amount of relational information at a glance, but that same power can be a weakness rather than a strength. Informational excess, for example, is often the result of poor visual design. To modulate such excess, clarify ambiguity, and make manifest what is latent in a graph, table, or diagram, representations often need "highly nuanced thick and rich text to reduce the noise level," visual design scholars James Carifio and Rocco Perla note.[37] But when separated from such text, they point out, visuals can be both "seed and fuel to a whole host of potential unintended and unwanted consequences through unwarranted and often unconscious inferences, deductions, and interpretations, which are broadly referred to as misunderstandings, misconceptions, or alternative conceptions."[38] The meaning of the data presented, in other words, is not necessarily stable and thus "authoritative" when these unwanted consequences come into play. Such unintended outcomes have significant implications for the visual presentation of human rights facts, which can easily become "facts" depending on the graphic techniques used. A table without verbal commentary, for instance, leaves the analytical work to the reader, which means the intended takeaway finding, the "memorable abstraction of the data" as one technical expert put it, may go unnoticed or misunderstood by the viewer.[39] The complexification of TBBC's IDP maps over time provides a representative example of how visual displays of famine crimes fix and unfix meaning in paradoxical fashion through the use of colors.

The story of complexification begins with TBBC's first IDP report, published in 2002. The report had three goals. First was to count the number of IDPs in relocation sites in brown areas, and in temporary settlements, known as "hiding villages" (*ywa pôn*), in black ones. Somewhat confusingly, the report routinely included what I call "specific estimates" (i.e., approximations in numerically precise form), as was the case with TBBC's conclusion that at least 632,978 people were displaced in southeastern Myanmar during 2002.[40] Second was to map the location of these sites and villages using data collected between 1996 and 2002. Third was to convince donors that the scale of the humanitarian crisis in brown and black areas warranted significant financial support despite the security risks to their staff and reputational risks to the funders.[41]

Ashley South, a consultant who helped research and author TBBC's first IDP report, said that the mapping effort was done with "good will." "They [the local partners] did the field research and helped to plot the locations . . .

which were hand-drawn and then transferred to Excel . . . so the maps were a rash of [color-coded] dots across southeast Myanmar, but it did the job."[42] (The desktop survey claimed to have identified the approximate location of 2,536 destroyed, abandoned, or forcibly relocated villages over the course of this seven-year period, which TBBC stated was likely an underestimate. Notably, the report did not elaborate upon the methodology used to compile this total, making it a numerical "black box" reconstruction of the past violence.)[43] "It was an accurate reflection of what was on the ground," he told me. "We may have missed some and had some in the wrong place, but . . . we cleared the minimal level of credibility."[44] South was correct when his assertions are assessed in terms of financial outcomes. International donors did begin to markedly increase their funding to TBBC and, by extension, its cross-border partners, following the publication of the report.

The number and types of maps grew steadily and improved in technical quality over the course of subsequent annual IDP reports, with most of them focusing on the demarcation of conflict-induced displacement and militarization of the region at different spatial scales. Paradoxically, these same developments made the regional-scale maps of affected villages less legible over time. The maps TBBC published that overlapped with the Northern Offensive exemplify this outcome. The 2006 map portrayed the conflict-affected villages using differently colored circles that corresponded to the years documented: 2002–2004 (dark purple), 2004–2005 (light blue), and 2005–2006 (orange).[45] By visual necessity, the map did not distinguish destroyed, relocated, or abandoned villages from one another, even though these distinctions reflect different forms of and responses to preemptive Tatmadaw violence. Similarly, this map, which is a composite of three periods in time, makes it impossible to discern which conflict-affected villages were subsequently rebuilt, reestablished, or returned to since they were spatially plotted. The 2007 map further complexified the representation of conflict-induced displacement by increasing the number of colored circles to five, each of which covered a different period (1996–2002, 2002–2004, 2004–2005, 2005–2006, 2006–2007), along with the inclusion of colored triangles to indicate the geographic location of the IDP and refugee camps.[46] The 2008 map simplified visual matters somewhat by reducing the colored depiction of the conflict-affected villages back to three periods of unequal length (1996–2002, 2004–2007, and 2008), again with triangles marking the location of the IDP and refugee camps. By the time of publication, the

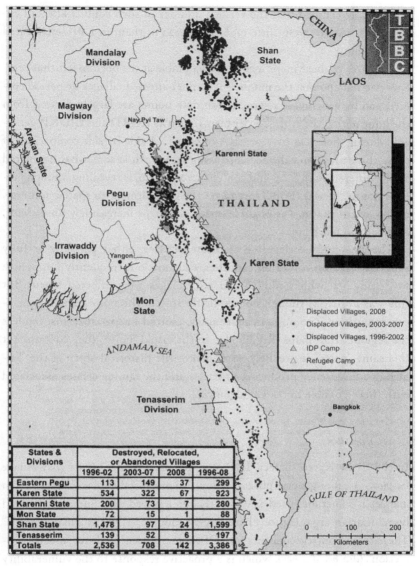

States & Divisions	Destroyed, Relocated, or Abandoned Villages			
	1996-02	2003-07	2008	1996-08
Eastern Pegu	113	149	37	299
Karen State	534	322	67	923
Karenni State	200	73	7	280
Mon State	72	15	1	88
Shan State	1,478	97	24	1,599
Tenasserim	139	52	6	197
Totals	2,536	708	142	3,386

MAP 2. Abandoned, displaced, and destroyed villages, 1996–2008. SOURCE: TBBC (2009).

2008 report claimed that the verified number of such conflict-affected villages had risen to 3,386 since 1996, with 1,222 of them in KNU-delineated Karen State.[47]

All three of these maps include a small table at the bottom left that presents two data points: the number of conflict-affected villages by period covered and by geographic region. (Both data points are largely derived from the information the cross-border teams, such as KORD and CIDKP, generated during their year-by-year ERA missions.) A side-by-side comparison of these three maps and the accompanying tables, while somewhat hampered by the differences in form and content across them, is revealing, though perhaps not in the way TBBC intended. The commitment to spatial accuracy, to the extent that it was possible, made the maps increasingly unreadable, especially in black areas.

The clustered overlayering of colored circles, either partially or fully superimposed on top of one another, thus made it frequently impossible to distinguish which conflict-affected villages were affected when. But this was arguably, though not explicitly stated, the point. The mapmakers' commitment to numerical accuracy, plotted in spatial terms, renders the regional IDP maps illegible due to the visual "noise" they contain. Yet this same "noise" is precisely what makes the historical story of the Tatmadaw's insurgency-producing practices and the famine crimes associated with them possible to read at a glance.

CONCLUSION

In the S'gaw Karen dialect, IDPs are "people who flee" (*bwa ghay mwyee ha plot*). A more general phrase, "people in an unstable place" (*pwa lo o ga mwyee*), is sometimes used as well.[48] (Karen involved with human rights and humanitarian organizations have largely adopted "IDP" as a loan word.)[49] These two idiomatic concepts for IDPs intersect with a third, "evasive protection" (*dta bee dta ber*), which is a proactive response to the vulnerability the Tatmadaw's insurgency-producing practices create for Karen civilians in conflict areas. *Dta be* means "to be hidden," and *dta ber* translates as "to be covered."[50] To survive as an IDP, in other words, requires one to remain invisible.

The desire for physical invisibility did not include a concomitant desire for political invisibility, however. Successive military regimes, both the State

Law and Order Restoration Council (1988–1997) and the State Peace and Development Council (1997–2011) repeatedly denied the very existence of IDPs.[51] The annual IDP reports that TBBC and its cross-border partners published challenged this official denial by making the IDP crisis visible to different constituencies in a position to act in response to it (e.g., UN bodies, foreign governments, and donors). "Numero-politics," a concept that is at the heart of the fixing and unfixing of quantitative-based meaning, shaped this political visibility. *Numero-politics* refers to contexts in which "what is at stake are both methods of counting as well as contestation over what the objects in question are being counted *for*," according to Aryn Martin, a sociologist, and Michael Lynch, a science and technology studies scholar.[52]

Returning to the conference, the former Australian ambassador's questions to me regarding the methodological validity and factual credibility, and thus the "authoritativeness," of the statistics that cross-border humanitarian organizations produced about IDPs directly concerned the relationship between the "for" and "how." He insinuated that the "for" of the ERA field documentation and annual IDP surveys biased the "how" toward MSF-like political advocacy, which he viewed as a violation of the humanitarian principles of neutrality and independence. He also suspected, or so I gathered from his tone, that greater IDP numbers translated into more foreign donor funding, which might not always be directed to relief activities. In their conversations with me, KORD, CIDKP, and TBBC staff strongly refuted such accusations, citing annual audits and long-term funding from the same donors as evidence to the contrary. The content of the ERA *fonds* in TBBC's extensive archive of conflict-induced displacement, which I carefully reviewed, further supported their claims due to the clearly evident combination of similarity and variation that existed in the *fonds*. (Similarity was due to common fact-finding methods over time, and variation was due to the differing details of what occurred during each individual attack over space.) But the broader point that Martin and Lynch raised remains valid. Statistics, when connected to a processual "event," such as the Northern Offensive, which unfolded over the course of three years, do not merely consist of a series of stand-alone facts. Rather, the statistics compiled—in this case, the famine crimes allegedly committed and the number of people reportedly displaced that appear in the separate ERA *fonds*—only become meaningful when understood as part of a larger, overarching narrative.[53] This narrative did not easily emerge.

In February 2006, shortly after the Northern Offensive started, the military regime issued new guidelines for international humanitarian organizations operating inside the country. The guidelines effectively placed the organizations directly under ministry-level control, which gave military officials the authority to oversee all hiring decisions, purchasing arrangements, and project implementation, as well as the ability to restrict travel. MSF-France was one of the very few organizations to operate in Karen State, where the Northern Offensive was well underway. The NGO's director, Dr. Herv Isambert, accused the regime of wanting "to get rid of all humanitarian workers in these politically sensitive regions . . . the restrictions imposed on us reduced us to the role of specialist contractors subjected to the political will of the military junta." "The Burmese [authorities] don't want anyone to witness how they organize the forced displacement of the population, the burning of villages, and forced recruitment," he added.[54] MSF left the country in protest in March, and surprisingly, the International Committee of the Red Cross, which is periodically criticized for being "excessively" neutral and refusing to speak out in such situations, did as well. The work of cross-border humanitarian organizations, such as KORD and CIDKP, was thus even more critical for documenting, if only partially, what was happening on the ground and for supplying assistance to the IDPs as the security situation permitted.

The practical use of this information has broader significance as well where the shaping of human rights "facts" is concerned. My attention to one aspect of the ERA fact-finding process, the construction of "authoritative" IDP numbers and then their visual elaboration in TBBC's maps of conflict-affected villages, has highlighted the ways in which such representations "blend[ed] aesthetics, utility, and politics" into communicative acts.[55] These acts clearly had an important story to tell.[56] But what that story was meant to communicate was not always straightforward. The ERA requests, for example, doubled as human rights field reports as a result of the detailed military-related information they contained, though that was not their intended purpose. On the contrary, the inclusion of such information was meant to provide evidentiary support for the humanitarian "facts," that is, the reported scale of the famine crimes and the resultant need for aid in cash-based form. But the cascades of numbers that filled the ERA *fonds* were not as self-evident as they first appeared to be either; rather, they were provisional, which meant the numbers were instead "of the moment." Tatmadaw battalions, for instance, often returned to the affected areas, where they committed further famine crimes, details of which appeared, albeit in less elaborated form, in the subsequent ERA distribution reports and ERA impact assessments. In other words, the three different kinds of ERA documents constituted three separate, reconstructed snapshots in time. So, the numbers they contained, although fixed on the page, were in reality continually in flux. As a result, calculating the scale and scope of the famine crimes reportedly committed during the Northern Offensive cannot be reduced to a simple additive exercise—one in which all of the food "objects" seized and destroyed listed in each ERA request can be simply totaled together. Instead, the individual *fonds* must be disassembled and then reassembled by documentation type (request, distribution report, and impact assessment, respectively) to identify what happened when and where according to the cross-border teams "speaking" on behalf of the IDPs themselves. Only then will it become possible to narrate the Northern Offensive in a more "authoritative," albeit still hearsay rather than verbatim, form.

The TBBC annual reports also revealed the extent to which IDP profiles are "things of measurement," to borrow anthropologist Sally Engle Merry's phrase. "The survey forms, the classifications, the boxes to be checked, the continuum of possible answers, the sequence of questions, the technologies of graphic representation," she explains, "are all part of the technology of statistical knowledge production, developed in a collaborative process by a series of actors, backed by institutions with incentives and money, over a long period of time."[57] In short, surveys produce "facts" through the structured questions asked (as well as not asked) and procedures used to gather answers, both of which are informed by particular and often multiple organizational agendas.

My analysis of TBBC's surveys was narrower in focus, however. It chiefly concerned TBBC's visual mapping of conflict-affected villages across southeastern Myanmar, a task that relied heavily on the underlying ERA request data. As I have explained, these specifics took two main forms: approximate locations and specific IDP head counts. The former consisted of small color-coded circles that corresponded to TBBC-determined time periods (2002–2003, 2003–2004, etc.). The latter appeared in the guise of IDP totals by region, enumerated in tables that accompanied the maps. The villages as circles were approximations, something similar to but not exactly equal to something else, because the ERA teams did not at the time have GPS

units in their possession. And without GPS coordinates, the plotted location of the conflict-affected villages on the maps was, in fact, a "best guess."
A "best guess" does not mean false, however, as approximations may be the
only option depending on the available information, the degree of accuracy
required, the sensitivity of the problem to these data, and the savings (usually in time and effort) that can be achieved by it. In this setting, the degree
of geographic accuracy, defined here as precision, was not critical. Instead,
I argued, though TBBC staff might not agree with me, the approximations
served a different purpose, which was to make years of conflict-induced displacement legible through the very illegibility of the published maps.

Finally, both the ERA numbers and TBBC maps, as human rights in
the guise of humanitarian "facts," foregrounded another important point,
namely, the making of what theorist Georgio Agamben refers to as "bare life."
The concept, he argues, is one of the defining features of the contemporary
moment as more and more sovereign states devise ways to strip vulnerable
populations of their rights and the legal protections associated with them.[58]
"Bare life" is omnipresent in southeastern Myanmar, but with an important qualification. The nonmajority ethnic populations in conflict-affected
areas, such as Karen ones, historically enjoyed neither rights nor protections after the country's independence. Therefore, the political question of
how life should be lived, a key component of the KNU/KNLA's struggle,
was always already replaced with the biological one of how to survive as a
result of decades of Tatmadaw's preemptive violence against civilians. The
widespread and systematic famine crimes reportedly committed during the
Northern Offensive were neither the first nor the last time Tatmadaw units
targeted civilians as part of its war of attrition against the KNU/KNLA.[59]
The Northern Offensive was simply the largest and best documented. It also
produced more than one archive. Testimonies regarding willful killings of
and indiscriminate attacks on civilians by Tatmadaw units, the subject of
the next chapter, are another.

CHAPTER 4

Killing Bodies

Narrativity Transcribed

The event is not what happens. The event is that which can be narrated.

—Allen Feldman

By definition, mass atrocity narratives rely on large numbers. But these numbers cannot be taken at face value, even when they are credible, explains Bridget Conley, the research director at the World Peace Foundation. "Most research that cites a fatality figure is not actually concerned with the fatality figure, but how that figure enables the researcher to do something else: tell a story, chart correlations, deliver aid, influence policy and so forth. The number is rarely *the thing*," Conley points out.[1] "Decisions about the beginning, the ending, what is included, what is excluded, what constitutes an authoritative account, and which numbers are to be questioned, and which accepted," she continues, "do not boil down to the science of statistics— although certainly this is not an irrelevant matter—but it also always a matter of how the story of violence is told."[2] Conley's argument, which is centrally concerned with issues of narrativity and the instrumental uses of it with regard to mass atrocity figures, also applies here, but in a conflict context where large numbers of civilian deaths are notably absent, in the Burma/Myanmar Online Library, the country's meta–human rights archive.

Evidence of mass killings, conventionally defined as four or more individuals in a single incident, appears very infrequently in the documentation on human rights abuses in KNU-delineated Karen State. The KNU/KNLA keeps track of Tatmadaw casualties, in addition to its own, but the NSAG has never published figures on the number of civilians killed, if indeed it collects them. Several Karen human rights and humanitarian organizations (e.g., KHRG, FBR, KORD, and CIDKP) do document civilian deaths to the best of their ability; however, no single database exists to track totals. But even if such a combined database existed, the numbers would undercount the total for a simple reason: the geographic areas under KNU/KNLA control declined dramatically from the late 1990s onward due to a series of large-scale Tatmadaw offensives that continued into 2011. The loss of territorial control, coupled with the traditional civilian response to military operations—flight to more remote areas—made it successively more difficult to document civilian death tolls. IDPs, when fleeing Tatmadaw patrols, often break into small groups of several households to take temporary refuge in spatially scattered hiding sites. "It means that if [they are] killed, there is no one to report it," one humanitarian aid worker explained to me.[3] Underreported tragedies thus pose a narrative problem, in addition to an evidentiary one. Nevertheless, the story of the willful killing of civilians in conflict areas, which is both a war crime and a crime against humanity under the Rome Statute, can be narrated, though not without considerable difficulty. Indiscriminate attacks on civilians, unlike willful killings when the soldier has a degree of control over the person (e.g., an extrajudicial execution), also produced a steady number of civilian deaths. Such attacks are much better documented, yet they too pose narrativity challenges, as the comparison of the two demonstrates.

Surprisingly, a sustained focus on narrativity as it relates to "fact" production is largely absent within the literature on human rights fact-finding, even though the collection and analysis of testimonies remains fundamental to this process.[4] Narrativity matters greatly, however. *Narrativity* is an umbrella term for diverse and sometimes conflicting approaches to understanding meaning-making. Broadly speaking, the concept can be divided into two basic components: narrative content (i.e., what is conveyed) and narrative discourse (i.e., how it is conveyed). Human rights organizations rely almost exclusively on the "what" to advance their "truth" claims, while the "how" is typically rendered invisible in their reports and subsequent advocacy efforts. The invisibility is problematic. The question of "what" to transcribe during an interview, to offer one relevant example, is an interpretive decision, whereas "how" to transcribe it is a representational decision, according to Mary Buscholz, a sociolinguist. "These decisions," she writes, "ultimately respond to the contextual conditions of the transcription process itself, including the transcriber's own expectations and beliefs about the speakers and the interaction being transcribed; the intended audience of the transcript; and its purpose."[5] But in fact-finding contexts, the question of how representational decisions are made is only rarely made explicit, even though no transcription is "disinterested," Buscholz notes.[6]

Transcription practices, to elaborate further, produce several types of erasure both during and after interviews. Fact finders generally do not utilize conventional notational practices to indicate points of emphatic stress, exhalations (laughter or sighs), expressions of strong emotion (tears or anger) in a testimony, and so on. They very rarely do so because such notations require technical familiarity on the part of not just the fact finder, but also the reader, who would need to be able to decipher testimony filled with abstract symbols, such as: < > for uncertain word, ( ) for transcriber comment, and — for self-interruption. Without these notational elements, the testimony becomes little more than words on a page, especially if there are no additional comments indicating changes in the person's body language, which may be of considerable significance. Such notations are important because firsthand testimonies of violence are almost always fragmented, double back to prior points, contain asides and digressions, include silences and omissions that may or may not be deliberate, and so on. These patterns reflect not only how people typically recall violent episodes, but also the redirection of the informant's testimony by the interviewer's follow-up questions, the purpose of which is to fill in gaps as they relate to the who, what, where, when, and how of the violent incident(s) that reportedly occurred.

However, human rights organizations almost never publish such transcripts in their original form for reasons of readability and, arguably, credibility, in addition to personal security. (Badly disjointed accounts can raise concerns about the factual accuracy and veracity of the statements, as lawyers often do during adversarial legal proceedings.) Instead, organizations transform the testimonies by editing statements and reorganizing passages, while trying to stay as close as possible to the original, into more coherent and linear narratives—a practice sometimes referred to in transcription studies as "Englishing."[7] Such forms of erasure, while generally limited and usually well intentioned, can have an outsized impact on meaning-making because these interpretive decisions (the precursor to the representational "how" of narrativity) occur behind the scenes. The extent to which an informant's testimony is mediated after the fact by those who collected it remains hidden to the reader as a result.

The same constitutive elements of narrativity—the "what" and the "how"—can also reveal something else of significance regarding human rights "fact" production. To quote Ann Stoler, who works at the intersection of the disciplines of anthropology and history, narrative similarities and differences additionally provide an opportunity "to explore the kinds of stories people told about violence, the sorts of cultural knowledge on which those stories were based, and the 'storeyed' levels through which those accounts . . . should be read."[8] In her view, the resulting "hierarchies of credibility" are based on widely held assumption that it is relatively easy to distinguish truth from fiction and news from rumor.[9] But as Stoler points out, the boundaries conventionally thought to separate facts from nonfacts are not always clear, especially in contexts of violence, as the degrees of difference and the contours of both categories are, in reality, typically fluid rather than fixed and thus disputed rather than agreed upon.

Stoler, to elaborate further, focused on acts of violence in a colonial context wherein Dutch plantation owners, journalists, and colonial officials in Indonesia struggled to determine whether the incidents were isolated and hence solely criminal in nature, or part of an identifiable pattern and thus an emergent organized threat to continued economic profit and political rule. She examined how colonists sought to discern the "true" intent of unknown perpetrators by analyzing the claims that the authors of personal letters, newspaper articles, and government correspondence put forward in written form. My analysis is similar in that it examines how a team of fact finders sought to determine the "true" intent of unknown perpetrators by analyzing oral testimonies from Karen civilians who claimed to have firsthand knowledge of willful killings and indiscriminate attacks. Both accounts, Stoler's and mine, contain stories within stories (source narratives, investigative narratives about the source narratives, and our respective narratives about both narratives), which when taken together bear some semblance to the genre of detective fiction in terms of narrativity. (I return to this issue at the end of the chapter.) But the subject positions of "the State" within our respective accounts are reversed. The written documents Stoler examined represented the colonial state and its interests as the "victim" of violence. By contrast, the oral testimonies from IHRC named "the State," headed by the Tatmadaw, as the "perpetrator." And it is the "how" of the perpetrator stories upon stories (i.e., the testimonies, IHRC's representation of them, and my analysis of both) that is the focus of this chapter.

IHRC's main objective was to determine whether sufficient evidence existed to prove long-standing NGO claims that willful killings of and indiscriminate attacks on civilians were not isolated incidents, but rather reflective of intent, that is, official Tatmadaw policies. Two concepts require further elaboration here, given IHRC's research focus. One concept concerns the principle of distinction, which consists of a set of international humanitarian norms and laws that parties to an armed conflict are supposed to follow so as to differentiate combatants from civilians. Where one episto-ontological category ends and the other begins is often very unclear in conflict contexts, however, and this lack of clarity has a bearing on whether or not official policy, and thus command responsibility, exists. (Command responsibility is framed as an "omission mode" of individual criminal liability, meaning the superior is responsible for crimes committed by their subordinate(s), which includes failing to prevent and/or punish such acts.)[10] Another concept is that of the "victim-witness." The hyphen that both visually separates and connects the two types of informant (i.e., the victim and the witness) is an important reminder that each subject position has a different relationship to the "facts" of violence. The experiential difference, in turn, has implications for the ways in which "hierarchies of credibility" are constructed and maintained by NGOs, assessed by their targeted audiences, and questioned by their critics. A biographical overview of the archive in question then follows. The archive consists of more than one thousand pages of testimonies concerning different aspects of the Northern Offensive, including statements from former Tatmadaw soldiers who had defected. The contents of the archive provided the evidentiary basis for two influential policy memorandums IHRC published in 2014 on willful killings and indiscriminate attacks on civilians in one township of KNU-delineated Karen State. The testimonies and the transcriptions practices that shaped them highlight how the representational strategies (i.e., the "how" of narrativity) profoundly affect what we are able to know in epistemological terms about such reported incidents.

THE PRINCIPLE OF DISTINCTION

From a historical perspective, the principle of distinction initially took shape in the Saint Petersburg Declaration of 1898, in which delegates affirmed that weakening the military force of the declared enemy was the only legitimate object of war. The Hague Conventions of 1899 and 1907 further refined the principle by providing the first formal statements on the laws of war and war crimes. The regulations contained in the Conventions did not explicitly specify how the distinction between combatants and noncombatants should be made, however. But Article 25 provided some broad guidance. It prohibited "the attack or bombardment, by whatever means, of towns, villages, dwellings, or buildings which are undefended."[11] It was only with the 1949 Geneva Convention relative to the Protection of Civilian Persons in Time of War (commonly known as the Fourth Geneva Convention) that the category of "civilian" became an identifiable subject position in treaty law. This Convention defined "protected persons" in negative terms, that is, anyone not party to the conflict or occupying power.[12] Protocol II, which supplemented the 1949 Geneva Conventions, further delineated the principle of distinction in noninternational armed conflicts. Protocol II entered into force in 1978, and it specified a number of protections to be afforded to civilians. The protections included prohibitions on the destruction of "objects indispensable to the survival of the civilian population" and the "forced movement of civilians," two violations discussed in the previous chapter on famine crimes.[13] The protections are not portrayed as absolute in these documents, however. Rather, the documents call on combatants "to refrain from directly attacking civilians . . . and to take reasonable precautions to avoid and minimize civilian deaths," verb choices that underscore the absence of any legal enforcement mechanisms.[14] The situation changed somewhat in 1998 when the Rome Statute codified the distinction, stating that "intentionally directing attacks against the civilian population as such or against individual civilians not taking direct part in hostilities" may constitute a war crime.[15] The odds of this occurring are extraordinarily low, however. In the twenty-eight cases that have made it to the ICC's courtrooms since 2002, its judges have issued a total of eight convictions, only one of them for attacks on civilians.[16]

The point at which a civilian becomes a combatant is often ambiguous, which has given rise to the so-called naked soldier debate among military philosophers, but not among international lawmakers. The question of how to determine whether a naked man taking a bath is a soldier when there are no visible weapons or uniform present highlights the instability of the conceptual and normative criteria traditionally used to differentiate "civilians" from "combatants."[17] The problem is especially apparent in the context of asymmetric warfare, such as a (counter-) insurgency, where identifiable uniforms are not always worn and civilians may carry out some noncombat support duties normally performed by soldiers. The problem, one further step removed, concerns the provision of material aid (e.g., food, money, medicine, and temporary lodging) to members of an NSAG. Does the provision of such aid transform someone into a legitimate target of attack? If so, what is the threshold; that is, how much aid and of what type qualifies as "direct" participation? The co-optation of humanitarian actors into contemporary counterterrorism laws since 9/11, including those that ban material support regardless of whether or not it is given knowingly, is a prime example of how elastic the definition of "direct" participation has become.[18] To help clarify the situation, which many humanitarian advocates regard as military overreach (especially by the United States), the International Committee of the Red Cross issued further interpretive guidance on the meaning of "direct" in 2008.[19] But a globally recognized standard remains elusive, which means humanitarian organizations in active conflict zones often find themselves delivering aid and services in a legal gray zone that may or may not be operationally advantageous to them.[20]

In KNU-delineated Karen State, civilian support for the NSAG was widespread, though far from universal.[21] But the nature of the assistance, especially for the KNLA, varied tremendously, from the minimal (e.g., serving as a guide on a one-time basis) to the extensive (e.g., serving as a soldier). Paying taxes, historically in the form of paddy, was by far the most common form of direct assistance, and for this people gained access to basic social services (e.g., education and health care), in addition to a measure of armed protection.[22] The provision of material support, when viewed from the perspective of customary international humanitarian law, would not qualify as "direct participation," the point at which a civilian risks becoming a combatant. Yet the distinction between the two categories was an uncertain one in contested areas. Karen civilians, simply by virtue of their ethnicity, were often always already "pre-insurgents," that is, potential enemies, in the eyes of Tatmadaw soldiers.[23] A man in his sixties, [name redacted], made this point quite clearly during an interview. "One time, the soldiers told us that we Karen have to come back and surrender to them. If we do there will be peace. If we [continue to resist] the problem will happen again and again." The villager told the soldiers, "'This conversation, you have to use it with your enemy [KNU/KNLA]. I am an ordinary man. I am not a soldier.

I don't carry arms. Why don't you go and talk to those who carry arms?'" The Tatmadaw soldier responded, "'If one fish is rotten in a sack of fish, all of the fish will also go rotten.'"[24]

Accounts of willful killings permeate the Burma/Myanmar Online Library meta-archive of human rights reports on the country, but mass atrocities, such as the massacre of hundreds of inhabitants of a village during a single incident, do not. The near complete absence of such alleged mass incidents, which were historically routine in counterinsurgency campaigns elsewhere around the world, is surprising given the size of many of the Tatmadaw's military operations. During the Northern Offensive, for example, dozens of Tatmadaw battalions depopulated at least 430 Karen villages between late 2005 and late 2008 using Four Cuts tactics, according to TBBC's local partners, CIDKP and KORD among them.[25] However, the offensive did not produce high civilian body counts. FBR, for example, claims to have documented a little more than 370 deaths over a two-year period. Other data sets, covering a larger geographic area and longer period of time, indicate that the civilian death total was likely higher, but by how much remains unknown.[26] The "relatively" low mortality number overall reflects, at least in part, the finely honed ability of Karen civilians in black areas to flee in advance of Tatmadaw units. But the low number also raises the question, which fact finders have long sought to definitively answer, of whether the reported accounts of willful killings, including alleged "shoot-to-kill" incidents, were due to the isolated acts of individual soldiers or a pattern indicative of official policy.

By contrast, the Tatmadaw's Four Cuts approach configured the "principle of distinction" in territorial rather than ontological terms. An extensive body of human rights documentation shows that Tatmadaw units viewed people in brown areas as pre-insurgents (i.e., potential combatants). Hence the tactics Tatmadaw units used to erode the ability of civilians to provide material assistance to NSAGs, all of them based on the act of seizure: time through forced labor, food and money through extortion, and homes and food sources through forced relocations. A far less voluminous body of human rights documentation suggests that the Tatmadaw units regarded people in black areas as "insurgents" (i.e., combatants) simply by virtue of their physical presence in those areas, meaning that the principle of distinction did not, from their perspective, apply. The next section recounts how the IHRC archive came into being, followed by an analysis of its published memorandums as they relate to the problematics of narrativity in human rights "fact" production.

THE MEMORANDUMS

IHRC published an influential legal memorandum in 2014 concerning the willful killings of Karen civilians, as well as indiscriminate attacks on them, primarily during the Northern Offensive.[27] The field research upon which the legal memorandum was largely based sought to determine whether the abuses committed during the Northern Offensive were patterned or violated international criminal law, and if so, whether sufficient evidence existed to allege that high-ranking Tatmadaw officials could be charged with these crimes. The team carried out eleven field missions to the Thailand-Myanmar border region, during which its members spoke with more than 300 individuals. They completed in-depth interviews with 150 of them, which generated more than one thousand pages of testimony containing varying degrees of knowledge regarding the attacks. (Ten of these individuals were village heads, who had extensive contact with military personnel prior to the offensive, and seven were former soldiers, who, although they did not directly participate in the Northern Offensive, shared detailed information about military structure, operational procedures, and reporting protocols.) Based on its analysis of the testimonies, IHRC claimed that three senior commanding officers, all generals, could be charged with crimes against humanity and war crimes, as defined in Articles 7 and 8, respectively, of the Rome Statute of the ICC.[28] These officers, IHRC further asserted, could be held legally responsible for alleged crimes under two theories of liability: individual criminal liability under Article 25 and command responsibility under Article 28.[29] In IHRC's concluding view, the evidence its fact finders had gathered from multiple sources was "sufficient to satisfy the standard required for the issuance of an arrest warrant by the ICC as set forth in Article 58 of the Rome Statute."[30] Later sections of this chapter will explore the evidentiary assumptions behind IHRC's legal reasoning.

Given the temporal length of the Northern Offensive (nearly three years) and its scope (large swaths of KNU-delineated Karen State, as well as parts of neighboring southwest Kayah State were affected), the research team faced the challenge of where to begin. "We originally started with Thandaung, Mu Traw, and Luthaw [Townships], but we decided to narrow down—to concentrate on either a Tatmadaw unit or a geographic region," the human rights lawyer, the principal researcher for the memorandums, as well as the primary narrator of the archive's biography, explained to me.[31]

His retrospective account was, as interviews always are, socially produced. Transcribed by me, then corrected and confirmed by him over email, the text of the interview represented here takes altered form: some details of the process and key events are paraphrased, additional background information has been added, and the quotes strategically chosen to underscore particular aspects of his account were not always emphasized above others in the original interview. The "how" of representation, in other words, matters here in this case as much as the "what" was recorded.

"We were in the northern Karen [refugee and IDP] camps, which led us to focus on Thandaung [Township]. It was easier to isolate [identify] people who had left between specific dates. We could isolate a target population much more easily." Local partners helped them do so and, in the end, the IHRC team conducted interviews with more than 160 people (villagers, village leaders, former porters, and former soldiers) who had fled Thandaung Township and could report on events that occurred primarily between January 2005 and December 2006, the end of the first year of the nearly three-year Northern Offensive. The majority of the incidents, as recounted by the informants, centered on two military units, Southern Regional Military Command and Light Infantry Division 66 (LID-66), both of which were named in dozens of the testimonies. The fact finders supplemented the testimonies with expert declarations obtained from four individuals with extensive knowledge of Tatmadaw strategy and tactics, the impacts of the state-sponsored violence on civilian populations in the affected area, and international criminal law. IHRC additionally referenced reports prepared by FBR and KHRG, two internationally known and respected local NGOs. Both NGOs conducted human rights fact-finding in some of the affected areas during the Northern Offensive, and their field documentation corroborated many of the patterns that emerged in the interview data according to IHRC.[32] But it was the testimonies that formed the evidentiary core of both the policy and legal memorandums.

In terms of process, the IHRC fact-finding team generated the testimonies using semistructured interviews that followed standard protocols, including informed consent and guarantees of anonymity. (The complete transcripts, which I was given permission to review, remain confidential for this reason, only appearing in the memorandums as strings of numbered references to specific interviews and incidents in the footnotes, a practice that produces a particular form of narrativity of its own.) The teams conducted the interviews in various Karen dialects and/or Burmese with the help of translators, who later retranslated the English version back to the interviewee to determine accuracy and completeness, making corrections and additions to the original statement entered directly into an encrypted laptop until an agreed upon transcription was reached. The final transcribed version of each testimony included some basic metadata, such as biographical details regarding the affiant (i.e., the person interviewed), the names of the people who conducted the interview, and the date and location where it was carried out. Many, but far from all, of the testimonies also included a brief statement at the end indicating whether the interviewee granted permission to share, either in part or in full, their testimony in the event that a future investigation with the goal of criminal prosecution ever became a possibility. In short, the process was consistent with best practices according to the lawyer, and when compared with leading fact-finding manuals, this was indeed the case. But upon closer examination, the transcription process was far from straightforward. As previously mentioned, it involved multiple steps, with the result being a socially produced testimony, an outcome that has important effects upon "fact" production.

I spoke with the lead researcher in 2017 about the impetus for the project. "We initiated it [the fact-finding project] at a time when threats of accountability in international forums were the only way to influence the regime's behavior," specifically, threats of further sanctions. But "by the time we were ready to publish [the legal memorandum], the context had changed." The election in 2011, which resulted in a semicivilian government taking power after decades of direct military rule, was the change to which he referred. The election raised hopes that genuine political and economic reforms would follow, and with that in mind, countries quickly lifted existing sanctions, flooding the country with foreign investment and development aid. However, current and retired high-ranking members of the Tatmadaw continued to control key positions in the new government, and rumors that a military coup would occur if the reforms moved in a direction not to their liking were widespread.

The changed but still fluid situation prompted the IHRC fact-finding team to debate whether to carry through with the project on the Northern Offensive or to pursue a more contemporary issue, specifically, the continuance of large-scale violence in Kachin State and northern Shan State. In 2011, the cease-fire between the Tatmadaw and the Kachin Independence

Organization, a major NSAG in the northern part of the country, collapsed after having lasted nineteen years. Smaller NSAGs in neighboring areas of northern Shan State also entered into the conflict, which the Rohingya crisis has since overshadowed, even though more than ninety thousand people remain displaced in Kachin State today as a result of the ongoing fighting and the convincingly documented mass human rights violations associated with it.[33] Ultimately, the team opted to pursue the Karen case. "We saw it as a transitional justice project through an international law lens," he explained.

With the ultimate goal of determining whether or not criminal accountability could be proved, the IHRC fact-finding team completed a full draft of the legal memorandum in 2012. But IHRC continued to make edits as they received feedback from third-party organizations (FBR and KHRG), as well as experts at Human Rights Watch, the International Center for Transitional Justice, and other prominent advocacy groups. Several UN bodies, including the office of the Special Rapporteur on the Situation of Human Rights in Myanmar, the US State Department, and foreign diplomats, as well as several Myanmar experts, also shared their confidential views on the draft. Some in-country experts had significant reservations about the legal memorandum, pointing to the possible political ramifications of asserting that several high-ranking Tatmadaw commanders had committed war crimes and crimes against humanity. Many diplomats and other pro-engagement figures, the lead researcher told me, similarly felt that "if we tried to hold them [the commanders] accountable, then they would be less likely to concede things," which might then stall substantive reforms. Given that possibility, the team spent much of 2012 trying to arrange meetings with senior government officials, and with Aung San Suu Kyi via her legal adviser, Robert San Pe, in 2013, to obtain their opinions.

These outreach efforts were not successful, so in March 2014 IHRC decided to release its policy memorandum, which focused on the need for security sector reform due to the failure of the Tatmadaw to respect the principle of distinction, as repeatedly claimed in the transcripts of the testimonies. IHRC's purpose in publishing the policy memorandum before the legal one was to prompt high-ranking government officials to actually engage with the substantive issues raised.[34] The head of the Myanmar Peace Center, Aung Min, reached out on IHRC's behalf to promote such engagement, "but we weren't getting any meetings," the lead researcher stated. During these efforts, Aung Min, himself the former South-East Regional Tatmadaw commander, discouraged the team, as reported to me by the researcher, from trying to speak to representatives at the Ministry of Defense. "They can't deal with it," said Aung Min (again as stated by the researcher, "quoting" him in this case), who attributed the lack of response to the initial efforts, with the backing of the European Union and other international donors, to start a nationwide peace process.[35] "Whether this was true or not, I don't know," the researcher told me. Regardless, IHRC moved forward and released its legal memorandum in November 2014. The purpose of the legal memorandum was dramatically different from that of the policy one on security sector reform, however. The central point, as outlined in the executive summary of the memorandum, was to make a fact-based case that Tatmadaw battalions had committed international crimes during the Northern Offensive on a widespread and systematic basis. The battalions did this to such an extent, IHRC argued, that three high-ranking commanders (Major General Ko Ko, Brigadier General Khin Zaw Oo, and Brigadier General Maung Maung Aye) could conceivably be arrested under the terms of the Rome Statute.

IHRC unexpectedly succeeded in obtaining a meeting with the deputy defense minister, Major General Kyaw Nyunt, and several other senior officials, after the legal memorandum's release. (The meeting was so unexpected that the IHRC lead researcher, clearly amused by the memory, had to rush out to buy a suit and arrange a long-distance taxi ride with Golden Harp, a company founded and run by former political prisoners, to get to the capital, Naypyidaw, a five-hour drive away, on extremely short notice.) The meeting, for which Soe Thein, the incumbent minister of the President's Office was also present, lasted for more than an hour and was "cordial and substantive," the researcher recalled. However, "the Ministry denied everything; [it was] a point-by-point refutation," all the while stressing "the difficulty of war and the difficulty of distinguishing between civilian and military targets." Furthermore, ministry officials complained that the report focused only on the Tatmadaw and did not examine the human rights abuses that NSAG groups had committed, an issue that several foreign pro-engagement reviewers of the draft had raised earlier. "He essentially said, 'You got it wrong and your sources are all one-sided.'"[36]

"We had no problems" at the press conference when they released the legal memorandum, the researcher said, still a little surprised even years after the fact. (My interpretation of his body language and tone.) "There probably was a lot of military intelligence in the room, and we had the US Embassy on the line while *en route* to the airport in case anything happened, but nothing did." (The presence of military intelligence is the norm for such events, and his decision to keep a member of the embassy staff on the phone was reasonable rather than self-aggrandizing, in my view, especially given the allegations IHRC publicly made.) What transpired afterward in terms of impacts, I asked. U Zaw Htay, an official in President Thein Sein's office, tried to deflect the legal memorandum's conclusions, the researcher stated. "'In civil war, both the Tatmadaw and ethnic armed groups might have violated human rights. . . Even America violates human rights in war,'" U Zaw Htay said, as told to me by the memorandum's lead author. (U Zaw Htay's statement, while indisputable, nonetheless utilized "whataboutism," a rhetorical device to accuse others of crimes while deflecting attention from those the Tatmadaw is alleged to have committed.) "'We must not play the blame game,'" U Zaw Htay stressed, reported the lead researcher.[37] "The diplomatic response was mixed," he continued. "It certainly made peoples' jobs harder. We had identified the Home Affairs Minister [Lieutenant General Ko Ko] as a war criminal [in the legal memorandum], which made meetings harder. [Our goal] was to send a clear signal that being a war criminal is not healthy for one's career. We explicitly strategized on this issue," he emphasized. (The minister did not suffer any noticeable consequences as a result of the accusation, however. He continued to serve as the minister of home affairs until his retirement in 2016.)

The response to the legal memorandum from Karen organizations varied. The KNU did not issue an official statement even though IHRC had met with its head officials during the early stages of the research process. The lead researcher attributed their silence to the hesitations that some officials had about naming specific people, a point that IHRC was fully cognizant of from the start. "Too many names," he said, "could raise concerns that we were going after 'everyone' in the Tatmadaw." By contrast, other NGOs, such as the Karen Women's Organization and the Karen Relief Center, fully supported naming names. Other ethnic groups, long subject to preemptive violence by the Tatmadaw, "talk[ed] about the report all of the time. The Kachin and the Shan, for example, and the Rohingya as well," he added. "They regard it not just as a Karen report. They see it as standing up to the Tatmadaw. They see the memo as a model, even though we did not achieve accountability. It showed what could be done." Several fact-finding organizations in

Kachin State and Shan State have since adopted IHRC's model, which supports the lead researcher's assessment of the memorandum's broader impact. With the assistance of foreign experts, these organizations are now developing their own respective case files on alleged international crimes (past and present) in the hopes that the prosecution of Tatmadaw commanders will become possible in the future.

THE VICTIM-WITNESS

The effects of narrativity on "fact" production are further complicated by the fact that the relationship of the "how" to the "what" in the two memorandums, and human rights reports more generally, is not always self-evident or transparently disclosed. According to Hayden White, history only emerges when events have been "emploted," that is, given "the formal coherence that only stories can possess."[38] Without such narrativity, the "data of experience," as another historian phrases it, will remain little more than a list of successive incidents.[39] Human rights reports are no exception; they share a common narrative regardless of conflict context and utilize a range of literary conventions to persuade the audiences that read them of their authoritativeness.[40]

Three related but different subject positions—the "victim," the "witness," and the "victim-witness"—are central to the "emplotment" of human rights facts/"facts" into recognizable narratives. "A victim is anyone who has suffered a human rights abuse, while a witness is someone who has knowledge about the violation based on his senses and can provide information on what is alleged," explains Théo Boutruche, an expert on international humanitarian law.[41] Boutruche's professional interest, however, lies in the liminal space where the two subject positions overlap, creating a hybrid that he terms the "victim-witness." Joining the two positions opens up new avenues of inquiry into how "victim-witnesses" understand and later narrate direct and indirect experiences of abuse that occur, often concurrently. Yet the same hyphen that links the two different subject positions (i.e., the "victim" and the "witness") poses challenges to the stability of human rights facts/"facts," and thus to narrativity more generally. The verification of such facts/"facts" relies heavily on three concepts—credibility, competence, and reliability—to assess the accuracy and value of a person's testimony. The three concepts, although they appear to overlap, are actually quite distinct, though fact finders rarely reflect publicly on the significance of the differences for the legitimacy of their "truth" claims. "Credibility refers to how believable a witness is," explains legal scholar Robert Rosenthal. "Competence," he continues, concerns "the personal characteristics of [the] witness." "Reliability," by contrast, revolves around "the inherent quality of the evidence."[42] How these concepts are weighted relative to one another varies depending on what they will be used for, however.

Human rights fact finders focus on establishing empirically, to the extent possible, what happened: the who, where, when, how, and why. For these reasons, they generally give greater value to the victim-*witness*, that is, those aspects of a person's testimony that contribute to answering such questions. The weighting happens because the need to corroborate testimony from multiple sources is central to the fact-finding process. But the preoccupation with whether or not victim-*witness* testimony satisfies the threshold for being sufficiently "truthful" diverts attention away from the motivations of the same *victim*-witness. The *victim*-witness may have very different reasons for sharing their testimony. Similarly, they may have very different expectations of how their testimony should be used. Moreover, neither of these desires may have anything to do with criminal prosecution. Truth commissions, "facing history" initiatives, and collective memory projects, all of which rely heavily on *victim*-witness testimony, are common examples of nonlegal, narrative storytelling and, in many cases, more accurately reflect the person's desired outcomes.[43] The tensions between the motivations and the expectations of fact finders and victim-witnesses thus raise a range of psychological and ethical, in addition to legal, issues. And yet these tensions receive very little attention, according to Boutruche.

Moving forward, in the next section I put Boutruche's category of the victim-witness into conversation with the points Conley and Stoler made concerning the need to read the accounts of willful killings of civilians both with and against the grain. A comparative reading of two sets of testimonies in terms of what was said (i.e., with the grain) and what went unsaid or was erased through transcription (i.e., against the grain) points to an important interpretive difficulty, however. The category of the victim-witness is not a stable one. The same informant can, over the course of their testimony, be a victim at one moment, a victim-witness at another, a witness at still another, and a hearsay source in yet another. The evidentiary weight we afford an account, either in whole or in part, thus must take into account the source's changing epistemological relationship to the facts/"facts" reported *and* the subsequent presentation of them to others, as the two are not always the same. A comparative discussion of victim/victim-witness/witness testimonies regarding the widely feared but poorly documented Tatmadaw unit known colloquially as the "Short Pants," which reportedly operated much like a death squad, follows. Attention to these same issues then shifts to alleged shoot-to-kill incidents, which is a particular genre of indiscriminate attacks on civilians.

SHORT PANTS

Accounts of "death squads" moving from village to village killing people—purportedly because they were suspected of either being actual KNU/KNLA members or having ties to the NSAG—began to circulate in eastern Bago Region in September 1998, where Tatmadaw battalions had been conducting Four Cuts operations for more than a year. (The west side of the Sittaung River, which divided Bago from north to south, was a brown area, while the east side was a black one.) Victims, Karen sources said, were typically murdered with knives, often beheaded afterward, and then dumped, typically in rivers and streams, for others to find. KHRG collected these accounts and then published them in 1999 as a lengthy section subsumed within a larger fact-finding report on human rights violations in the eastern Bago Region. (The "what" and the "how" of these particular accounts provide context for the evaluation of IHRC's later documentation and representation of willful killings during the Northern Offensive.)[44] KHRG's reporting on the Short Pants is based on fifty interviews, with the details regarding their actions divided into four parts: structure and purposes, methods, killings, and other activities (e.g., demands for forced labor and extortion). A close reading of the source quotes and KHRG's interpretations of them indicates that the report's narrativity was structured not only around direct, first-person accounts, but also on statements of conjecture, supposition, hearsay, and rumor, such as those quoted here, with emphasis added, which KHRG did not explicitly flag when making its claims of "fact":

> I've *heard* that they kill the people whose names are in the book . . . to cut all connections [with the KNU/KNLA]. To threaten the public so they won't dare contact them in the future and won't dare to give them rations. This is the main objective of their killing.[45]

They go to houses and ask the names of the people, and if the person is on the list, they kill them. They were given special authority and a license to kill. . . . With the authority they have, *people have said* that even Operations Command can't comment on their work.[46]

I've *heard* that they have already killed 30 people between Shwegyin and Kyauk Kyi [two towns]. When the group commanded by Bo Nagah [Commander Dragon] came, they said they are supposed to kill 70 villagers in the area. . . . They must kill exactly 70 people, the group that comes when they rotate their troops will also kill 70 people. Each of the groups must kill 70 people.[47]

Now *they have said* that they plan to kill 30 people per month between Shwegyin and Mone [Townships], and 30 more between Mone and Tantabin [Townships]. Among the 30 that they kill, one will be a bad person and the other 29 will be good [innocent] people.[48]

Despite numerous references to written kill lists, KHRG was not able to obtain one during its field research, and no copies have since emerged. Similarly, it was not possible for KHRG researchers to independently verify evidence of official kill quotas either. If anything, the opposite appears to have been the case. Of the 151 civilians reportedly executed in Nyaunglebin District (eastern Bago Region) between March 1997 and April 1999, the local sources KHRG interviewed for the report attributed only 35 to the Short Pants. (Tatmadaw and DKBA troops were allegedly responsible for the remainder of the willful killings.) Yet KHRG analysts did not raise questions about the veracity of these and other difficult to substantiate claims about the Short Pants' strategy and tactics. But a narrow focus on the credibility of some of the statements, while not unimportant, misses a broader issue of importance here—namely, the effects of what anthropologist Michael Taussig refers to as "epistemic murk" on fact-finding and reporting. According to Taussig, such murk arises in extremely violent contexts where fears and fantasies come to define the "social being of truth." In his view, the resulting murk requires an analytical shift from the question of "whether [or not the] facts are real, [to] . . . what the politics of their interpretation and representation are."[49] (Such a shift is antithetical to fact-finding as a project, but epistemic murk nevertheless needs to be taken into account when making "truth" claims based on victim/victim-witness/witness testimonies in very violent contexts.) In the case of the Short Pants, the murkiness is not limited to interpretations and representations of "facts" in the collected accounts, but extends to those of KHRG and, by extension, my own.

Officially named "guerrilla retaliation units," the "death squads," as KHRG dubbed them in the title of its report, are known to have operated out of the Bureau of Special Investigations of the military government's Directorate of Defense Services Intelligence (DDSI). The companies, which typically consisted of small sections (groups of no more than ten soldiers), preferred to employ their own self-declared names, such as Monsoon (Mouq thon), Lightening (Moe kyo), and Sweeper (D'myet hleh), as overheard by several witnesses while listening to them interrogate villagers. But Karen speakers generally referred to them more simply as Baw di boh (a name the soldiers allegedly did not like) because of the short pants they wore.[50] Unlike regular soldiers, the sources for the report repeatedly mentioned, the Short Pants units eschewed standard issue uniforms. Instead, they wore ordinary civilian clothing during the day and changed into guerrilla camouflage gear, including short pants, at night, when they reportedly sought out their victims, though many of the first- and secondhand accounts actually concerned daytime incidents. The units carried AK-47 and AR assault rifles, eyewitnesses also said, which are better suited for combat in the jungle than the ones rank-and-file troops use, yet they did almost all of their killing by hand with knives. Separate estimates of the number of people executed, according to these same local sources, generally fluctuated between fifty and one hundred, though KHRG claimed that the actual total was significantly higher, quite possibly double or triple this figure, because many people allegedly disappeared during the time period studied but were never found.[51]

While the empirical basis for KHRG's (guess-) estimate is unclear—no explanation was provided—the reported killings did fall into one of two clear categories based on the details in the excerpts from the interview transcripts. The first category was ad hoc in nature. Short Pants sections reportedly killed people who were going about their daily business outside the village (cultivating fields, fishing in streams, walking on paths, and so on). The victims, typically no more than one or two at a time, simply had the misfortune to be in the wrong place at the wrong time, according to accounts by people who did not personally witness the events. The second category was targeted. "When they target a specific person for execution, a [Short Pants] section usually enters the village sometime in the night, surrounds the person's house and orders them to come out, then takes the person away and executes them outside the village." (It was unclear whether the claim was based on firsthand or secondhand knowledge, as well as the extent to which the pattern was the same where other targeted executions reportedly occurred.) "On occasion," this particular source continued, "they will have another villager go to fetch the suspect or will call the suspect to go with them as a guide and then execute him or her once they are outside the village."[52] Regardless of whether or not the killings were random or targeted, they almost always occurred out of sight according to the account, after the victim was led away. The statements are thus limited to what happened prior to the killing, as described previously, or after the killing, as described later. No direct eyewitness accounts of a killing appear in the report, which is a curious omission if the goal of the Short Pants was to generate widespread terror.

The after-the-fact accounts focus on the material evidence left behind—most commonly, desecrated corpses. "They cut out people's tongues, cut their ears off and cover their faces with their own intestines," stated one witness, whose description was echoed by others. "They do that so the villagers will be afraid. Now if we hear their voices, our hands and knees tremble and we can't do anything."[53] "They hung one of the heads on the path out of the village that goes to Mone [Township] and another on the path to Ler Doh [Kyaukgyi Township]," a different victim-witness explained, relating the Short Pants orders in his own words. "We had to cut bamboo and weave it into stands like those used [to support containers of] drinking water and then put the heads on them. . . . They ordered people to do sentry duty around those heads and if the heads disappeared, they said the villagers would have to replace them with our own heads. They kept them there for over a month and then another army group came and forced the villagers to bury the heads."[54] But unlike regional offensives, the executions and the desecration of corpses did not produce the large-scale forced migration of civilians out of the affected areas, which had long been the primary goal of the Tatmadaw's Four Cuts strategy. The difference begs a larger question: What was the larger purpose of the Short Pants?

One speculative claim, presented as a theory in the KHRG report, links the establishment of the Short Pants companies to widely known rivalry between Lieutenant-General Khin Nyunt, then the head of Military Intelligence, and Vice-Senior General Maung Aye, whose strong preference for regional offensives had failed to end continued KNU/KNLA resistance to centralized military rule. According to this theory, Khin Nyunt formed the Short Pants to accomplish what Tatmadaw battalions could not on their own: terrorize civilians into permanently breaking all contact with the NSAG regardless of whether or not they fled the area, an explanation that several of the local sources voiced themselves. The theory proffered by KHRG arguably explains why the units operated independently of the normal chain of command, were active only in areas where battalions were not present, and roamed the township in ways inconsistent with normal troop rotations—claims that appear in many of the interview excerpts.[55] Thus it became impossible to predict when and where the Short Pants companies might target someone for execution.

After-the-fact evidence, not available to KHRG at the time, complicates the NGO's speculations, however. The rivalry between the two generals did not end until Khin Nyunt's enemies placed him under house arrest in 2004. Reports of killings by Short Pants companies appear to have largely ceased by 2001, though they reappeared during the Northern Offensive, which I discuss in the next section. In fact, the 1999 KHRG report, with its lengthy section on the death squads, remains the only one dedicated to the Short Pants in the vast human rights section of the Burma/Myanmar Online Library meta-archive. The absent presence of the Short Pants in this meta-archive plausibly suggests that the units may have instead been a short-lived experiment under the supervision of Brigadier General Tin Aye, then the head of the Southern Regional Command, and not, as KHRG feared at the time, a model that would be replicated in other townships.[56]

Details on different aspects of the Short Pants in the KHRG report were not limited to the killings that sources claim the sections committed or to suppositions about their origins and objectives. But the decision to focus on these two specific issues is useful in that they return us to the problem that epistemic murk poses for fact finders and their subsequent narration of what allegedly occurred. The "what" and "how" of documentation and analysis in contexts of considerable epistemic murk, such as those involving the Short Pants, requires very careful attention to how the boundaries between fact and fiction, as well as news and rumor, are often intertwined rather than distinct. Such attention necessitates careful parsing of the documentation and nuanced qualifications of "truth" claims—two things that are not always present in human rights reports like KHRG's one on this form of violence: summary executions. The repeated shifts back and forth between individual accounts, presented in the excerpted form of quotes, as reproduced earlier, and the report writers' representations of them as part of its overarching narrative about the Short Pants, is a case in point. The repeated shifts in "voices" between the two are not always clearly demarcated, making it difficult, in the absence of the full interview transcripts, to determine when KHRG is speaking on behalf of its informants and when its fact finders are speaking on behalf of the organization. As a result, the boundary between what is conveyed (narrative content) and how it is conveyed (narrative discourse) is blurred, further adding to the epistemic murk that already surrounds the origins, purpose, and actions of the Short Pants. A strikingly different form of narrativity characterizes the testimonies in IHRC's archive on the Northern Offensive, including the Short Pants, and their representations of them in its two memorandums.

THE QUASI-AFFIDAVIT

IHRC's interview process and transcription procedures produced an unusual type of narrativity, which I term the *quasi-affidavit*. An affidavit proper, which means "he has declared on oath," has its origins in medieval law. Today, an affidavit is a written account of someone's statement of facts, usually as it relates to a legal proceeding. As a general rule, these facts are limited to matters within the person's firsthand knowledge, which may also include their actions, thoughts, and intentions at the time. But in practice, hearsay often appears in affidavits, although it may or may not be admissible in legal proceedings. Typically, an affidavit has three parts: a commencement, a statement that swears that everything is true under threat of penalty; an attestation clause, which certifies who made the oath and the date; and signatures of the author and the witness(s), often notarized or otherwise authenticated. The 150 testimonies IHRC's researchers gathered are quasi-affidavits, with the prefix meaning here "partly but not fully." That is, the transcribed testimonies exhibit some of the formal properties of this genre of documentation but not all of them.

The testimonies, stripped of interview questions and devoid of transcription notes, begin with a brief biography of the affiant and include a statement of facts (direct knowledge) and "facts" (indirect knowledge) on violent incidents, with the focus on the Northern Offensive, and in many cases, an acknowledgment of consent, such as this one: "I consent to having my name be put on a witness list for a future investigation (e.g., UN process), but please do not use my name in any public documents. You can use any of the other [information] in any public document."[57] But the testimonies were not sworn under oath, nor were they notarized by an independent third-party witness. Nevertheless, the testimonies, in terms of the "what" they contain and the "how" of their representation both within IHRC's archive and its published memorandums, were fashioned with this future possibility in mind. As a consequence, the epistemic murk that explicitly characterized but was not acknowledged in the KHRG-collected accounts of the Short Pants is not self-evident here. Instead, the narrativity of the quasi-affidavit, presumably as shaped by the interview questions, largely restricts the testimony to the source's basic senses—what they physically saw, heard, and felt—though many examples of hearsay and speculation can easily be found in the archive as well.

Interestingly, several of IHRC's sources claimed to have had contact with Short Pants sections well after 2001, years after they reportedly ceased operations in areas where KHRG had collected testimonies. The sections were also active in townships farther north than the ones KHRG documented in 1999.[58] One source, Number 52, reported periodic encounters, approximately ten in number, with Short Pants soldiers in 2003. Some of the details are consistent with the information KHRG gathered five years earlier: the sections consisted of four to five men drawn from different infantry battalions, and they wore civilian clothing, shorts, and jungle boots. But in sharp contrast to the KHRG accounts, the soldiers made no effort to hide their individual identities, he said, speaking as a *victim*-witness. Even five years after the fact, he was able to recall the names of four of the officers who beat him, three times in total, as well as their favorite dish: a special local curry. "They were there [village name redacted] for about a year, and then I heard they were disbanded. . . . They killed villagers a lot, so the officers decided to order them back to their [Tatmadaw] units and not to go further [i.e., continue]."[59] But specific details on the killings in the quasi-affidavits, such as this one, which the interviewer did not explore further, were very rare. The reasons are unclear, with the most likely explanation being the primary purpose of the interview, which sought to identity whether broader patterns of violence against civilians during the Northern Offensive existed. Willful killings that occurred prior to the Northern Offensive simply may not have been subject to follow-up questions.

Another source, Number 142, a former village head, provided a similar account, but in much greater detail than was the norm in the majority of the interviews IHRC conducted. A Short Pants section arrived in his area in January 2006, just as the Northern Offensive was getting underway, and remained there well into 2007. The soldiers, three of whose names became known to him, again wore camouflage clothing, short pants, and black jungle boots, which the informant compared to those worn by "American soldiers." They carried some rocket-propelled grenades in addition to AK-47 rifles, but he made no mention of combat-style knives, the signature weapon of the Short Pants.[60] No one in the village knew anything about the Short Pants sections when this one entered the village, he explained. The eight-man section announced its presence by seizing five villagers, including the headman and the secretary, whom they then tied against the posts underneath the church. Number 142, now speaking as a witness, who had been away collecting vegetables, returned to find a soldier beating one of the older men. The source, again in his role as a witness, intervened by speaking to the soldier in Burmese, stating, "'You should not do this.'" Number 142 then explained that he had waved a logging permit he had received earlier from the local government authorities, which he believed gave him some official standing in the eyes of the soldiers. "'It is not your business,' one of the soldiers said, but after that, they released the people from the church," recalled Number 142.

Not surprisingly, everyone refused to serve as the village head following this incident. But rather than forcing someone to serve, the Short Pants section organized a public meeting and required one person from each household to come and write down numbers on a piece of paper. The villagers had to take turns selecting a piece of paper, Number 142 recalled. "Whoever selected number one was the village chief," number two would be the second, and so on up to five, with each person required to serve a three-month term in succession. Number 142 selected number one, but the other household heads refused to take the position after his term expired. Inexplicably, there was no stated retaliation in response to the refusal, an important nonevent that went unexplored by the interviewers.

For reasons not specified in this testimony, Number 142, now recounting this incident as a victim and a witness, agreed to continue as village head until he eventually fled the area for the border in 2007, even though the soldiers beat him on numerous occasions and burned his cardamom gardens, an important cash crop, well before then. The soldiers beat other villagers as well, typically following an attack by the KNLA when the section was out on patrol, but they did not torture or kill anyone, he said. That only occurred when people ventured outside the village alone or in small groups. "They would rape or kill them," he claimed, but without providing an estimated number, even though village heads are expected to keep detailed lists of who lives in the village. "For this reason, . . . they [the villagers] would go in groups of five or more. If the soldiers see more than five, they might not do anything," the former village head stated. "If there was a group, they would tell them to sit down and put their heads down. They would say, 'Do not look at our faces.'"

He closed his testimony regarding the Short Pants section with another incident, the details of which originated with someone else and thus were hearsay. Four women from another village reportedly had the misfortune to encounter this section while walking along a path about one hour away. The soldiers beat all four of them, he had heard, but stated this as a fact to the interview team. "One escaped, but the other three were killed. The woman that escaped ran back to my village but did not say what happened." Another villager later found the bodies and asked some women 'to go cover the bodies because they had no clothes.'" The village head helped bury the bodies afterward, he continued, noting that the Short Pants section's soldiers left their signature behind: all of their throats had been cut.

Number 142's testimony warrants the space given to it for several reasons. Perhaps most obviously, it has a clear plotline with a beginning (church incident), middle (village headman system and periodic beatings), and end (rape and then murder of the women). The full narrative arc distinguishes it from the briefer accounts of the Short Pants in the IHRC archive and, of course, the highly abbreviated examples in the KHRG report, which only appear in the form of block quotes excerpted from the interview transcripts. But the details, elements of which are also found in other testimonies in IHRC's archive, indicate that the Short Pants sections used a particular village as a base of their operations for extended periods of time and rarely killed any of the inhabitants, and the number executed elsewhere was not known. These patterns, if representative of those in areas during the Northern Offensive not documented by IHRC, depart significantly from their conduct during the late 1990s, when terrorizing rural populations through a combination of violence and rumor was the primary objective of the Short Pants, according to KHRG. The IHRC research team struggled to interpret the significance of the sections as a result, stating in its policy memorandum that the Short Pants could variously be a "highly trained special force, a mobile hit squad, and/or a special reconnaissance force."[61]

The "and/or" is important here because it avoids the common tendency in human rights reports to provide definitive answers without any qualification, even in contexts where epistemic murk is pervasive. Further research, should future investigations into the international crimes the Short Pants allegedly committed occur, may provide more insight into the primary purpose of the sections. But in the interim, what tentative conclusions can be reached? The accumulated facts and "facts" present in IHRC's interview transcripts suggest that the Short Pants killings were neither widespread nor systematic in nature. Yet similarities (e.g., the "uniform" worn, the intimate nature of the killings, and the subsequent desecration of the corpses) do indicate that the different sections appeared to share a broad goal, namely terror through willful killings, and the soldiers employed the same methods to accomplish it. These patterns by themselves, however, do not provide sufficient evidence to determine whether the creation and deployment of the Short Pants sections at various moments in time was a matter of state policy or an experiment by a single Tatmadaw regional commander, a claim that is, without further support, speculation as well. By contrast, the details of "shoot-to-kill" incidents present in dozens of the quasi-affidavits, despite their fragmentary nature, more fully support long-standing NGO allegations that such a policy existed, though the type of narrativity used in the memorandums necessitates a qualification of IHRC's claim.

PERFORMING DISTINCTION

An overwhelming body of documentation, collected by many different fact-finding groups over the course of decades, shows that Tatmadaw units employed a standardized set of tactics to coerce everyday "compliance" in brown areas where they had established permanent bases or camps near villages. Forced labor, which "seized" villagers' time and thus their agency, was one. Travel restrictions, which "seized" time, and by extension agency, in a different manner, was another. The restrictions could last anywhere between several days to several weeks, and they limited the ability of villagers to work their rice fields, cultivate cash crops, and gather forest products, as well as engage in upland-lowland trade. Their labor time, rather than being actively redirected to serve military-related purposes (e.g., building perimeter fortifications, delivering messages between officers, and carrying rations as well as ammunition), as was often the case with routine forced labor, was instead consumed by inactivity. Simply, villagers, trapped behind a bamboo fence with only one exit guarded by soldiers, could not freely come and go as they pleased. The restrictions were also expensive. Villagers were generally able to obtain permission to engage in their everyday livelihood activities unless a total ban was in place, but only after paying a fee, without which getting a travel pass was impossible. Such fees, which the village head gathered and then gave to the local commander, quickly became extremely burdensome for people living on the margins of the cash economy.[62]

Normally, a Tatmadaw officer conveyed the details of any travel restrictions or total bans to village heads at a face-to-face meeting. Written instructions, unlike forced labor orders, were thus uncommon. KHRG was able to obtain a rare written example, however, and assuming the document is representative of what was said during face-to-face meetings, it communicated an important element of the travel restrictions in brown areas:

Stamp   Frontline #XX Infantry Battalion
Frontline #XX Infantry Battalion   Column X Headquarters
Column X Headquarters   Letter Number: XXX/Co. X/ OoX
                                                  Date: 1999 September XX

To: Village Head
    XXX village

Subject: To inform all villagers who live in villages [redacted]
1) We, the Army Column, are searching out and fighting the Nga Pway ["ringworms," derogatory slang for the KNLA] in the jungle, in the mountains, in the rivers and the valleys by day and night. We, the Army, have mistakenly shot the villagers.
2) We, the Army, do not want to shoot innocent villagers. We inform the villagers as follows so that this will not occur again.
   (a) Do not hunt or beat the bush [to flush out game] with guns in the jungle.
   (b) Do not run away when you see the Army. If you run away, we will consider you to be Nga Pway and you will be shot.
   (c) Do not go from one village to another at night. If it is an emergency matter, go along the path using a lamp or firebrand. Do not use a flashlight. If the lamp suddenly goes dark, you must continue on by singing a song.
3) We inform you that action will be taken against villagers and villages who do not follow the above.

                                                        Signature
                                                        XXX XXX
                                                   Column Commander
                                                     Column X H.Q.
                                         Frontline #XX Infantry Battalion[63]

The written notice makes the rules of engagement clear, at least in cases of 2(a), 2(b), and 2(c). Villagers were responsible for performing the principle of distinction in these particular ways in these specific contexts. Otherwise, a soldier, declared the column commander, could "justifiably" shoot to kill without making any further effort to determine whether the person was in fact a civilian or a combatant. The logic of the written notice thus reflects the predisposition of Tatmadaw soldiers to view Karen in brown areas as "pre-insurgents" whose mobility must be regulated to protect themselves against "insurgents" (i.e., the KNLA). One example, interviewee Number 146, speaking at this moment as a witness, emphasized this point. "[General] Tin Aye said," in idiomatic terms, "'when you pick mangos with the stick, you are able to identify the ripe mangos, but if you do not have a stick, then you cannot tell which mangoes are ripe. In this case you have to pick all of the mangos,'" Number 146 recalled. "This means that the leaders of the villages, who are the sticks, have to help identify the KNU. Without the leaders from the villages, if the army goes to the area and sees a civilian, they will consider them as members of the KNU and will shoot them, because they will not be able to identify them," Number 146 explained. "He [General Tin Aye] said that we had to go back and tell the villagers very well, until they understand, that this is the last warning and if they do not listen this is the choice they have made. He [the General] said, 'if you do not go back and inform the villagers, it is your fault,'" reemphasizing the point that the burden of distinction was upon the civilian, not the soldier.[64]

Testimonies regarding the pass system, which was possibly created in part to reduce the frequency of such shootings as well as generate income for soldiers through the imposition of fees, date back to the first generation of human rights reports in the early 1990s. The system effectively linked individual identity to geographic place in a manner recognizable to bureaucrats everywhere. In many brown areas, it was not possible to obtain a travel pass without first acquiring a recommendation "letter." According to former village head, interviewee Number 100, the township government designed the template, which the village head had to complete by hand every time a person requested a pass; it required basic information about the applicant: name, father's name, age, and place of residence, as well as the destination, purpose of the trip, and the amount of time needed. The letter closed with a simple attestation, which the head of the village would then have to sign: "I certify that this is my villager and I recommend my villager."[65] (Village heads had to fill in and sign their own letters, he added, but without transcription notes it is impossible to discern whether he said so with irony, frustration, and/or exhaustion.) The person then had to obtain an additional stamp (the Tat Kwe seal) and signature from the infantry battalion based in the area; otherwise the pass was not valid. The number of days permitted varied, with one being the most common length of time granted, according to the IHRC quasi-affidavits. Very few livelihood activities could be completed in one day, so the limited duration forced villagers to devote additional time and funds to obtaining letters on a regular basis. "Sometimes, I would have to write recommendation letters all day," said Number 100, speaking as another victim-witness in terms of his time and labor consumed by the task, to one IHRC interview team.[66]

Compliance with the system, outlined here using excerpts from some the transcripts, was difficult, as its implementation could be arbitrary, which often made advance planning impossible. Again, Number 100 recalled, "I don't remember how many times the letters were closed in 2005," the year prior to the start of the Northern Offensive. "They would close and open them for very short periods of time (a few days or one week), and then switch back and forth. If the village chief allowed a two-day permission during a month when only a one-day permission was allowed, the village chief was punished as well. . . . The military came to me and said, 'If you break the rules again, you will be punished. You get one warning.'"[67] Village heads could also be punished if the people they vouched for did not follow the terms of the pass, by traveling to a different place, failing to specify all of the goods taken to market for trading, overstaying the time limit, and so on. But the primary responsibility rested with the villager, numerous people said. "If a villager was caught without a pass, they would be accused of being KNU," explained one village head, Number 146, speaking from experience.[68] "They would beat you, and if you weren't beaten you would be sent to the Taw Oo [Toungoo] army base. If you had money, you would have to bribe them to be safe. If a person didn't have money, they might be killed. This happened to people in my village," he continued, again speaking as a witness.[69] Another villager echoed the village head's claim through a series of if-then statements of his own, which indicated in his mind that arbitrary violence against civilians was permissible: "If we were caught without a travel pass, if they wanted to kill us, they could. If they wanted to torture us, they could. If they wanted to send us to jail, they could. If had a travel pass, it was evidence that I was going the right way."[70]

Such statements, when viewed in the aggregate, support IHRC's claim that the use of travel restrictions was widespread and systematic in Thandaung Township, if not brown areas more generally, which many fact-finding organizations, including the ILO as part of its 1998 CoI, have also concluded, referencing interviews of their own. However, the footnoted examples of the organization and implementation of the travel pass system in the memorandum, when compared against the full quasi-affidavit transcripts in IHRC's archive, provide few details as to whether the first- and second-hand accounts of violence were or were not affected by other contextual elements, for example, recent violations of the rules by fellow villagers or recent KNU/KNLA activity nearby. The absence of such details makes an independent assessment of whether the incidents of violence reported were wholly dependent on the soldier's discretion or dictated by official policy, an important distinction that circles back to the question of whether higher-level commanders bear criminal responsibility for violence committed by their subordinates. But in so called free-fire (i.e., black) areas, no direct communication between soldiers and civilians was reportedly needed. Many of IHRC's victim-witnesses (i.e., people fired upon) and witnesses (i.e., people who saw that occur) stated that soldiers simply shot at them without making any effort to determine whether they were combatants. The narrativity of these accounts, which IHRC described as "shoot-on-sight" incidents, is highly fragmented in nature to begin with, and appears even more so in the memorandums as result of what is erased through citational practices.

FREE-FIRE ZONES

Typically, KNLA activity in brown areas led to a complete travel ban. Such bans, which could last for considerable periods of time, transformed everyday places outside of villages in brown areas—rice fields, gardens, bamboo groves, forest paths, and so on—into spaces where the principle of distinction temporarily disappeared. But black areas were always already lethal spaces according to many of the people IHRC interviewed—one of whom, speaking as a witness, bluntly put it in causal terms: "If the military saw us, they would shoot us."[71] During the Northern Offensive, Tatmadaw battalions treated most of Thandaung Township, the geographic area IHRC studied, as a black area, a conclusion the researchers reached based on the extrapolation of statements made in many of the quasi-affidavits. When taken together, the statements, as interpreted by IHRC's researchers, led them to assert that Tatmadaw soldiers made no concerted effort to differentiate civilians from combatants regardless of their "age, sex, proximity to opposition forces, and whether they [were] carrying weapons."[72] All told, IHRC's researchers calculated, while attempting to avoid double counting, that the "shoot-on-sight" incidents resulted in at least thirty separate deaths.

[22] Clinic Database, Interview Nos. 1, 4, 8, 12, 26, 31, 33, 35, 47, 49, 51, 52, 57, 58, 61, 76, 80, 82, 84, 89, 90, 92, 97, 99, 100, 105, 107, 109, 114, 118, 120, 132, 133, 136, 139, 142, 146, 147, and 151.[73]

The "limited geographic and temporal scope of its investigation," IHRC added, meant the fatalities "represent only a small fraction" of the total.[74] IHRC's claim regarding fractionality is, without question, true. The qualified figure of "at least" thirty is based on recollections provided by a small number of informants (39 out of the 150 people interviewed), who separately shared details regarding indiscriminate "shoot-on-sight" incidents that occurred both in the year prior to (2005) and during the first twelve months of the Northern Offensive (2006) in one specific township (Thandaung). According to TBBC's local partner ERA surveys, Tatmadaw operations in this township displaced more than 5,000 people in 2006, adding to the more than 13,000 IDPs already in hiding areas outside of their abandoned villages, whose own experiences, if interviewed, would presumably raise the total number of incidents and civilian deaths significantly.[75] (TBBC did not publish Thandaung-specific IDP figures for 2007–2008, the final two years of the Northern Offensive, however, which makes it impossible to use the stated scale of the conflict-induced displacement as a potential proxy.)

Moreover, Tatmadaw operations displaced tens of thousands of civilians not just in Thandaung, but across at least five townships in KNU-delineated Karen State, as well as two more in neighboring Kayah State, which again suggests the total number of civilian deaths was far more than 370, as reported by FBR. But what "factual" significance should be attached to the fractional figure IHRC reported in the memorandum?

Reliable models for estimating excess population mortality rates, developed by epidemiologists, certainly exist. Patterns, based on decades of accumulated data from conflict settings and humanitarian emergencies around the world, indicate that a two- to tenfold increase over baseline mortality rates, when they are known, is common. IDPs almost always experience

FIGURE 4. Internally displaced persons at momentary rest. SOURCE: Photo by Ken MacLean.

higher mortality rates than do populations that remain "in place," including refugees in camps. Additionally, most of the crisis-attributable morality is indirect, with the exception of high-intensity armed conflicts, such as Syria. Further, children under five generally have much higher death rates, which may lead to overestimates for the population as a whole, while the elderly tend to be undercounted, which can result in the opposite problem. And precrisis vulnerabilities, such as food insecurity, play a significant role in shaping mortality outcomes, but are often difficult to incorporate into models.[76] These well-documented epidemiological patterns return us to the point that Bridget Conley made at the outset of the chapter—namely, the significance of excess mortality statistics is not simply the number; it is also crucially about "how the story of violence is told."[77] In the case of humanitarian crises, the story is typically about real-time "pathways to action," specifically, what resources need to be mobilized immediately and how civilian protection can be improved now.[78] By contrast, human rights fact finders seek to document, to the extent historically possible, conflict-related mortalities, if not in total, then with regard to patterns, with the ultimate goal of criminal accountability in mind. The question then becomes, what kind of story was IHRC trying to tell by restricting its claims about the existence of a shoot-to-kill policy to an unspecified fraction?

Narratives in IHRC's quasi-affidavit archive concerning shoot-on-sight incidents involving civilians varied, but they shared enough features that their storied accounts can be categorized into genres, though IHRC did not do so itself in the memorandums. The most common accounts were what appear on the page, because they lack transcription notes, as matter-of-fact statements concerning the incidents that people personally experienced and/or witnessed. Not surprisingly, most of these accounts described momentary, unexpected encounters with Tatmadaw soldiers who then reportedly opened fire upon them while they were going about their daily lives or attempting to flee from attacks on their villages.[79] But many other accounts provided broader, reportedly patterned context for such incidents. However, these quasi-affidavit claims often relied on a mix of direct knowledge, conjecture, supposition, and hearsay, which are not explicitly acknowledged in the memorandums due to the transformation of the transcripts, some of which are excerpted from the archive here, into interview numbers.

"I was afraid of the Burmese military. They were very active. The villagers couldn't farm or do any work peacefully as normal, and I was very afraid. By very active, I mean the Burmese military came into the jungle, and if they saw villagers, they [would] shoot at villagers."[80] "I was a young child when I first heard it [the term black area]," another person stated. "If the military goes to a black area, they can do whatever they want, and villagers will run away whenever they hear the military is coming. Villagers do not want to face the military in a black area. The military will arrest people and kill the people they catch."[81] "When the Burmese military came into a place, I would leave, so I didn't see it myself," said another. "I heard from others that the Burmese would execute them and thrown them away 'like a leaf.'"[82] "In the black area, we were mixed with KNU, and the military did not differentiate between the KNU and Karen people," explained one more source. "Their enemy should have just been the KNU, but the military did not care. . . . Whenever you heard or saw the military, you had to focus on escaping the military to save your life."[83] Similar statements can be found throughout the archive, giving credence to IHRC's claims of differential rules of engagement whereby the principle of distinction disappeared in black areas. But again, it is impossible to parse these statements for readers who only had access to the memorandums, because they only appear as interview numbers in the documents' copious footnotes.

Spatialized representations of shoot-on-sight stories constituted another genre. By 2004, the year before the Northern Offensive started, Tatmadaw units had established two parallel lines of control stretching north to south. The western line ran through lowland areas of the townships along the Sittaung River Valley.[84] The eastern line included townships approximately one hundred kilometers from the border with Thailand. IDP hiding areas were located in the rugged mountains between these two lines and the small number of military access roads that crosscut this sizable black area. The frequency of conflict-induced displacement was high in these areas (reportedly three times per year on average), and food security, which poor soil further exacerbated, was low (harvests of only 40 to 50 percent of what was planted were stated as common).[85]

Some of the accounts from people who fled these areas identified long-standing black areas in geographic terms, the most frequently mentioned being areas east of the Day Loh River, which bisects Thandaung Township on a north-south axis. "The military side [i.e., west side] was called 'our land' by the soldiers. The soldiers said that when we enter black areas, if we see anyone, we can do anything we want," said one interviewee. "That is why people dare not hide outside the villages. If they see you, they can kill you. It applied to everyone that was here [as] the military would consider you KNU."[86] Other accounts identified the contours of particular black areas and could name which villages fell within them.[87] These areas also appeared on military maps, according to one former soldier. The maps, he explained, delimited "enemy controlled territory," in this instance in the form of red ink.[88] An officer reportedly told him that "all of the people who stayed in the red area, they are all enem[ies]. . . . Even if they are not soldiers, they are enemies. That means you can shoot someone. We are allowed to shoot if we saw someone in this area." The officer, he continued, "told [this] to us face to face. It was never written down. It [the policy] had a name: It means kill all the people in the area."[89] But as was the case with the prior genre, these details only appear in summarized form without excerpts from the transcripts.

The last genre consisted of "defector" stories provided by former Tatmadaw soldiers. IHRC spoke with seven such individuals, several of whom had served in either Bago Region or Kayin [Karen] State prior to the

Northern Offensive, where large-scale multibattalion clearance operations later took place. Collectively, their testimonies contributed significant background details on the command structure of the Tatmadaw and its operational field practices, including reporting protocols between soldiers in the field and their commanding officers in the rear.[90] One soldier was very blunt when the interview turned to the topic of shoot on sight. "We were told that if we captured someone during the fighting, we should kill them."[91] Who they should kill was somewhat less clear. At one point during the interview, he stated, "The KNU was the enemy." But he then immediately when on to generalize who fell into this category: "The ethnic groups in Burma were our enemies. There are the Kachin, Shan, Arakan, Karen, Kayah, Chin . . . because these groups do not obey the ruling system; they are the enemy." Yet at another point, he again narrowed the category to include only those people in the "front lines," a shorthand phrase widely used to refer to contested areas where Tatmadaw and NSAG troops regularly engaged with one another. "My own captain told us, 'Every enemy who you see in the front lines area, kill them all.'" The varied references to who constitutes the enemy make it difficult to determine whether they were specific to the commander in charge or reflective of Tatmadaw policy, however.

A different soldier, Number 90, after discussing his experiences in the army, also turned to the alleged shoot-on-sight policy, noting that rules of engagement changed after the 1997 offensive. "Before you had to shoot only KNU, but after that you had to shoot anyone. It did not matter who you were. . . . All Karen people you have to kill. If you do not want to you still have to. The rules are only in the town, but in Karen villages there are no rules." The soldier again returned to this issue after recounting his frontline experiences. "The order is if you go the village and you see someone, whoever it is, whether it is KNU or a villager, you kill them. . . . The order came from the three officers" whom he had directly named earlier in the interview. "There were other times where soldiers shot people," he continued, again returning to the topic. "I saw it all the time. . . . Shooting people with the gun is not serious. Most of the time we entered the village, we saw people and they ran away, and we shot at them. In a week, maybe ten people we shot, and they died."

The soldiers' statements, assuming for the moment that they are disinterested (i.e., without the desire to impress) and factually accurate, are damning, though it should be recalled that none of them were operational during the Northern Offensive. Nonetheless, their statements do raise a serious question not explicitly addressed in the methodology sections of either memorandum, namely, acquiescence bias. Such bias occurs when respondents give researchers the answers that the researchers seem to expect. Leading questions are the most common, but not sole, cause of this problem. IHRC employed triangulation, the use of multiple data sources to corroborate findings and to test the validity of conclusions, to avoid this type of bias. (IHRC, citing declarations from Tatmadaw experts and leaked military documents, in addition to the statements made by the former soldiers, led its researchers to assert that "the use of geographic delineation, color-codification, and corresponding differential rules of engagement" provided sufficient evidence to conclude that the willful killings of and indiscriminate attacks on civilians reflect long-standing operational policy, tactical level practices, and enlisted soldier–level discretion.)[92] But without full access to the quasi-affidavits in IHRC's confidential archive, readers of the memorandums are yet again faced with a difficult interpretive decision: to accept on faith or not the conclusions based on strings of interview numbers in the footnotes.

In IHRC's view, that faith was warranted, though the two memorandums did not explicitly frame its reasoning in such terms. IHRC asserted that, as part of its narrative regarding the number of deaths in the archive, the testimonies provided sufficient prima facie evidence for the ICC to issue arrest warrants on three connected grounds. First, IHRC argued, the generals named had knowledge of the international crimes committed due to Tatmadaw reporting protocols. Second, the generals failed to prevent the crimes' continuance, as evidenced by the incidents recounted in the quasi-affidavits. And third, the generals took no subsequent steps to refer the perpetrators of shoot-on-sight incidents to the relevant authorities for punishment.[93] Prima facie, Latin for "at first glance," has an unusual meaning in this context, however, as an ICC arrest warrant is an initiating document (i.e., a summons), not a judicially authorized act. The evidentiary threshold is as a consequence low, set at "reasonable grounds to believe" rather than "substantial grounds to believe," which is what is needed for conviction should the ICC's Office of the Prosecutor bring the case to trial.[94] The testimonies, transcribed and narrated in quasi-affidavit form, were thus meant to provide not a conclusion per se, which is how most people are highly likely to read them, but rather a starting point for a future criminal investigation.

CONCLUSION

Martin Smith, the leading expert on the history of internal armed conflicts in Myanmar following independence, estimates that ten thousand people died annually during the 1950s, 1960s, 1970s, and 1980s. As noted in an earlier chapter, Smith concludes that this figure is "probably fairly accurate" but does not provide any details as to how he arrived at it.[95] Unfortunately, no estimates on the average death tolls since then exist, which is why Bridget Conley's point about the different purposes that fatality figures serve is useful. "The number," she explains, "is rarely *the thing*."[96] In addition, what matters is how the statistic is emploted into a broader story and the instrumental purposes to which the story is then put.[97] Conley's point returns us to the larger issue of narrativity, which is central to "fact" production regardless of whether or not the authors of fact-finding reports and those who conduct advocacy using them acknowledge it. Two types of narrativity, a shorthand term for the analytical examination of storytelling that includes the "how" of representation in addition to the "what," critically shaped the form and content of both memorandums. One type was based on closure, while the other relied on erasure.

Literary scholar Peter Hühn has pointed out that "the plot of the classic detective novel comprises two basically separate stories—the story of the *crime* (which consists of action) and the story of the *investigation* (which is concerned with knowledge)." "In their narrative presentation, however, the two stories are intertwined," he states. "The *first story* (the crime) happened in the past and is—insofar as it is hidden—absent from the present; the *second story* (the investigation) happens in the present and consist of uncovering the first story."[98] Human rights reports, IHRC's memorandums among them, evince some striking similarities to inverted detective stories, in which the identity of the perpetrator is revealed at the beginning, with the remainder of the story devoted to the effort to solve the mystery of how we know they are "guilty." In terms of plot, such reports begin with an executive summary followed by a set of recommendations. The former section identifies the alleged perpetrator and summarizes the alleged crimes committed, while the latter lays out the appropriate actions to be taken in light of the investigative findings: policy changes, institutional reforms, economic sanctions, and/or prosecution. The core of the human rights report thus concerns the "uncovering" (i.e., the story of the investigation) by the "detective" (i.e., the fact-finding organization), with whom the burden of proof resides.

The report, if persuasively presented by the "detective," will convince the reader that the intertwined first and second stories constitute an evidence-based and well-reasoned whole, a marriage of the two that is crucial to establishing credibility and persuasiveness with targeted audiences. In this chapter, the first investigative story concerned willful killings by Shorts Pants, as separately narrated by KHRG and IHRC. The second investigative story concerned spatially and temporally circumscribed shoot-on-sight incidents, with the question of policy at the center of the analysis. Such a policy, if it existed, would potentially make the commanding officers criminally responsible for the actions of their subordinates during the Northern Offensive, which is what IHRC ultimately concluded after completing its investigative review of the quasi-affidavits. But the broader issue of human rights narrativity, to the extent that it resembles the plot of a detective story, includes another "storied" layer that involves disclosure as well.

Ann Stoler, in her examination of violent outbreaks in colonial Indonesia, draws attention to the ways in which plantation owners, journalists, and government officials sought to discern the "intent" behind the incidents, and what types of responses were warranted depending on whether or not they were random or organized in nature. The diverse answers to both questions, she argues, highlight how preexisting forms of cultural knowledge shaped the credibility of different hypotheses concerning motive. I have made a similar analytic move with regard to IHRC's memorandums, albeit with one important difference. "Epistemic murk," to again invoke Michael Taussig's concept, suffused both investigative settings. But in Stoler's case, the patterns of violence (or lack thereof) meant "closure"—a definitive ending to the detective story, a key feature of the genre—was impossible. Simply, no consensus emerged as to what was happening and why. While open endings are possible, albeit rare, in detective stories, they are not acceptable when transposed into human rights contexts. Closure—a definitive statement of who, why, and how (i.e., the means, motive, and opportunity in detective novels)—is required. Otherwise, the document fails to satisfy the traditional conventions of a human rights report.[99]

But upon closer inspection, the traditional representation of closure in the memorandums, and in human rights reports more generally, is somewhat misleading when the commonly used practices of erasure are taken into account. The transformation of the semistructured interviews into quasi-affidavits required the erasure of the informants' body language and tone of voice and the wording of the questions and the follow-up ones, as well as the reworking of the answers into a coherent, linear narrative, sometimes described as "Englishing." The result was a socially produced document rather than a straightforward transcription of what was said, much less how it was said. Due to the need to protect the identities of the informants as well as their relatives inside Myanmar from possible retribution, IHRC employed an additional form of erasure in the memorandums: complete redaction.

With the exception of the very occasional quote, no verbatim traces of the testimonies appear, aside from the long strings of interview numbers in the footnotes, which are meant to function as evidentiary anchors for the "truth" claims made in the body of the text. But without full access to the unredacted quasi-affidavits, the reader has no way to determine the positionality of the informant (i.e., when they are speaking as a victim, victim-witness, witness, or a combination thereof over the course of the interview), or, for that matter, to differentiate direct, firsthand from indirect, second-hand knowledge in the statements. I raise these points not to cast doubt on the credibility of IHRC findings. The contents of the testimonies, even with their limitations, support its conclusions, which other reports on the Northern Offensive, including the one I wrote based on ERA documents in TBBC's archives, further corroborate.[100] Rather, these various points are meant to once again draw attention to the importance of the representational practice of "stockpiling."

Human rights reports purportedly "let the facts speak for themselves," and Ron Dudai's concept of stockpiling helps establish the authority of these "facts" in visual terms in the case of the memorandums. Stockpiling thus relies on the steady accumulation of information to persuade readers that the report is factually accurate, the data objectively interpreted, and the findings contextualized within the appropriate legal frameworks.[101] Consequently, report writers often use stockpiling to convert "subjective" information (e.g., the experiences of individuals in testimonial form) into ostensibly more "objective" quantitative modes of representation (e.g., statistics embedded in tables and charts). Extensive footnotes, one of the defining features of the IHRC memorandums, similarly stockpile "evidence," but do so through the practice of erasure. The legal memorandum, focused on war crimes and crimes against humanity allegedly committed during the Northern Offensive, contains nearly four hundred footnotes, a substantial percentage of which identify other interviews that also "speak to" the same issue:

[83] Clinic Database, Interview Nos. 16, 27, 58, 118, and 139.

[84] Clinic Database, Interview Nos. 2, 5, 11, 13, 16, 27, 30, 37, 39, 44, 49, 59, 87, 89, 92, 93, 114, 115, 122, 124, 128, 136, 141, and 146; Clinical Expert Declaration, Expert 1., para. 90, Clinic Expert Declaration, Expert 4, para. 32.

[85] Clinic Database, Interview Nos. 51, 52, 62, 69, 100, 103, 106, 112, 115, 118, 120, 125, 129, 139. 145, and 146.[102]

The page-after-page accumulation of such lists in both memorandums tells "the story of violence" in a manner that the main text does not by visually bridging the epistemological gap between a particular incident (e.g., a willful killing or an indiscriminate attack on civilians) and an identifiable pattern (i.e., official policy). The extent to which the gap is closed is always contested and thus unfinished, however, as was also the case here. The same is additionally true of the recursive archive examined in the next chapter, which concerns a transnational NGO-led campaign to convince the UN Security Council to initiate an investigative CoI into the long-standing human rights and humanitarian crisis in Myanmar.

CHAPTER 5

Investigating Bodies

The Recursive Logic of Citations

Law rarely engages with its textuality.

—Renisa Mawani

Texts do not exist in isolation; rather, they emerge out of, become embedded in, and then contribute to larger referential ecosystems, a dynamic process that complicates the "what" and "how" of human rights narrativity. Literary scholar Gérard Genette offers a useful way to disaggregate these dynamics in spatial terms. The *peritext*, he explains, includes elements inside the confines of a bound volume, such as the title, cover art and illustrations, frontmatter, and backmatter, as well as the formatting and typography. Such elements "often pass unnoticed due to familiarity or by the inconsequential role they are usually assigned," yet they inflect the meaning of the narrative in numerous ways.[1] By contrast, the *epitext* includes elements outside the text in question, such as interviews, reviews, and commentaries, in addition to the author's own drafts, correspondence, and diaries. These concepts, when taken together, constitute the volume's *paratext*, which Genette describes as "a zone not only of transitions but also of *transaction*: a privileged place of a pragmatics and a strategy, of an influence on the public, an influence that . . . is at the service of a better reception for the text and a more pertinent reading of it."[2] The goal of the paratext, in other words, is to direct the reader's interpretation of a text—for example, a human rights report—in specifically desired ways.

In this chapter, the paratextual transactions under investigation arise out of a transnational NGO-led advocacy campaign that sought to convince the

UN Security Council to authorize a CoI into alleged international crimes in Myanmar. The pragmatics involved and strategies used by the participating NGOs relied heavily on footnotes, which cited previously published documentation, especially that of the UN, to help legitimate overlapping findings and to justify shared policy recommendations. This paratextual practice of quotation, both inside and outside the documentation presented, produced a recursive archive over time, the significance of which highlights yet another modality of human rights "fact" production.

Traditionally understood, the primary purpose of footnotes is "to give as a reference" or "to cite as an authority." The capacity of footnotes to serve in this referential manner complicates Genette's definition of the paratextual, however. As historian Elise Garritzen has noted, the "prime function [of footnotes] in historical discourse is to provide evidence for arguments or to comment on the text." "This renders notes an integral part of the text and disqualifies them as paratexts," Garritizen explains. But at the same time, she continues, "notes perform another function which gives enough reason to classify them also as paratexts: they identify the text as scholarly narrative," which links them to other texts.[3] Thus, she points out, "long lists of sources not only provide sufficient proof for arguments and a testimony of the hard work that the historian had done, but they also revealed the origins of his thoughts by indicating the previous research he had consulted."[4] As a consequence of this dual functionality, footnotes both are and are not paratextual elements because they perform referential work both inside *and* outside the main text.

Why does this dual functionality matter in a human rights context? Many kinds of specialists, most notably lawyers, employ footnotes to buttress arguments regarding existing case law, as well as competing interpretations of it. As legal scholar Renisa Mawani explains, "law's self-generating truth claims are vividly apparent in the recursive, accumulating, and discriminating paper trails of statute and precedent." "By referencing statutes and judgements that came before and by determining which are apposite," she continues, "law cultivates its meanings and asserts its authority while at the same time concealing and sanctioning its material, originary, and ongoing violence."[5] Human rights organizations employ a similar tactic. Their reports often contain hundreds of footnotes citing other publications, especially relevant elements of international human rights, humanitarian, and refugee law. But the epitextual practice of citing other reports, policies, and laws carries with it a number of complications beyond the one voiced by Garritizen.

On the one hand, the footnotes in human rights reports are intended to help legitimate an organization's assertions of expertise, states Ron Dudai.[6] Footnotes in a human rights context thus represent claims that the factual and legal sources "are presented in a transparent way, open for independent review [i.e., fact-checking] by the reader."[7] (Though, as the previous chapters made problematically clear, the underlying sources of the footnotes themselves, where they reference fact-finding data, are often redacted and/or unavailable for review for reasons of confidentiality and security.) On the other hand, the social construction of this expertise rests upon an unstated assumption that provides the basis for assertions of objectivity. Dudai explains, "The Archimedean point of departure for the whole project, is the presentation of these human rights conventions as self-evident, their validity and authority axiomatic."[8] For this reason, he argues, mainstream advocacy-oriented recommendations are presented "not as a moral condemnation or emotional, nationalist claims, but a reference to this or that international convention."[9] Of course, not everyone holds these "ethico-onto-epistemological" positions, which assume that all three concepts (ethics, ontology, and epistemology) should be inseparable when engaging in "responsible" forms of knowledge production.[10]

Critics of human rights as a universal project, for example, maintain that its underlying principles, beliefs, and values are inescapably Western in origin, inform self-interested demands for foreign interventions in the internal affairs of non-Western states, and facilitate the imposition of neoliberal reforms in their wake.[11] But government resistance to human rights claims that run contrary to one's self-interest are, importantly, not limited to pariah states such as Myanmar. The United States, which has long presented itself as a champion of human rights globally, continues to refuse to become party to the Rome Statute on multiple grounds, one of them being the forcefully stated, self-interested need to prevent persecutions of American officials and service members in the name of protecting the country's sovereignty. (The ICC's decision in early 2020 to open an investigation into alleged war crimes in Afghanistan, which would include any American soldiers may have committed, is a direct challenge to US exceptionalism.) The point here is that calls by Western governments for the UN to intervene in Myanmar's internal affairs, while arguably justifiable from a moral perspective given the volume of documentation on the country's human rights situation, were always rejected by successive military-led regimes as being politically hypocritical.[12]

Dudai's observation about the paradoxical nature of footnotes in human rights discourse, although helpful, nonetheless requires further delineation. It does so because Dudai does not differentiate between two forms of indexicality, around which my discussion of paratextual forms of human rights narrativity revolves. Each type of quotation, due to the performative role of indexicality, enjoys a different epistemological relationship with "fact" production. "We know what we are talking about because we cited the UN Special Rapporteur on the human rights situation in Myanmar who has demonstrated X to be true in their report" is one form of indexicality. "We know what we are talking about because our fact-finding proves our reports to be true" is another form of indexicality.[13] The first example quotes others, whereas the second one quotes oneself and thus is self-referential, meaning that the basis of the two respective "truth" claims importantly differ. The interplay between the two forms of indexicality, which is common but rarely acknowledged in human rights reports, was also central to the transnational advocacy campaign (ca. 2003–2011).

The discussion that follows unfolds on two levels simultaneously. First, the chapter provides an abbreviated history of the campaign to convince the UN Security Council to authorize a CoI to investigate the human rights and humanitarian crisis in Myanmar on the grounds that it posed "an international threat to peace and security. (A CoI, like other forms of UN-sponsored fact-finding missions, is organized in response to serious violations of international human rights and humanitarian law to document what has occurred, with the broader goal of promoting accountability and countering impunity.)[14] The historical details require me to again write both with and against the grain to avoid a teleological narrative, as the campaign did not have a clear leadership structure or mutually agreed upon coordinating mechanism. Instead, different NGOs joined in the advocacy effort at different moments and in different ways over the course of nearly a decade. Nevertheless, the key recommendations, later supported by more than a dozen governments, eventually coalesced around a common investigative focus: a set of international crimes that reportedly took place in Myanmar after the Rome Statute entered into force in July 2002, the starting date for which ICC prosecutions became possible.

Second, the chapter also analyzes the campaign in terms of how paratextual documentation practices informed the epitextual, after-the-fact production of "facts" that cite prior ones, as well as the varied responses to this type of human rights narrativity. (Put another way, consider theorist Judith Butler's phrasing, which is a modified extension of Jacques Derrida's arguments regarding deconstruction: "A structure gains its status as structure [its structurality]—only through reiteration, through repeated restatements and reinstatements, which means that there is a substantial measure of performativity at work.")[15] The performative similarities that came to exist across the reports highlight an important but often unnoticed feature of human rights reports in general. Reports routinely "quote" other reports in a variety of ways and, in doing so, produce new referential meanings beyond what is contained in them separately. The practice of "quotation," deliberate in some instances but not in others in the case of the CoI campaign, created a recursive archive, the significance of which in terms of narrativity extends beyond the case of Myanmar.

RESOLUTIONS AS A REFERENTIAL GENRE

UN resolutions, which featured prominently in the CoI campaign, are peculiar documents. The word *resolution* does not appear in the UN's Charter, but the resolution has become the primary genre through which UN bodies make their respective positions known. Regardless of length, UN resolutions follow the same format and consist of three parts linked together, through a series of commas and semicolons, into a single sentence. The heading identifies the specific body, such as the Security Council, that issued the resolution. Preambular clauses follow, the contents of which frame how that body views the problem, such as a "threat to international peace and security," while the operative clauses that form the third part of the resolution outline the specific course(s) of action to be taken in point-by-point fashion. (Gerunds, such as "recalling" and "reaffirming," in the preambular clauses typically refer back to prior resolutions to assert the legitimacy of the subsequent gerunds, such as "acting" and "authorizing," in the operative clauses.) "Decides to remain actively seized of the matter," the phrase that closes nearly all Security Council Chapter VII resolutions, announces, in shorthand diplomat-speak fashion, that other UN bodies shall not make any recommendation with regard to what the Security Council refers to as the "dispute" or "situation" in question until it so requests.

The Security Council has the sole power to define a "threat" and then authorize binding enforcement measures "to maintain or restore international peace and security" under Article 24 of the UN Charter. These measures, as set out in Chapter VII of the charter, permit the use of coercion, including military force, to enforce compliance.[16] However, the framers of the charter did not explicitly define what the concept of "threat to international peace and security" meant, leaving this instead to the discretion of the Security Council to determine on a case-by-case basis.[17] Given this discretion, it is perhaps unsurprising that a comparative analysis of past cases indicates the existence of what one legal scholar described as "a subjective sliding scale of evidence that the Council believes it must articulate in order to legitimize its initial threat to peace determination."[18] Due to this sliding scale, NGOs and several UN bodies have historically cited a diverse array of "threats" to convince the Security Council that the evidentiary threshold has been met and coercive action is now politically as well as morally acceptable.

Since the end of the Cold War, Chapter VII resolutions have become commonplace, leading some observers of the Security Council to argue that their "value" (i.e., symbolic import as well as the likelihood of a targeted state changing its behavior in constructive fashion) has decreased over time.[19] This claim may or may not be true. But as one possible sign of this decrease in value, Article 39 determinations, the threshold that triggers Chapter VII action, routinely stand on those that preceded them, meaning that the determinations are recursively linked to prior ones to justify them. Security Council resolution no. 1127 on Angola (1997), regarding the country's stated "threat to peace and security," is a good example. The final resolution in this epitextual chain of referencing reads: "United Nations Security Council resolution 1404, adopted unanimously on 18 April 2002, after reaffirming Resolution 864 (1993) and all subsequent resolutions on Angola, particularly resolutions 1127 (1997), 1173 (1998), 1237 (1999), 1295 (2000), 1336 (2001), 1348 (2001) and 1374 (2001), the Council extended the monitoring mechanism of sanctions against UNITA [National Union for the Total Independence of Angola, a rebel group] until 19 October 2002." Such exceedingly long recursive sequences, legal scholar Patrik Johannsson notes, are comparatively rare, but he adds that there is a "clear pattern in Security Council practice."[20] The significance of the Security Council–related issues—the absence of a clear definition of what constitutes a "threat to peace and security," the mutable nature of the evidentiary threshold that must be met, and the nonstandardized invocation of precedent—has a direct bearing on the Myanmar CoI campaign, which did not begin as a planned campaign, but instead evolved into one over time.

CAMPAIGN 1.0

Precedent is an earlier event or action that is regarded as an example or guide to be considered in subsequent similar circumstances. The National Coalition Government of the Union of Burma (NCGUB), which styled itself as the government-in-exile after the military regime overturned the results of the 1990 elections, published an important desktop study in October 2003. The study, "The Crisis in Burma: An Agenda for the United Nations Security Council," both cited precedent and set precedent for the CoI campaign that slowly took form in its wake, gained strength in 2008, and effectively ended in 2011 when a quasi-civilian government finally took power. By 2003, in the NCGUB's own words, conditions in Myanmar had become such that it posed a "threat to international peace and security." (Notably, this report and the others that followed did not seek to explain how it was that several neighboring countries, especially China and Thailand, continued to maintain normal economic and diplomatic relations with Myanmar's military-led government during these years.) The NCGUB made its case over the course of forty-seven pages, supported with 181 notes to other documents, more than half of them UN Security Council resolutions concerning other conflicts, the result being a veritable cascade of citations.

To make its case, the NCGUB focused attention on three criteria that its researchers stated the Security Council had referenced in successive Article 39 determinations since 1992: "disruption to democracy," "internal conflict and gross violations of human rights and humanitarian law," and a "dire humanitarian situation." The report's four authors then provided summaries outlining how two or more of these criteria were present in past Chapter VII resolutions concerning the "threats to peace and security" that the former Yugoslavia, Sierra Leone, Haiti, Somalia, Liberia, Rwanda, Burundi, Zaire, Albania, the Central African Republic, and East Timor had presented at various moments in time.[21] The organizing logic of the NCGUB's argument thus rested on an indexical argument; that is, because the Security Council had issued resolutions in these prior instances, Chapter VII action was similarly justified in the case of Myanmar, as all three "threat" criteria were present and UN documented. That such action had yet to occur in this situation (as well as analogous situations), the NCGUB argued, was "primarily due to a lack of political will on the part of the Council members, and/or the obstruction by one or more of the five veto-wielding permanent members."[22] But the NCGUB, after acknowledging the reality of Security Council dynamics, nonetheless pushed forward by detailing a plan titled "Options for Coercive Measures." The plan included a range of political, economic, and military policies that, if seriously implemented, the government-in-exile believed, would force positive behavioral change on the part of the military regime.

Precisely why the NCGUB decided to make its case for Chapter VII action at this particular moment in time remains unclear. (I was not able to reach the authors for comment.) Broadly speaking, the "threats" had not significantly worsened during the year leading up to the report's publication. In fact, the regime had actually agreed to cooperate with the ILO on the issue of forced labor, and it also released, with much fanfare, a seven-point "Road Map to Discipline-Flourishing Democracy." Political opposition groups promptly rejected the "Road Map" on multiple grounds, but many NSAGs welcomed it, on the assumption that they would be directly involved in the promised national convention to discuss the process. Their hopes proved to be misplaced, as also happened to be the case with the NCGUB's recommendations. The Security Council did not issue a Chapter VII resolution on Myanmar. (Of the two dozen such resolutions it authored that year, nearly all of them concerned major conflicts in the Middle East and sub-Saharan Africa.)[23] And unsurprisingly, the regime made no substantive effort to improve its conduct where human rights and humanitarian affairs were concerned. (The UN Commission on Human Rights resolution no. 2003/12 regarding Myanmar, which "recalled" numerous prior resolutions, expressed a long list of "grave concerns" about the situation.)[24] Nevertheless, the NCGUB report provided, without the intention of doing so, the conceptual framework for the narrativity of subsequent reports arguing for a CoI.

CAMPAIGN 2.0

The September 2005 report "Threat to Peace: A Call for the UN Security Council to Act in Burma," picked up where the NCGUB's 2003 report had left off in paratextual terms.[25] The report, commissioned by former president of the Czech Republic Václav Havel and Nobel Peace laureate Archbishop

Desmond Tutu, was intended to provide an "objective and definitive report on the threat that the Government of Burma poses both to its own people and to regional peace and security," as the two luminaries explained in its foreword. DLA Piper Rudnick Gray Cary (DLA et al.), one of the world's largest multinational law firms following a recently completed three-way merger, agreed to prepare the report. In some respects, the law firm was an obvious choice. The then chair of the board, former US senator George Mitchell, was committed to peaceful forms of conflict resolution. (Mitchell had served as the special envoy for Northern Ireland, during which he had helped negotiate the Good Friday Agreement, and several years later he had acted as the special envoy for Palestine-Israel.) The firm, immediately upon its creation, also launched New Perimeter, a first-of-its-kind initiative to support international pro bono efforts for social causes. (The report was one product of this initiative.) But the choice was an odd one in one important respect. The firm specialized in a wide range of corporate, legislative, and regulatory law, but had no demonstrated expertise on human rights, humanitarian, or refugee issues at the time. The lack of such expertise constituted an absent presence in the report's narrativity, as none of its findings were explicitly framed within these international legal frameworks.

As is the case with all desktop studies, the research team's fact-finding efforts were inevitably limited to the conclusions prior reports had reached. In this instance, the focus was on the Security Council. "To guide our work," the report's authors wrote, "we first reviewed initial Security Council resolutions that were adopted in response to internal conflict situations (when a government was in control of the country) that the Security Council deemed a threat to the peace. This review enabled us to identify the criteria that helped the Council make its decisions."[26] The criteria the team identified included the overthrow of a democratic government, conflict among factions, human rights violations, refugee outflows, other (drug trafficking), and other (HIV/AIDS). In the team's assessment, "no single factor was dispositive," that is, decisive, "to [the Security Council's] decision to intervene. Instead, the Security Council considered the totality of the circumstances of each country's situation in determining that a threat to the peace existed."[27]

But, as Garritizen points out in her discussion of paratexts, "notes unveil only some of the material historians have investigated, not how they have reflected this material within the context of their entire source base and the ideological and cultural framework of their own era."[28] In other words, footnotes, as well as endnotes, disclose sources, but only those selected for inclusion, which is the case here, as evidenced by several readily identifiable lacunae, specifically, sources that one would expect to be included but were not. The research team, for example, did not explain the thought process by which they selected these specific seven countries for examination, some of which, such as Cambodia, have very little in common with Myanmar. (Ethnonationalism was not an issue in Cambodia, whereas it was one of the driving forces of the armed conflicts in Myanmar, for example.) Nor did the research team elaborate on why their efforts to determine the primary criteria the Security Council had used did not include any of the other "threats to peace and security" situations that resulted in Chapter VII resolutions after 1997. (The Security Council issued several dozen such resolutions between 1998 and the publication of the 2005 report.)[29] Equally curiously, the research team made no epitextual reference, over the course of sixty-nine pages and 711 footnotes, to the 2003 NCGUB report, even though it employed the same research methodology and arrived at the same conclusion. In conceptual terms, the two reports, the latter of which evokes but does not mention the existence of the former, mirror one another in terms of indexicality. Both of the reports recursively cite Chapter VII resolutions to justify their respective calls to action—namely, that the situation in Myanmar "checked" all of the boxes, plus an additional one specific to it (HIV/AIDS), and thus warranted concrete Security Council action beyond a resolution, in the firm's professional assessment.

International intervention, the report writers continued, would accomplish three critical tasks: "restore the peace, promote national reconciliation, and facilitate a return to democratic rule."[30] The irony here, from an epitextual point of view, is threefold. First, there had been no national peace since independence in 1948. Consequently, there was no prior peace to restore. Instead, concrete steps, including political dialogue with the NSAGs, were needed to create it. Second, reconciliation was and remains today understood by minority populations to mean assimilation and domination by the majority population, which runs counter to the law firm's desired outcome. And third, democratic rule without the decisive role of the Tatmadaw being maintained within it was an impossibility then and continues to be so today due to the terms of the pro-military 2008 Constitution, which enshrines the armed forces' place in the political order. The report's authors either were unaware of these ironies or sought not to complicate the "how" of their narrativity by acknowledging these obstacles, emphasizing instead the extent to which the UN's relevance was at stake. "In short, the United Nation's efforts to date have failed," they wrote. "The statement is not designed to place blame on any individual or international organization. Indeed, the blame for a lack of progress lies solely with the Government of Burma." Nevertheless, they continued, "Whether the UN can find a way to deal with the Government of Burma is in many respects not only a question for Burma, but a question of the United Nations' ability to carry out the UN Charter."[31]

The conclusion reflects a widespread liberal assumption that intervention in the name of human rights and/or humanitarian grounds would serve to "(re) establish 'rule of law' and to (re) build the nation, in this case Myanmar, and thus avoid the greater evil of 'doing nothing' in response to a crisis."[32] Given this assumption, it was unsurprising that the question of the UN's ability, which in this case meant political will, was at the center of the critical epitextual responses to the report. At the mid-September 2006 meeting, the US and UK representatives to the Security Council requested that the "situation in Myanmar" be added to the provisional agenda on the grounds that the country was "likely to endanger the maintenance of international peace and security."[33] Therefore, the representatives asserted, further discussion was needed to determine whether Security Council action, on top of what other UN bodies were already doing in Myanmar, was warranted. According to the meeting minutes, the Chinese representative, Wang Guangya, opposed the request on the grounds that a discussion of a country's internal affairs would not only exceed the Security Council's mandate but worsen the situation it was meant to improve. "External interference" at this time, he declared, could destabilize the region as a whole, giving rise to a genuine threat to peace and security that in China's view did not then exist. For this reason, he asserted, the international community should support the "progress [that] is undeniably being made, slowly but steadily. As an old Chinese saying goes, one cannot enjoy eating hot bean curd if one is too anxious."[34]

The cited proverb, which calls for patience now to experience pleasurable benefits at a later date, is consistent with the Chinese government's policy of "constructive engagement" that many Southeast Asian and East Asian countries maintained with Myanmar for decades. Proponents of this policy position asserted that foreign investment, combined with little to no criticism of the military regime's human rights record, would gradually result in positive change.[35] (Opinions were divided as to whether such change would include a transition to democratization, including full civilian rule.) Despite Chinese opposition, ten of the fifteen Security Council members voted to add Myanmar to the provisional agenda. A closed-door Security Council meeting occurred on 29 September, which included the UN under-secretary-general for political affairs and the Myanmar representative to the UN, Kyaw Tint Swe, as an observer.[36] The substance of the discussion remains confidential, but the outcome was not.

Diplomatic representatives from the United Kingdom and the United States submitted their joint draft resolution at the next Security Council meeting, held on 12 January 2007. Curiously, the draft did not cite prior Myanmar-specific resolutions from the General Assembly, of which there were many, or reports from other UN bodies, of which there were again many more. Instead, the draft indexed other resolutions: "*Recalling* resolutions 1325 (2000) on Women and Peace and Security, 1612 (2005) on Children and Armed Conflict, and 1265 (1999) and 1296 (2000) on the Protection of Civilians in Armed Conflict, and the Statement of its President of 28 November 2006 (S/PRST/2006/48)." Citing these resolutions framed the rationale for Security Council action in terms that the international community had already accepted as appropriate responses to "threats to peace and security" globally.[37] (The draft did, however, go on to cite some specifics, including ongoing attacks against civilians, especially in KNU-delineated Karen State, where the Northern Offensive was then taking place.)[38] The content of the draft was disappointing, according to the head of the US Campaign for Burma (USCB, an NGO that had extensively lobbied UN representatives to get Myanmar added to the Security Council's agenda. Despite their efforts, the director told me, the draft resolution, which largely reiterated the recommendations proposed in the DLA et al. law firm's 2005 report, failed to make any explicit reference to war crimes or crimes against humanity, which many fact-finding NGOs had pushed hard to have included.[39] Instead, the text of the draft resolution: "urged" the military regime to cooperate with the UN; called on it to "cease" violations of international human rights and humanitarian law; to "cooperate" with the ILO with regard to its efforts to eradicate forced labor; and to begin a "genuine" dialogue with the political opposition, with democratic transition as the goal.[40]

Despite the anodyne nature of the recommendations, Vitaly Churkin, the Russian representative and serving president of the Security Council, disagreed with the proposed resolution. In his view, there was no clear proof of a "threat." Therefore, it was not acceptable to use the Security Council to discuss the allegations. (Churkin preferred, and not without some justification, the Human Rights Council as the appropriate venue, for this reason, as its mandate is to promote "universal respect for the protection of all human rights and fundamental freedoms for all," as well as "to address situations of violations of human rights, including gross and systematic violations, and make recommendations thereon.")[41] The Chinese representative made a similar case. Again, according to the meeting minutes, he stated that, first, the ongoing conflict between the Tatmadaw and multiple NSAGs was "mainly the internal affair of a sovereign State" and, second, the governments of the neighboring countries, including his own, which had major economic investments in Myanmar, did not believe the situation consisted a regional "threat to peace and security." So although "the international community could offer all kinds of constructive advice and assistance," he stressed, the Security Council needed "to refrain from arbitrary interference."[42] (However, he did so without explaining in specific terms what he meant by "arbitrary.") The Security Council met again in early October to vote on the draft resolution, no. S/2007/14, which "recall[ed]" resolution A/RES/61/232 of the General Assembly "expressing deep concern at large-scale human rights violations in Myanmar, as cited in the report of the Special Rapporteur of 21 September 2006."[43] But the Russian and Chinese representatives to the Security Council killed the draft resolution by issuing a joint veto, their first since 1972.

CAMPAIGN 3.0

Two different advocacy tracks emerged between 2008, when the Northern Offensive in KNU-delineated Karen State was still raging, and 2011, when the final offensive against the NSAG ended in an unofficial cease-fire. First-track reports reproduced long-standing advocacy strategies, as several prominent human rights NGOs released new fact-finding documentation regarding ongoing Tatmadaw operations against not only Karen civilians affected by the Northern Offensive, but also Rohingya, Chin, and Kachin civilians elsewhere around the country.[44] Collectively, these field-based reports came to share, without direct evidence of deliberate coordination, a high degree of discursive coherence and unity in terms of their structural form, rhetorical style, and analysis informed by international human rights, humanitarian, and refugee law. In short, the reports adhered to the classical

conventions of the genre and thus functioned as contemporaneous case studies that other reports could cite as "evidence" of ongoing gross breaches of
human rights and humanitarian law around the country. The reports were
not epitextual (i.e., commentaries on one another) for this reason; nevertheless, they created a larger discursive context for advocacy efforts that
reinforced their common but separately stated message: the Tatmadaw's
concurrent use of large-scale preemptive violence against civilians was, in
their respective views, further exacerbating the "threat to peace and security" the country allegedly already posed to the region.

By contrast, second-track efforts built on the advocacy strategy that
the NCGUB and DLA et al. reports had earlier pioneered, in the hopes
that the international context was more receptive and the domestic situation had worsened to the point that a CoI was now politically feasible. For
this reason, second-track reports continued to draw upon the UN's archive
in indexical fashion to assert that the organization's own documents demonstrated that the country genuinely presented a "threat to international
peace and security."[45] In visual and compositional terms, the paratextual
elements structuring second-track reports increasingly emulated the form
and content of legal briefs, although they were not explicitly styled as such.
The briefs, which were simultaneously matter of fact in tone but written to
be rhetorically persuasive in style, also included repeated references to UN
"facts." Specifically, the conclusions of various UN bodies were expressed
through citations to past resolutions and special rapporteur reports to
construct their respective arguments. The IHRC report is exemplary in
this regard, particularly as it relates back to broader questions of recursive
narrativity.[46]

In early 2007, the director of the USCB approached the clinical director of IHRC to commission a report. The intended goal was both to draw
attention to the scale and severity of the human rights situation and to demonstrate that legal action was possible at a future date. However, the violent
suppression of the Saffron Revolution, a series of peaceful demonstrations
led by Buddhist monks protesting the political-economic crisis during the
fall of 2007, redirected energy away from efforts to get the UN to take up
the CoI issue and toward appropriate international responses to the crackdown itself. The January 2008 elections for the nonpermanent members of
the Security Council again delayed forward movement, as advocacy groups
had to devote significant amount of time to educating and lobbying the five

new members after they assumed their seats before they could raise the possibility of a CoI.[47]

Despite these setbacks, IHRC continued its archival research for the remainder of the year and published its report, "Crimes in Burma," in early 2009. The preface, a common peritextual element in general, played a particularly important signifying role in this instance. Several leading jurists, including prosecutors and judges previously involved in the International Criminal Tribunals for the Former Yugoslavia (1993) and Rwanda (1994), commissioned the report.[48] (Both ad hoc tribunals, created by the UN Security Council, were forerunners to the establishment of the ICC.) The involvement of these jurists, the director of the USCB told me, was part of a broader strategy to involve other "notable" persons, such as Nobel Peace Prize winners, to forestall criticism that the campaign did not have outside support but was instead driven by Burmese activists and Western governments hostile to the military regime.[49] (Six Nobel Peace Prize winners and representatives of two Peace Prize–winning organizations served a similar function in 1993 when they gathered in Bangkok to call for the release of Aung San Suu Kyi, who had won the prize in 1991 but was still under house arrest.) The military regime was not persuaded by this rhetorical move, but then its leaders were arguably not the primary audience. Instead, it was the Security Council members whom IHRC presented with an advocacy report that relied exclusively on UN-produced "facts" to support arguments for a CoI.

The "Crimes in Burma" report, much like the DLA et al. and NCGUB ones before it, continually mirrored back the UN's own findings on the human rights situation in Myanmar—an epitextual move it foregrounded at the very start of the executive summary by quoting strikingly similar conclusions written years apart by two different special rapporteurs to the country:

> These violations have been so numerous and consistent over the past years as to suggest that they are not simply isolated or the acts of individual misbehavior by middle- and lower-ranking officers, but are rather the result of policy at the highest level, entailing political and legal responsibility.
> —Rajsoomer Lallah (1998)

> As noted by the Special Rapporteur in his previous reports, the above-mentioned serious human rights violations have been widespread and systematic, suggesting that they are not simply isolated acts of individual misconduct by middle- or low-ranking officers, but rather the result of a system under which individuals

and groups have been allowed to break the law and violate human rights without being called to account.
—Paulo Sérgio Pinheiro (2006)

IHRC made several strategic choices to frame the UN's own consistent conclusions in ways the researchers thought would be the most persuasive. First, IHRC's researchers devoted special attention to the UN resolutions and reports its bodies had issued after the Rome Statute entered into force in 2002. They did so because the Rome Statute permits the ICC, under certain circumstances, to prosecute individuals for international crimes regardless of whether or not the state is party to the statute. (Myanmar is not.) With the goal of possible future prosecution in mind, IHRC further opted to limit the subject matter to violations that were "well-established and representative of the egregious nature of reported abuses" in the country *and* fell under ICC jurisdiction.[50] (The four crimes examined, within the confines of the relevant UN documents, included forced deportations, sexual violence, extrajudicial killings, and torture.) Second, IHRC also chose to limit the geographical area under discussion to eastern Myanmar, where the Northern Offensive had just ended.

The region, IHRC's researchers argued, was a "representative sample" of the preemptive violence directed against nonmajority ethnic populations in conflict areas nationally—a point that the track one reports made separately. The extent to which this region is an exemplar is not clear, however, because the depth and breadth of credible fact-finding is so uneven in other conflict areas. So, although clear patterns of violations exist in the meta-human rights archive on Myanmar, the intensity of the violence in KNU-delineated Karen State and its duration, nearly seven decades, raise unanswered questions about its representativeness.

The issue of representativeness aside, the report, by narrowing its investigative focus in these stated ways, identified three subsets of "evidence" from the UN's own archive: eighteen General Assembly resolutions, sixteen Commission on Human Rights (now Human Rights Council) resolutions, and seventeen reports of the special rapporteur.[51]

Of these, the seventeen special rapporteur reports hold additional significance that the thirty-four combined resolutions issued by the General Assembly and the Human Rights Council do not. Special rapporteurs are independent experts with a UN mandate to examine, monitor, advise, and

TABLE 2   HUMAN RIGHTS VIOLATIONS LISTED BY COMMISSION
ON HUMAN RIGHTS AND HUMAN RIGHTS COUNCIL RESOLUTIONS

Year	Resolution Number	Forced Displacement	Sexual Violence	Extrajudicial Killing	Torture	Arbitrary Detention
1992	✓i	✓9*	—	—	—	✓2
1993	✓ii	✓P*, 13*	✓P, 6	✓P, 6	✓P, 6	✓P, 9
1994	✓iii	✓7, 16*	✓7	✓7	✓7	✓10
1995	✓iv	✓P*, 11	✓11	✓11	✓11	✓4
1996	✓v	✓10, 17*	✓10	✓10	✓10	✓10
1997	✓vi	✓2, 2*	✓2	✓2	✓2	✓2
1998	✓vii	✓3, 3*	✓3	✓3	✓3	✓3
1999	✓viii	✓4, 4*	✓4	✓4	✓4	✓4
2000	✓ix	✓6, 6*	✓6	✓6	✓6	✓5
2001	✓x	✓4, 4*	✓4	✓4	✓4	✓4
2002	✓xi	✓5, 5*	✓5	✓5	✓5	✓5
2003	✓xii	✓3, 3*	✓3	✓3	✓3	✓3
2004	✓xiii	✓3, 3*	✓3	✓3	✓3	✓3
2005	✓xiv	✓3, 3*	✓3	✓3	✓3	✓3
2006	✓	X	X	X	X	X
2007	✓xv	X	X	✓1	X	✓1
2008	✓xvi	✓6	X	X	✓6	✓6

SOURCE: IHRC (2009).

NOTES: Numbers are the paragraph numbers where documents refer directly to a certain crime.

✓ = Abuses constitute a crime against humanity as defined in Article 7 of the Rome Statute.

* = Reference to forced displacement and refugee flows to neighboring states.

P = Statement in the preface of the resolution (i.e., before the numbered paragraphs start).

X = The resolution does not refer to the specific crime but refers to human rights or humanitarian violations in general.

publicly report pursuant to Human Rights Council resolutions on human rights problems in specific countries or on broader thematic areas. The mandate for the first special rapporteur on the situation of human rights in Myanmar was established in 1992, and it has been extended annually since then, again performatively by resolution, indicating both the intractable nature of the problem and the seriousness with which the UN continues to regard it. (Myanmar is one of only thirteen countries globally today where a special rapporteur is currently in place.) But more importantly here, the special rapporteurs' reports were based on a combination of direct and indirect fact-finding (self-generated documentation in the case of the former, and documentation produced by others and determined to be credible by the special rapporteur in the case of the latter), whereas General Assembly and Human Rights Council resolutions, passed via majority vote, are not. The respective conclusions of the latter two bodies arguably (but not necessarily) carry much less evidentiary weight as a result, even though they represent the position of State members to the UN as opposed to a specially appointed individual expert.

IHRC's selection of these documents as a whole shifted the nature of the discussion from one in which archives, in this case those of the UN on Myanmar, are conventionally understood to be repositories of "facts," to ones that are productive of them. Restated, the conclusions found in the relevant UN-authored documents mirrored back what IHRC believed the Security Council members already knew to be true. As IHRC put it, "sufficient *prima facie* evidence of grave violations of human rights and international humanitarian law, including contravention against crimes against humanity and war crimes," as defined in the Rome Statute, already existed and warranted a Security Council–mandated and fully resourced CoI.[52] "Failure by the UN Security Council to take action and investigate these crimes," stated Tyler Giannini, the director of IHRC and one of the coauthors of the report, "could mean that violations of international criminal law will go unchecked."[53] His claim proved to be factually accurate, though the phrasing could be deemed problematic by some because it framed this body of international law as the "victim" in need of defense rather than the actual victims themselves. The Security Council did not authorize a CoI, however, and grave breaches of human rights and humanitarian law continued, as the UN once again later concluded.

CAMPAIGN 4.0

A series of other organizations—especially the International Federation for Human Rights (FIDH); ALTSEAN-Burma, which campaigns for human rights and democracy in Southeast Asia but especially Myanmar; and the Burma Lawyers' Council—issued their own advocacy documents during 2009, also calling for a Security Council–authorized CoI.[54] These advocacy documents adopted the same recursive approach, repeatedly referencing IHRC's recent report and the UN's own previously stated conclusions on the human rights and humanitarian crisis in Myanmar.[55] Tensions existed behind the scenes, however, particularly over what time frame and types of abuses a potential CoI should investigate, a problem future transitional justice initiatives will also face. Some groups, such as Karen ones, wanted to go back in time as far as possible, explained Debbie Stothard, the secretary general of FIDH. Other groups, she continued, thought 1962, when the Tatmadaw first seized power in a coup, would be an appropriate starting point. Others identified 1998, when the ILO released its CoI on forced labor, as the best starting point. In all cases, she noted, the groups were supportive of a CoI, but only to the extent that it would not implicate the NSAGs that claim to represent their own ethnic communities. Participating in fact-finding efforts on this controversial issue, they explained to Stothard, would place them in an untenable position with the NSAGs.[56]

The comments Special Rapporteur Tomás Ojea Quintana made in March 2010 as part of his periodic report to the Human Rights Council, pursuant to its resolution no. 10/27, raised hopes that substantive progress toward a CoI was finally imminent. (By the end of the year, sixteen separate governments had publicly issued calls for one.)[57] Quintana's report, based heavily on three recent fact-finding trips by the special rapporteur over the previous six months, presented a detailed picture of the situation, as seen through his eyes.[58] (Prior resolutions—no. 64/238 of the General Assembly, which concerned the need to protect a wide range of civil and political liberties as set out in Security Council resolutions nos. 1325, 1820, 1888, and 1889, regarding "women's right to equality and justice both during and after the conflict"—as well as continued concern about "serious human rights abuses against civilians" in border areas, helped shape the framework of his investigations.)[59] The special rapporteur concluded that "a pattern of gross and systematic violation of human rights which has been in place for many years still continues." "Given the extent and persistence of the problem, and the lack of accountability," he stated, "there is an indication that those human rights violations are the result of a State policy."[60]

His conclusions reaffirmed those that prior special rapporteurs and special envoys had previously submitted to the Commission on Human Rights pursuant to its first resolution, no. 1992/58, concerning Myanmar. One of Quintana's recommendations was new, however, and it proved to be highly controversial. "According to consistent reports," he explained, "the possibility exists that some of these human rights violations may entail categories of crimes against humanity or war crimes under the terms of the Rome Statute of the ICC."[61] "The mere existence of this possibility," he asserted, "obliges the Government of Myanmar to take prompt and effective measures to investigate these facts." "There have clearly been cases where it has been necessary to establish responsibility, but this has not been done," he continued. "Given this lack of accountability, United Nations institutions may consider the possibility to establish a commission of inquiry with a specific fact-finding mandate to address the question of international crimes."[62]

His Excellency U Wanna Maung Lwin, the permanent representative and leader of the Myanmar delegation to the United Nations, issued a formal statement one week later that sought to reframe the report in an epitextual manner that would prompt a majority of the Human Rights Council members to reject Quintana's conclusion. In his response, U Wanna Maung Lwin explained that he wanted "to set the record straight" with regard to three issues, about which in his view the special rapporteur's comments displayed a "lack of objectivity." The issues he identified concerned the purported (1) lack of progress toward a political transition, as set out in the regime's own "Seven-Step Roadmap to Democracy"; (2) absence of judicial independence and impartiality; and (3) failure to stop increasingly violent ethnic and religious discrimination against Rohingya Muslims.[63]

His Excellency presented his counterarguments at some length. Curiously, he did not devote similar space to a point-by-point response to the much more serious allegation of "possible" war crimes and crimes against humanity. Instead, U Wanna Maung Lwin emphatically stated that the special rapporteur's conclusions "did not reflect the real ground situation," effectively dismissing Quintana's own fact-finding as lacking any "truth" value. Furthermore, the report was based on "disinformation emanated from unverifiable and unreliable sources and anti-government elements," meaning that the documentation lacked credibility in the eyes of the military regime.[64] Thus, he declared, the report "contravene[d] the Code of Conduct for Special Procedures Mandate-holders of the Human Rights Council Resolution 5/2 Article 6," which concerns the prerogatives of the special rapporteur. (One of the four prerogatives listed in this resolution includes the requirement that the mandate holder "take into account in a comprehensive and timely manner, in particular information provided by the *State* concerned on situations relevant to their mandate," and do so "without prejudice.")[65] U Wanna Maung Lwin additionally stressed that the "Special Rapporteur made inappropriate demands and prejudgements to the political process by linking the human rights issues with the hidden political agenda," but he did so without specifying to which "sources" or "elements" he was referring. Such an approach was "not in line with the principle of the Human Rights Council, which is to eliminate a double standard and politicization," U Wanna Maung Lwin stated. Finally, the report, His Excellency concluded, "falls outside the purview of the mandate of the Human Rights Council"; consequently, the "line of action recommended, [the CoI] is unjustifiable and disproportionate."[66]

Epitextual comments, such as the ones U Wanna Maung Lwin submitted to the Human Rights Council via his written response, are meant to shape how a text is received, and they do so quite often in ways that do not correspond with the original author's intent, in this case, that of the special rapporteur. Hence U Wanna Maung Lwin's decision to cite the Human Rights Council's resolution no. 5/2, Article 6, to undermine member support for the special rapporteur's report, a key goal of which was to convince its members to refer the matter for further investigation into possible war crimes and crimes against humanity. But the pragmatic effectiveness of such a strategy in terms of achieving the goal of interpretive foreclosure (here, invalidating the special rapporteur's report on procedural grounds) is dependent on a number of factors, such as "the nature of the addresser, of the addressee, degree of authority and responsibility of the first, [and] illocutionary force of his message."[67] In this regard, His Excellency U Wunna Maung Lwin offers a complicated example of pragmatic effectiveness through the practice of citation.

U Wunna Maung Lwin, a former active military officer, directly took part in a series of Tatmadaw offensives against the KNU/KNLA from the late 1980s through the mid-1990s, generating the first large-scale waves of refugees into Thailand, which incidentally led to the formation of the TBBC shortly afterward. He later joined the diplomatic corps and served several stints as an ambassador before becoming the country's permanent representative to the UN (2007–2011), where he quickly gained a reputation for effectively defending the military regime's policies and actions. (The newly elected quasi-civilian government immediately promoted him to minister of foreign affairs in 2011, which further suggests his reputation was warranted.) U Wunna Maung Lwin was thus adept at representing the interests of the military regime, which lent his public statements significant credibility among its leadership and, perhaps, with other country members of the Human Rights Council that have similarly problematic human rights records, but that is conjecture on my part. But the manner in which he sought to undermine the special rapporteur's recommendations was also reflective of the military's discursive defense of itself whenever it faced external criticism: denial.

Denial can take different forms. Stanley Cohen, writing about human rights violations, distinguishes literal denial (nothing happened) from interpretive denial (what happened is really something else) and implicatory denial (what happened is justified).[68] A close reading of His Excellency's counterarguments reveals elements of all three forms of denial. First, U Wunna Maung Lwin asserted that the scheduled November 2010 elections would be, despite substantial evidence to the contrary, free and fair. (The NLD, the main opposition party, boycotted the election due to the way the military regime structured the process in its own favor.) "Regrettably," he said, "the Special Rapporteur has made prejudgments on the ongoing home-grown political process and setting preconditions [by the military regime] on the upcoming general elections" (literal denial).[69] Second, His Excellency dismissed accusations by the special rapporteur that the judiciary was neither independent nor impartial. "It is functioning in accordance with the existing laws, legal procedures, and administrative measures," he asserted, neglecting to acknowledge that the military regime created the judicial framework and closely directed the legal process for the duration of its period in power (interpretive denial).[70] Third, the communal violence, most of it directed toward Rohingya Muslims, was in his view understandable given their alleged provocation, which from the regime's perspective meant the inflammatory habit of referring to themselves as "Rohingya." "In our view, the accusations in the report," he emphasized, "[are] an attempt to deliberately frame Myanmar and to create misunderstanding between our country and international community. In my country, there is no discrimination whatsover on grounds of religion, races, and genders" (implicatory denial).[71] But the primary focus of U Wunna Maung Lwin's rebuttal of the special rapporteur's report concerned the many ways in which the recommendations purportedly "violated [the] sovereign right[s] of an independent State," which he stressed were protected under the terms of the UN Charter.[72]

His Excellency's opinion was not without merit in the eyes of some, one of whom provided his own epitextual commentary on the special rapporteur's report. Derek Tonkin, a former British diplomat to Thailand, Vietnam, and Lao concluded that the special rapporteur's recommendation, a proposal to consider establishing a CoI, "probably exceeded his mandate." The mandate does not include, he explained in proceduralist terms, the authority to make recommendations to other UN organs on what specific course of action should be taken as a consequence of the conclusions presented. Any effort to employ his proposal to strengthen a "world-wide campaign for a UN-led inquiry," Tonkin continued, was a "deliberate misrepresentation" of what the special rapporteur wrote in the report, a position open to debate when the exact words Quintana used are revisited.[73] Nevertheless, the mandate issue that Tonkin raised is an important one. (Notably, it was not the last time he did so. Tonkin criticized subsequent UN fact-finding missions on the Rohingya crisis, which he also dismissed as illegitimate due to "factual inaccuracy and historical bias," which has prompted some activist groups to accuse him of a being a genocide denier.)[74]

But the UN General Assembly did not provide a clear-cut answer on the mandate dispute in its annual resolution on Myanmar, no. A/RES/65/241A, in late December 2010, in which the General Assembly reaffirmed "its previous resolutions on the situation of human rights in Myanmar, the most recent of which is resolution no. 64/238 of 24 December 2009, those of the Commission on Human Rights, and those of the Human Rights Council, the most recent of which are resolutions nos. 12/20 of 2 October 2009 and 13/25 of 26 March 2010." The 2010 resolution instead urged, in recursive terms, "the implementation of the recommendations contained" in the special rapporteur's previous reports.[75] The resolution further expressed concern that the UN's "urgent calls . . . have not been heeded" and emphasized that "without significant progress heeding those calls of the international community, the situation of human rights in Myanmar will continue to deteriorate."[76] The statement includes an important footnote indicating that the recommendations include those drawn from the March 2010 report. But it is highly unlikely, for the reasons U Wunna Maung Lwin and Tonkin respectively stated, that they extended to Quintana's controversial suggestion that the Human Rights Council "may consider the possibility" of establishing a CoI.[77]

The government's (quite possibly valid) claims that the special rapporteur had exceeded his official mandate did not prevent "notable" individuals (e.g., internationally known jurists and Nobel Peace Prize laureates), advocacy groups, and at least sixteen governments from citing the IHRC report as part of the international campaign for a CoI. Many of these actors employed "implicatory denial" themselves. Some of them, for example, argued that there was a clear and pressing need to move forward with the special rapporteur's proposed CoI irrespective of whether or not it was in compliance with the Human Rights Council's special procedures. In other words, the mandate restrictions, which limit the special rapporteur's duties "to monitor, advise and publicly report," should be disregarded in the name of protecting human rights and establishing accountability—a position that was deeply problematic in its own right.

In late July 2011, the quasi-civilian government finally agreed to hold a sit-down meeting with Aung San Suu Kyi in mid-August. Some activists claimed that this was the result of the advocacy campaign, but no one with direct knowledge of the conversation has since confirmed or denied this assertion. Regardless of whether or not the CoI campaign, via the debate it prompted at the level of the Human Rights Council, contributed to this outcome, the new government did begin to release political prisoners, to permit the registration of independent political parties, and to create its own National Human Rights Commission. Again, it is not known whether any discussion focused on claims the special rapporteur had made regarding grave breaches of international human rights and humanitarian law in the country's contested border regions—allegations that dozens of UN resolutions support, according to IHRC's report. Nonetheless, some observers felt that the regime "did not want to become another Sudan," a conflict that did result in an ICC referral, and that its military leaders "feared The Hague," where ICC prosecutions take place, hence the concessions rather then further resistance.[78] The basis of this claim, which the director of the USCB relayed to me, is unclear, however. Her assertion is certainly a self-serving one in the sense that NGO campaigns always want to present their advocacy efforts as being effective. But then again, self-interest does not make the stated perception of the generals' fears of foreign intervention and potential prosecution false, either. Given the military regime's well-documented paranoia, especially where the preservation of state sovereignty is concerned, ICC action would certainly be anathema.[79]

The three main concessions, none of which were politically costly, were part of the newly elected quasi-civilian government's broader stated commitment to the democratization process. The concessions quickly succeeded in undermining the CoI campaign's momentum.[80] But the concessions did nothing to resolve the UN-documented practices driving the human rights abuses prohibited by the Rome Statute, again according to the director of the USCB, as well as staff at the Burma Partnership, an NGO that worked closely with Burmese civil society organizations during the CoI campaign.[81] "The CoI campaign did have some impact," the USCB director explained to me. "There was some movement on the political side. But the [ongoing conflict] in Kachin State and northern Shan State, and lack of military involvement in the ceasefire talks [was] a problem. The talks [were] over-hyped, overblown. There [was] not enough skepticism," which in her view distracted international attention away from the broader "threat to peace and security" the country purportedly posed beyond its borders.[82]

CONCLUSION

Anthony Grafton's magisterial account of the footnote marks an attempt to locate the "precise point when [the discipline of] history publicly doubled back on itself."[83] The doubling back produces a curious paradox. Footnotes, he explains, subtly raise epistemological questions about the very evidentiary points that they are intended to support. "In documenting the thought and research that underpin the narrative about them," Grafton points out, "footnotes prove that it is a historically contingent product, depending on the forms of research, opportunities, and state of particular questions that existed when the historian went to work."[84] Grafton's point, which concerns the paratextual nature of the footnote, is not to dismiss the historiographical project as a form of social constructivism without empirical basis. Rather, his goal is to focus scholarly attention on a documentary practice that is critical to the discipline and the kinds of "truth" claims it makes possible yet remains largely taken for granted as a legitimate object of analysis.

The eleven pro-CoI reports discussed or simply cited in this chapter contain a total of 2,461 footnotes. Many of these reports include dozens of additional endnotes, not enumerated here, plus appendices that refer to yet more documents. My examination of citational practices and the epitextual responses to them highlight what can be gained by taking the performative as well as epistemological function of footnotes in human rights reports, and UN documents more generally, as warranting analytical study.

Why is such study warranted? Footnotes, *pace* Grafton's insights, help shape perceptions of authoritativeness as well as the authorizing function of human rights reports. Sociologist Claire Moon makes an interesting distinction here. "If only people knew [the facts], they would act," she wrote.[85] This logic, which Moon refers to as the "knowing-acting nexus," has a "documentary" component and an "interventionist" one.[86] The first component, which is descriptive in nature, utilizes a combination of quantitative data to establish the "scope, intensity, and range" of abuses, qualitative testimonials from victims and witnesses to convey the "truth of suffering" to others, and footnotes to other sources.[87] The second component is prescriptive in nature and thus takes the form of recommendations that are supported through citations to either existing international law or calls for new law to address the issues not yet covered by precedent.[88] However, her point, as I interpret it, reflects liberal assumptions about what can be called the "narrative of choice," that is, the either/or belief that, as Elizabeth Bruch put it, we "must either stand by as atrocities occur or intervene militar[il]y to establish a new legal order."[89]

But this "choice" is problematic on another level as well. Human rights organizations must simplify, if not decontextualize, the historical, social, and political context in which the violence occurs to emphasize instead the technical issues concerning the patterns of abuse as defined by relevant international law, which privileges one form of "knowing" over another.[90] The process of decontextualization, which is critical to fashioning claims to objectivity and rights as universals, essential for legitimizing "acting," frequently obscures the "knowing" of the geographic scope, historical depth, and intersectional nature of the structural forms of inequality and injustice that perpetuate violations at different scales and degrees of severity.[91]

Resolutions, which are a peculiar example of the knowing/acting nexus, constituted one of the key citational practices featured in this chapter. Special envoys and UN special rapporteurs traveled to Myanmar more than forty times between 1992 and 2008 to gather information regarding the situation on the ground; to convey messages from the secretary general to high-ranking military officials; and to promote dialogue between the regime and the political opposition, the NLD, symbolically headed by Nobel Peace Prize winner Aung San Suu Kyi. The findings informed discussions in the General Assembly and the Human Rights Commission (now Human Rights Council), which issued nearly three dozen resolutions on Myanmar, most of them citing prior ones, during these years.[92] UN resolutions, except in rare circumstances, are not legally binding, however, and those issued arguably had no effect on the human rights situation in the country, which was among the worst in the world during this fifteen-year period, according to the organization's own special rapporteurs, whose work was in turn authorized pursuant to yet more resolutions.[93] The NGO-led effort to convince the UN Security Council to approve a CoI, if not an ICC referral outright, was thus an attempt to replace the symbolism of resolutions with concrete enforcement actions.

The NGO-led effort, as a result of the paratextual practices used, led to the emergence of a recursive archive. But an archive is not a collection of "things" (e.g., documents, images, and sounds), as French philosopher Michel Foucault has pointed out. Rather, an archive, he explains, is best understood as a set of relations and institutions that enable discursive statements of particular kinds to become parts of an archive.[94] Citation practices in the form of footnotes and recursive mirroring (i.e., the re-presentation of UN-authored conclusions back to the Security Council, typically through citations to prior resolutions) consequently produced a rich, intertextual body of statements that shaped the contours of the CoI debates inside and outside the UN.

The attempt to persuade the Security Council to intervene on the basis of what numerous UN bodies had already concluded was unsuccessful for many reasons. But the failure was fundamentally due to the ambiguity of the central claim itself—namely, that Myanmar posed a threat to international peace and security. Despite concerted advocacy efforts, the supposed "threat" remained an empty signifier, that is, "a signifier with a vague, highly variable, unspecifiable, or non-existent signified."[95] Put more plainly, the key players, both for and against the CoI, were able to define the phrase in ways that reflected their own self-interests because the phrase had no agreed-upon meaning. Given the absence of an official UN definition, it was unsurprising that realpolitik blocked the possibility of a CoI.

Human rights philosopher Frédéric Mégret underscores the complexity of this particular debate—to intervene through an official investigation or not—by differentiating between facts for the purposes of action and facts for the purposes of adjudication in UN fora more generally:

> We can think of facts as having two purposes, especially in the UN context: facts are needed for action, and they are needed for adjudication. The facts needed for each however are not the same. Facts necessary for action are merely quasi-facts, facts as they can best be ascertained in the circumstances; there is recognition that time is of the essence, that decision cannot afford to wait for certainty. Facts as needed for adjudication are more in the manner of incontrovertible, demonstrable, or highly probably truth because of the way the negative

consequences they portend for persons or institutions and because one does not have, unlike political action, the excuse that time is pressing. Human rights fact-finding, and therein lies some of its challenges, now more often than not occupies [this] dual space.[96]

The UN's own documentation on the human rights situation in Myanmar, which contained extensive collections of both types of facts (action and adjudication), was thus the condition of possibility for the NGO-led CoI campaign, which began in 2003 and ended in 2011 as the Tatmadaw's unofficial cease-fire with the KNU went into effect. The 2011 elections and promised reforms were not the only factor that contributed to the campaign's rapid denouement afterward, however. The Rohingya crisis, which began in 2012, was the primary reason international attention shifted away from the CoI campaign. (The intercommunal violence displaced more than 140,000 people, overwhelmingly Rohingya, according to the UN, which did not explain how it arrived at this figure.)[97] Advocacy groups and some governments promptly launched renewed calls for an independent CoI on the grounds that the violence demonstrably posed a "threat to peace and security beyond [the country's] borders," largely due to the potentially destabilizing effects upon Bangladesh, which is currently hosting more than one million registered and unregistered refugees. And once again, the government's counterclaims ranged from literal denial (nothing happened), to interpretive denial (what happened is really something else), to implicatory denial (what happened is justified).[98] Multiple UN-approved fact-finding missions, as well as Myanmar-based counter fact-finding missions, have since taken place. But Mégret's point about the difference between facts needed for action and those needed for adjudication, which is a key component of human rights narrativity in general, remains unresolved to this day with regard to Myanmar and the actions of its armed forces.

Conclusion

Just as it is often said that truth is the first casualty of war,
then maybe facts are the first casualty of politics.

—Frédéric Mégret

"Do human rights work? That is, have human rights law, institutions, and activism produced positive change in the world? And, if so, how do they work and under what conditions? How can we learn from past successes and failures to make human rights work better in the future?"[1] These questions originate with Kathryn Sikkink, a political scientist who has devoted much of her career to answering them. As a result of her data-driven, evidence-based approach, she arrives at a very different conclusion than that of critics who opine that decades of efforts to protect and to promote human rights globally have failed to deliver on what was promised.[2] Her argument, that human rights do indeed work, albeit slowly as a result of concerted struggle, centers on the need to distinguish between "those making empirical comparisons and those making comparisons to an ideal."[3] I agree with her overarching conclusion that there is "evidence for hope."[4] But I also share the view that our continued inability to overcome a number of foundational problems limits the emancipatory potential of human rights. Among these are the racist and sexist tropes that inform interventionism; the entrenched nature of realpolitik; the hegemony of legalistic approaches that crowd out other ones; and the failure of liberalism, with its narrow emphasis on rights-bearing individuals, to meaningfully address structural violence.[5]

I mention the debate (do human rights work?) because it has direct bearing on this book. My examination of how human rights "facts" are frequently fashioned rather than simply found, and the varied ways in which traces of this process are erased, however unintentionally, can easily be read as an attack on the legitimacy of human rights documentation more generally.[6] My intent is quite the opposite, as I deeply believe and personally participate in justice and accountability efforts. The legitimacy of human rights "truth" claims is instead, in my view, strengthened rather than weakened by making the interplay of facts and "facts" more transparent and thus open to examination and debate. Two citational practices, quotation and redaction, have figured prominently throughout this book, and I devote further discussion to them here to highlight what can be gained when critical yet constructive attention is devoted to their interplay.

QUOTATION: ADDING "FACTS"

The verb "to quote" has a curious history. The practice of quotation first emerged in fourteenth-century Europe, and it was originally restricted to visually distinguishing successive passages in a text through the addition of a *diple*, a type of symbolic marginalia. By the seventeenth century, the mark had visually evolved into the ones we use today to signal that the words inside of the open and closed quotation marks are reproduced from elsewhere. The practice solidified over the next century, in tandem with the spread of the idea of authors' rights as a form of intellectual property, whereby the words that appeared inside quotation marks had come to constitute an "assertion of private ownership."[7] From a more narrowly linguistic perspective, the utility of quotation marks lies in their ability to distinguish direct speech from indirect speech. (The former refers to verbatim speech, while the latter involves a description of what was said.) But the distinction between direct and indirect speech breaks down upon closer examination, explains Meir Sternberg, a literary critic:

> Quotation brings together at least two discourse-events: that in which things were originally expressed (said, thought, experienced) by one subject (speaker, writer, reflector) and that in which they are cited by another. In principle, these form—spatiotemporally, thematically, teleologically—two separate and independent events. . . . But once an act of quotation takes place and associates them as quoting and quoted event, their relationship so tangles as to need disentangling at a number of points.[8]

Sternberg's point, which has important implications for human rights practice, is this: that which is originally expressed and that which quotes it in verbatim form "can never fully be the same, [as] there is always some element of reformulation in the re-presentation of someone else's words."[9] These words, in other words, are lifted from one context and redeployed in another one, as I have done here, which allows me to make a different argument with Sternberg's words than he did in the original. In doing so, what would otherwise be ephemeral, from oral testimony to the printed page, becomes "circulable," "portable," or "reportable" across time and space.[10] The resulting mobility of quotations-as-verbatim-facts, which commingles two discourse events without making the semantic consequences of doing so explicit, takes two common forms in human rights documentation and advocacy.

Pull quotes, the first example, visually populate most NGO human rights reports. Such quotes have been "pulled" (i.e., excerpted) from their original context and transformed into a graphic design element to entice people to read the entire text, or to highlight a key element of it. Such quotes, usually no more than a couple of brief sentences, almost always presented in a larger and different style font, are drawn from a longer statement, such as a victim's interview or an expert's professional opinion:

> *Whenever SPDC [Tatmadaw troops] approach our village, we have to run away. Even if they do not reach us, they fire mortar shells at us. They steal our food and possessions, kill our animals, burn our houses and plant landmines. All we can do is run.*[11]

The pull quote here originates with a Karen woman who participated in a focus group held in Thandaung Township, which was, at the time, the epicenter of the Northern Offensive. The CIDKP conducted the focus group and then forwarded a copy of the transcript to its humanitarian partner, the TBBC; I featured these two organizations in chapter 3. TBBC later recontextualized the woman's statement in anonymous form as a pull quote in its 2008 annual report on internal displacement in southeastern Myanmar and the international law relevant to it.[12] The quote, reproduced in large-scale font, covers the entire bottom half of the report's executive summary title page, while a color photo of IDPs fleeing across a rapids-filled river dominates the top half. Pull quotes like this one may or may not reappear elsewhere in the text. But in every instance, the pull quote is excised from the context in which it was first expressed, meaning that a new element of epitextual interpretation is always added.

Why does this matter? As postcolonial critic Ella Shohat reminds us, "An utterance must be analyzed not only in terms of who represents but also in terms of who is being represented for what purpose, at which historical moment, for which location, using which strategies, and in what tone of address."[13] In this instance, the pull quote, like the many others that appear in the report, including ones from the UN special rapporteur, visually reinforced TBBC's concluding allegation, which it expressed in qualified form in its 2008 annual report. Namely, Tatmadaw battalions had very likely committed crimes against humanity on a widespread and systematic basis over the previous year, especially in Karen areas, where the TBBC's annual IDP survey calculated that more than sixty thousand villagers were hiding in black areas due to the Northern Offensive.[14] ("The evidence cited in this report," TBBC's researchers wrote, "appears to strengthen Amnesty International's recent assessment that the violations meet the legal threshold to constitute crimes against humanity.")[15] Because of its mission as a humanitarian organization, TBBC did not issue specific recommendations beyond this generalized call for the "international community" to hold the military regime "to account."[16]

But other actors went on to utilize TBBC's findings for their own ends: rights-based NGOs for advocacy purposes, development staff to justify further requests for cross-border aid to assist IDPs, and diplomats for high-level lobbying at the UN. None of these subsequent uses are unusual. They are instead the norm. Excerpts from testimonies combined with statistics become "facts," and the cumulative "evidence," typically encapsulated in report form, becomes an instrumental tool for use by others. However, these transformations highlight an important point. Quotations are more than words fixed in time by the quotation marks that bracket them. Quotations also possess a degree of agency and, as they circulate in other contexts, can effect change in ways independent of the source's original intent—in this case, the recontextualization of TBBC's apolitical statement of human rights and humanitarian "facts" into political ones.

The second example of addition involves what one cultural historian described as "harvesting others' words."[17] This evocative phrase, which I have harvested for my own purposes (the author originally used it to describe the practice of creating edited collections of quotations), illustrates how quotes can be utilized as rhetorical devices to link "facts" in strategic ways. Rhetoric, which is the art of effective or persuasive speaking, thus inescapably adds meaning to the quoted text because the intent behind it is to confirm a "fact" or to persuade someone of the credibility of the "fact" presented.

In chapter 5, for example, I detailed the efforts of an unsuccessful NGO-led campaign to convince the UN Security Council to authorize a CoI into alleged crimes against humanity and war crimes in Myanmar. The recursive use of quotations, I argued, provided a strategic way to link the production of "evidence" to the establishment of "authority." The NGOs participating in the campaign serially quoted sections of the UN's own published reports, resolutions, and voting records to establish the "factual" legitimacy of their calls for a CoI on the grounds that Myanmar posed a genuine "threat to peace and security." (The threshold, named but not defined in the UN Charter, that would trigger Security Council enforcement actions.) The recursive practice consequently put different temporalities into conversation with one another: the past (previously published UN documents), the then present (cited "facts," drawn from these same documents, detailing the purported nature of the threat Myanmar posed), and the then desired future (a UN Security Council decision to authorize a CoI, which could result in a referral of the case to the ICC for investigation and possible prosecution of its military leaders). In 2010, the successive NGO calls for action culminated in a form of verbatim-once-removed. With explicit reference to the reports human rights NGOs had submitted to his office over the course of many years, Tomás Ojea Quintana, the UN's special rapporteur on the human rights situation in Myanmar, reached the same conclusion they had, albeit with a degree of qualification. Quintana, in his report to the UN, said that its bodies *"may consider establishing a commission of inquiry with a specific fact-finding mandate to address the question of international crimes."*[18] "At this particular stage in the history of Myanmar," he added, "the State faces this critical assignment which must be addressed by this Government and by a newly elected Government as well."[19] In other words, the time for a CoI "may" (a word that both conveys possibility and invites permission) have finally come.

Quintana was not the only UN official to suggest that a CoI might be in order. Previous UN special rapporteurs to Myanmar, Paulo Pinheiro and Yozo Yokota, also called for a CoI in separate op-eds in leading newspapers, one of them *The New York Times*. In ordinary circumstances, their respective statements would have generated considerable attention, but not in this instance. Quintana's status as the current special rapporteur and the venue in which the official UN report was released, the Human Rights Council, guaranteed an international controversy, resulting from his breach of diplomatic norms and, as some critics asserted, his mandate. But the underlying point here is not whether Quintana's efforts succeeded or failed in moving the CoI issue another step forward. It is instead the cumulative power of recursive source citation, an abbreviated form of verbatim, to generate supporting "evidence" through stockpiling.[20] The process by which this occurs is far from straightforward according to linguist Mikayo Inuoe. It requires being able to identify "what kinds of social, technological/technical, and ideological practices are necessary to turn a particular text . . . into a credible or otherwise weighty copy of another text?"[21] Close attention to the biographies of quotations, which often involve all three of these practices, offers one way to understand how human rights "facts in the form of conclusions" are constructed, deployed, countered, and denied within and across reports, as well as among different audiences.

REDACTION: SUBTRACTING "FACTS"

The verb "to redact," like "to quote," also has an interesting history. "To redact" once meant "to arrange" or "to edit," particularly in circumstances where multiple textual sources were combined and altered slightly to make a single, coherent document, such as a religious text. But in common parlance, the verb more narrowly connotes obscuration, the act of hiding or concealing something for either legal or security purposes, creating an absent presence in the process. Thick black lines, followed by photocopying to make the original text harder to recover, is the typical tool of the censor, even today. Other, long-standing techniques are still used as well. Lacunae may be inserted, bracketed ellipses added, and pseudonyms given to help protect the contents of a document—all of which routinely appear in the archives examined in this book and the reports made possible by them.

The process of redaction, also known as "sanitization," is one of strategic removal so that sensitive information, once masked, can be distributed to a broader audience. As a result, who decides what is sensitive and how much text needs to be visually excised through masking are routinely disputed and, in some instances, challenged through legal action. In the meantime, however, the reader is left trying to make sense of the complex interplay between what is legible and can be known and what must, in the eyes of the censor, be rendered illegible and thus remain unknown.

Despite technological improvements, redaction remains a laborious process. Software developers are still struggling to bring programs to market that can reliably automate redaction, especially as born-digital materials pose technical challenges that paper documents do not. (In response, a group of historians, computer scientists, and statisticians are using natural language processing and machine learning techniques to carry out syntactic analyses of previously but now no longer classified government documents to develop algorithms to predict future redaction patterns.)[22] Regardless of the method used, the redaction process can be a highly fraught one because of the consequences of an unintended disclosure. Yet no best practices guidelines are available for human rights workers, which is surprising given that raw data, such as unredacted interview transcripts, can pose a serious security risk to victims and fact finders alike.

Sometimes the decision of what to redact prior to publication is an easy one, such as when very specific details appear in testimony. Such identifying details are most clearly evident in accounts of torture because of the specificity of what reportedly occurred. But potential identifiers also appear in other accounts that feature a singular event, such as the destruction of a church by arson, a land mine blast in which a precise number of soldiers are also injured or killed, and a rare case when someone files a human rights complaint with the local authorities. However, the risks disclosure poses are not always readily apparent, leaving the decision to redact or not, and to what extent, up to one's professional judgment, which may often be little more than a "best guess." (The precautionary principle, although not always followed, calls for more rather than less redaction, if there is any uncertainty.)

The resulting tension between transparency, which is essential to the credibility of a fact-finding organization's "truth" claims, and opacity, which is necessary to avoid causing harm to sources and staff, pervades every aspect of human rights documentation and, especially, advocacy. Jonathan Abel, in his study of literary censorship in interwar Japan, summarizes this paradox in a manner that is surprisingly relevant here:

> Archives and censors share a curious relationship. Although they serve vastly different functions in theory and according to common sense (one preserves, the other destroys), in practice censors and archivists engage in many of the same activities. Despite their stated institutional responsibility to remove and destroy, censors historically have collected and preserved for posterity the very material deemed dangerous to society. Conversely, despite their overt purposes

of collection and preservation, archivists have historically excluded, removed, and destroyed material deemed unworthy or unwieldy.[23]

From this perspective, human rights fact finders are archivists *and* censors. Fact finders generate immense amounts of raw data through their work. But an archive of everything is an archive of nothing, which is why data on some kinds of violations are inevitably not used or preserved. At the same time, the data that do reside in an archive cannot be released *in toto*. They must be censored in ways appropriate to the contexts in which the data are consumed. (UN investigators may see a fuller version of the underlying source documentation than general audiences, for example.) So, just as "secrecy must itself be performed in a public fashion in order to be understood to exist," redaction, which is a public representation of a secret, must also be performed to show that fact-finding organizations have yet more documentation that they could release, in uncensored form, in the future.[24]

As mentioned in the introduction, the perceived credibility of a fact-finding organization is partially a function of its brand recognition. Such recognition, which legal scholar Jennifer Mnookin refers to as "reputational knowledge," helps shape how field data are redacted when released in published form.[25] The KHRG, whose archive on forced labor I featured in chapter 2, maintains a network of trained volunteer fact finders across much of KNU-delineated Karen State, and they regularly contribute raw field documentation to KHRG's researchers. These direct connections enable KHRG to provide ethnographic insights into the lived experiences of civilians in conflict-affected areas that other organizations cannot. The level of detail consequently requires the extensive use of redaction to reduce the risk of retaliation, as explained by KHRG here:

> [We] blanked out the names of people, villages, Army camps, Army officers and other details where these could be used to track the villages involved. These have been replaced with "xxxx," "yyyy," "aaaa," etc. We have generally used "xxx" for numerals and general information, "xxxx," "yyyy," "zzzz," "wwww," "vvvv," etc. for place names, and "aaaa," "bbbb," "cccc," etc. for people's names. When an order refers to several people or places, we have assigned each person and place a specific string ("yyyy," "cccc," etc.) to keep the references consistent and avoid confusion.[26]

The patterned redactions of identifying details, which visually signal this ethnographic expertise, arguably bolster the credibility of KHRG's reporting with some audiences (e.g., other human rights organizations, governments that have imposed sanctions on the previous military regimes, and the relevant UN bodies). But the extensive redactions have also prompted questions that I have heard voiced over the years by skeptics regarding KHRG's claims of independence. The skepticism centers on two issues. First, KNU administrators and KNLA soldiers operate in the conflict-affected areas, where the worst violations tend to occur, which raises the possibility that at least some of KHRG's field sources are motivated to provide accounts that are supportive of KNU/KNLA agendas. Second, in most instances, it is not feasible for third parties to re-interview KHRG's sources directly, which makes independent verification of the source information extremely difficult, if not impossible. (Neither criticism, valid or not, applies to the forced labor orders KHRG collected. Tatmadaw soldiers personally wrote them, and the originals are available for review upon request, pending vetting by KHRG.) Nevertheless, doubts about KHRG's independence remain in some quarters, even though many other fact-finding organizations have documented similar abuses in conflict-affected areas across the country for decades. But the main point here is that too much information in redacted form can also be a liability, at least with some audiences.

The IHRC occupies a different position in the global hierarchy of "reputational knowledge." The clinic, headed by a leading Myanmar legal expert, has published an influential series of fact-finding reports and policy memos on the human rights situation in the country for more than ten years. The prestige of the IHRC is reflected by the fact that leading prosecutors and jurists (e.g., the first prosecutor at both the International Criminal Tribunals for the Former Yugoslavia and for Rwanda, and the former president of the Inter-American Court of Human Rights) write prefaces for their reports, which are read at the highest political and diplomatic levels.[27] By contrast, the IHRC rarely reproduces quotes from informants in the text of its publications, which instead focus on patterns of violations and the international criminal law that applies to them. IHRC's interview source material appears in more abstracted form in its footnotes as a consequence. The footnotes, such as the examples referred to in a previous chapter, contain strings of references to testimonies and expert declarations, in this case, the Tatmadaw's alleged shoot-on-sight policy, as coded in IHRC's confidential database of crimes troops reportedly committed during the Northern Offensive:

Clinic Database, Interview Nos. 68, 98, 125, 156 (shoot-on-sight policy in place at night only), and 157; Clinic Expert Declaration, Expert 1, para. 89, 96–97; Clinic Expert Declaration, Expert 2, para. 97; Clinic Expert Declaration, Expert 4, para. 31.[28]

Such citational practices help establish the authority of IHRC's "facts" via a redactive mode of stockpiling. The practice of stockpiling, as earlier described, utilizes the steady accumulation of information to persuade readers that the report is well researched, credible, and contextualized within the appropriate legal frameworks, even though none of the original source material appears in the text itself. In this instance, it is the visual act of enumeration that helps establish evidentiary weight through the repetition of numbered sources.

The 2005 report "Threat to Peace: A Call for the UN Security Council to Act in Burma" provides another example of human rights documentation at a yet further citational distance. Vacláv Havel, political dissident and former president of the Czech Republic, and Bishop Desmond Tutu, a Nobel Peace Prize winner, commissioned the report, which DLA Piper Rudnick Gray Cary, a multinational law firm with annual revenues in the billions, prepared on a pro bono basis. "Threat to Peace" helped accelerate the ultimately unsuccessful campaign to convince the Security Council to authorize a CoI, which I summarized earlier. This report, and the others that followed, pushed the stockpiling process yet further into abstraction. The eighty-page report contained 711 citations, a very substantial portion of which quoted the UN back to itself:

[540] See UN Doc. S/25942 (1993) (Letter from the Permanent Representative of Cuba).
[541] UN Doc. S/PV.3238 (1993).
[542] Id.
[543] Id.; see also UN Doc. S/25942 (1993) . . . .
[544] UN Doc. S/PV.3238 (1993).
[545] See Id. (commending His Excellency Mr. Dante Caputo, Special Envoy of the Organization of American States and the United Nations for its efforts in attempting to achieve a settlement with the regime).
[546] S.C. [Security Council] Res. [Resolution] 841, supra note 520 (imposing a trade embargo on the country).
[547] Id.
[548] Id.
[549] UN Doc. S/PV.3394 (1994).

550 UN Doc. S/1994/642 (1994).
551 Id.[29]

The purpose of this rhetorical tactic, as I have explained, was to persuade UN decision makers to act on what they had repeatedly concluded in prior reports, resolutions, and so on: that the human rights situation in Myanmar represented a "threat to peace and security" domestically, regionally, and, when drug trafficking was taken into account, internationally. But in doing so, the lived experience of the victims of the violence was entirely erased, which constitutes the ultimate form of redaction.

ARCHIVING A CRIMINAL CASE FILE FOR MYANMAR

Both citational practices, quotation and redaction, point to another question that haunts human rights documentation. In the most general sense, any archival document (or *record* to use the more general term) is "created naturally in the course of transacting of business of any kind, whether by governments, businesses, community organizations, or private individuals," information experts Sue McKemmish and Frank Upward explain.[30] In other words, there is nothing inherently special about such a record in ontological terms; however, this status importantly changes once the document/record enters into a recognized archival context. Belief in the trustworthiness of documents/records in archival contexts is intimately linked to confidence in their authenticity. Luciana Duranti, a theorist of archival studies, maintains that a record is authentic "when it is the document it claims to be." "Proving a record's authenticity does not make it more reliable than when it was created," she explains. "It only warrants that the record does not result from any manipulation, substitution, or falsification occurring after the completion of its procedure of creation."[31] The International Standards Organization (ISO) has globally formalized this definition under the terms of ISO 15489, which concerns the creation, capture, and management of records regardless of their structure or form.[32] The ISO principles, when properly implemented, are meant to guard against the unauthorized addition, deletion, alteration, use, and concealment of records.[33] Nevertheless, as James Rhoads emphatically puts it, "A *good* archivist must also be suspicious!"[34] A record's authenticity, in other words, cannot be taken at face value simply because it resides in an archive of some kind.

Critically, the definition of authenticity provided by Duranti and institutionalized by the ISO only applies *after* a record is created. The processes that occur prior to that point are not covered. But in the context of human rights documentation, the methodologies that fact finders utilize frequently require a degree of ad hoc creativity and tactical flexibility, as the efforts to identity the North Korean labor camps described in the introduction make quite clear. The examples presented in each of the chapters underscore this same point: authenticity, when understood narrowly as an ontological state that comes into being following a record's entry into the archive, fails to recognize the multiple ways human rights "facts" are fashioned as well as found before, during, and after entry into an archive.[35] Spreadsheets and databases, which change as new records are added and deleted from them in a digital archive, embody such malleability.

This malleability is not limited to computer software programs, however. Indeed, "the [very] plasticity of 'facts' themselves, and the negotiation of what is and is not accepted as being 'factual,'" human rights philosopher Frédéric Mégret argues, "is not subsidiary to conflict but central to it."[36] Mégret's observation about the centrality of negotiation to the determination of what is "factual" has important legal implications in the case of Myanmar. I elaborate on several of these later as they highlight issues regarding the mixed value of the archival "evidence" currently available for the potential future prosecution of international crimes. After all, as legal historian Cornelia Vismann has noted, jurisprudence "decides upon the conditions under which legal discourses must function to perform justice."[37]

The Ferencz International Justice Initiative works to empower victims of mass atrocities to pursue justice and to hold their perpetrators accountable. The initiative, housed within the US Holocaust Museum, hosted a meeting in October 2018. Present were a range of Myanmar country experts, human rights documentation specialists, and lawyers experienced with the construction of case files and the prosecution of perpetrators, as well as myself.[38] The overarching goal of the hackathon-style, daylong workshop was to identify what could be done to support efforts to enforce accountability for international crimes in Myanmar over short-, medium-, and long-term time horizons. The workshop organizers posed six orienting questions at the outset for the participants to consider. What has been done to date? What does a dream prosecution look like? What are the most viable cases? Who are the targets of possible prosecutions? What are the biggest challenges to putting together case files, and how do we best overcome them? And how do we design plans that have additional benefits beyond punishing perpetrators? The purpose of answering these questions was to generate ideas that organizations the participants represented could consider, vet internally, and then, ideally, take action upon.

The Regime Crimes Team leader for the Commission for International Justice and Accountability, an NGO, explained that the crime base is often easy to document and to present, that is, the what, where, and when of the violations committed. The challenge is to prove the responsibility of the accused, which he said is "the primary battlefield" in court. "Ninety-percent of the energy goes here," he emphasized. Four types of documentation, what he termed the "4 I's," can help prove responsibility. Defectors, testimony given during cross-examination, and the contents of plea agreements can provide insider witness information. Records of phone calls and radio communications can reveal command-and-control relationships. Internal documents, such as security services reports, can further corroborate coordination. And international materials, such as confidential minutes of peace negotiations and internal investigative deliberations, when obtainable and admissible, can help confirm the veracity of the preceding. But the most important source, he stressed, was internal regime documentation, with the military's archive as the "Holy Grail," as he put it.

A former member of the ICC's Office of the Prosecutor agreed, but pointed out that it was easier to prove that international crimes occurred during a clearly defined time period of "high-intensity" violence. In his opinion, the Tatmadaw's attacks on Rohingya civilians would be more attractive to a prosecutor than the decades of comparatively low-intensity violence in KNU-delineated Karen State in southeastern Myanmar for this reason. But in both instances, a central dilemma remained: whether to pursue a strategic prosecution (i.e., someone who can actually be arrested) or an emblematic one (i.e., the person most responsible for the crimes). The answer, he explained, was not always clear. "There are lots of views within the office of the ICC. It is not swinging one way or the other. [Differing] views are always present in every case." His view on the Rohingya was not universally shared, however. The Rohyinga case, one participant forcefully stated, would be "the least appealing in some ways due to the antipathy within the country; they would receive the least support or cooperation in terms of building a case."

Further conversation produced a general consensus around a hybrid approach, which could be termed an emblematic case with strategic characteristics. A clinical instructor at Harvard Law School, a refugee from Myanmar herself, summed up this strategy as one in which plaintiffs should "seek the highest level of 'arrestibility' at the international level *and* the lower level for domestic prosecutions." Two individuals quickly rose to the top of the list as emblematic cases, while it was recognized that their arrest would be impossible unless the individuals were detained while traveling abroad. Senior General Than Shwe, the former chairman of the State Peace and Development Council and commander in chief of the Tatmadaw (1992–2011), was the first. He oversaw the planning and execution of state-sponsored violence around the country and, although currently retired and now in his late eighties, continues to exert significant influence on affairs of state. Senior General Min Aung Hlaing, the commander in chief and following the February 2021 coup the chairman of the State Administration Council, was the second. He was appointed to the commander in chief position in 2011, and troops under his ultimate control have committed well-documented war crimes and crimes against humanity in Kachin State, northern Shan State, and Rakhine State, where the vast majority of Rohingya resided before large-scale ethnic cleansing began in 2017. In terms of high-level domestic prosecutions, participants additionally singled out commanders of the primary combat units, the LIDs, because they are directly responsible for the crimes their subordinates committed during field operations.[39]

But a Myanmar desk officer at the US Department of State underscored a central problem. Namely, there is a significant difference between a lawyer's understanding of documentation (what is needed to create a crime base) and the type of cataloging that Network for Human Rights Documentation Burma (ND-Burma) and other fact-finding NGOs carry out. "Their documentation is very broad and often spot reporting," she said. "It is not specific enough and does not meet legal standards in terms of a custody chain, time and date stamps, geo-locations, etc. These specifics are needed to meet prosecutorial standards." "That should be the lens and goal," she stressed. An associate director at Human Rights Watch agreed. But she also counseled caution in light of her experiences with the UN's International, Impartial, and Independent Mechanism on International Crimes Committed in the Syrian Arab Republic (IIIM). NGOs and international bodies, such as the IIIM, have different mandates, and the primary constituencies of the former are the victims and the sources. If the confidentiality of both is not protected, she emphasized, NGOs working to meet legal standards risk being seen as "the arm of the prosecution." "You should assume what you share with the prosecution will also be shared with the defense during discovery, which means it will enter the public domain," she continued. "What is not risky [to victims and sources] now, may be risky five to ten years in the future in terms of witness identification." The risk is not limited to victims. The risk extends to different visions for transitional justice in the future.

DEFINING TRANSITIONAL JUSTICE

Calculating future risks to victims if the relevant archival records are released is not a pressing issue currently in Myanmar. The obstacles to criminal proceedings, which are critical for ending impunity, are insurmountable at present. But in the meantime, transitional justice conversations are taking place about what might be possible in the still undetermined future. However, "the traditional focus on suffering is not appropriate here [in Myanmar]," explained a researcher with the Pyidaungsu Institute for Peace and Dialogue. "People do not want revenge. Instead, they want their lives restored. Most people find solace in their communities and in their religion. Not a commission," he explained. "So, it should be public and maybe have a legal component with support of the international community. But the process should help them build their lives and to live with dignity. Burmese people, especially the ethnics, never had dignity."[40]

Assuming for the moment that his view about the desire for restoration is widely shared, an overarching question remains: What model should be used? Transitional justice experts have presented several potential models in workshops with rights-based groups located in Thailand and Myanmar interested in the issue, with South Africa, East Timor, Guatemala, and the Philippines serving as case studies. But none of the models have gained traction due to a pervasive sense of exceptionalism among the participants (Burman and non-Burman participants alike). The common response is that the situation in Myanmar is unique and requires its own model. This position means that there is no general consensus as to how to move the conversation forward regarding possible approaches for the future.[41]

Some approaches are not possible at all in Myanmar, unfortunately. The transitional justice of restitution aims to restore the status quo before the violations occurred. However, state-sponsored violence continued for so long, for example for many decades in much of KNU-delineated Karen State, that it is not feasible to reestablish the state in which things were before the conflicts began. Other efforts are more realistic, provided that the Union Peace Conferences (known as the "21st Century Panglong") produce a meaningful resolution to the political disputes that underlie many of the conflicts.[42] ("When the landmines are pulled out of the ground, then that's an indicator of trust," as one humanitarian worker put it to me.)[43] Foreign donors have invested significant resources to support these conferences. The Norwegian government-led Myanmar Peace Support Initiative (MPSI) provided several million US dollars between 2012 and 2014 to strengthen the cease-fires and to promote dialogue between the armed actors by funding pilot projects in various former conflict zones, including the KNU-delineated Karen State. Many border groups, especially Karen CSOs, were highly critical of the MPSI, however, which they argued was not transparent, excluded their involvement, and prioritized neoliberal-style economic development over political dialogue. But not everyone agrees on the extent to which CSOs should be involved in current discussions. One critic of the Karen CSOs pointedly noted, "They do not understand that they have a right to be consulted and have their views represented, but not to have a seat at the table with the military and armed groups. They have gone beyond their missions."[44]

The United Kingdom went on to award the Myanmar Peace Center, which the MPSI created, more than US$22 million, to be spent over four years (2014–2018), "to build an environment more conducive to dialogue, tolerance, and create safer communities by supporting locally driven, catalytic initiatives and ideas which enhance social cohesion."[45] But the peace process, which is a prerequisite to moving forward with "national reconciliation," as it is called, remains stalled.

The impasse leaves reparations as the only acceptable topic of discussion, though the focus remains largely on compensation to former political prisoners. Several commemorative projects, such as museums and shrines, now exist as well.[46] Nevertheless, these initiatives remain very limited in number and scope, and thus impact. The initiatives lack broad impact in large part because popular understandings of transitional justice, where they even exist, are problematic, as the earlier statement suggests.

In Myanmar, "the concept [of transitional justice] is solely associated with courts and punitive action," explained a staff person at the Open

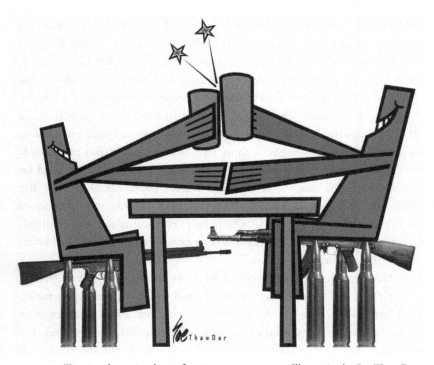

FIGURE 5. Toasting the national ceasefire agreement. SOURCE: Illustration by Soe Thaw Dar.

Society Institute, an INGO that supports the efforts of local CSOs and media leaders to promote democratization in the country.[47] Her observation echoed what the coordinator of the Alternative ASEAN Network on Burma and the secretary general of the International Federation of Human Rights told me during a separate interview. Her local partners work around this preconception by providing a basic introduction to transitional justice during trainings "to demystify it." "We work with them [CBOs and women's groups] to come up with their own proposals about what it would look like," she told me, rather than relying on international models that emphasize legal action. "It is the Voldemort strategy; we don't use the word [transitional justice]. Instead, we focus on helping people to understand the standard sequencing: 1) truth; 2) accountability; 3) reparations; and 4) institutional reforms." "But in Burma," she added, "We will need to do institutional reforms first to create opportunities and the ability to do [the] others."[48]

Her point about the need for reforms is widely shared. Parliament, which is structured in a manner that maintains impunity under provisions of the 2008 Constitution; the Myanmar National Human Rights Commission, which lacks adequate independence, resources, and investigative powers; and of course the Tatmadaw, which has so far resisted security sector reform, typically top the list.[49] The lack of progress in these areas, as well as the NLD-led government's increased use of repressive colonial-era laws to silence critics prior to the 2021 coup, have prompted activists to set aside any explicit references to transitional justice to focus instead on the need for "national reconciliation," a concept that is more politically acceptable. But the broader challenge, one expert explained to me after having interviewed the heads of thirty different CSOs, is that "reconciliation takes multiple narratives. They say that others don't have an understanding of our history of suffering, so there is mistrust."[50]

In this regard, "national reconciliation" is an empty signifier, that is, a phrase that points to no actual object and has no agreed upon meaning. Nevertheless, it is possible to categorize the narratives into two main forms: ethnic Burmans, who endured decades of political repression, and ethnic non-Burmans, who endured decades of widespread and systematic preemptive violence at the hands of the Tatmadaw. The question of reparations, which can be discussed more openly, thus takes different forms across these two groups. My point is not to deny cross-cutting commonalities; they exist.[51] But the experiences that inform these groups' views on justice can be broadly delineated in a manner that reflects their experiences of indirect and direct violence, respectively.[52]

Former political prisoners, who are predominantly ethnic Burmans, have been at the forefront of public efforts to promote reparations, which some groups would like to see enshrined into law. The Assistance Association for Political Prisoners (AAPP), a group formed by former detainees, has long struggled to identify where prisoners are held; to improve their conditions with "donations" (i.e., bribes to guards); and to arrange material, psychological, and vocational support for them upon release. AAPP gently advocates for the government to provide programs to help rebuild the lives of the thousands of political prisoners who spent years of their lives incarcerated in cruel and degrading conditions, many of them victims of torture as well. The documentation project on torture, which AAPP began in 2013, "could be linked with work that other groups are doing. It is not to equate them.

The situations are dramatically different. However, it helps establish a consistent pattern across time, space, and ethnic group. Again, it supports claims that these abuses are not only systemic, but state approved," the staff explained. "Such cross-cutting approaches will attract more media attention and international concern than if they are done in isolation."[53] But the problem of competitive victimhood, wherein representatives of different ethnic groups claim that their members suffered more than other groups, continues to make such collaborative documentation, archive construction, and advocacy efforts extremely difficult.

The political space with which to expand efforts beyond calls for reparations remains quite circumscribed today as well. "But in order to achieve national reconciliation, it is not possible to set aside transitional justice. Otherwise, genuine transition will not occur," the deputy in charge of foreign affairs for AAPP told me, quickly adding that further human rights documentation was needed for the latter to be achieved. "They [government and military officials] have not fully committed to the national reconciliation process because they don't understand that transitional justice is not directly concerned with you; rather, it concerns the institution. So, when we provide trainings with MPs and military representatives locally . . . we cannot call it 'Human Rights and Transitional Justice' trainings in the title. We can use 'Democracy and Human Rights,' and then smuggle some transitional justice into it."[54] Such efforts have yet to have an impact, however, as the NLD, which once counted dozens of political prisoners among its membership, was, prior to the coup, actively resistant to making transitional justice part of the political discussion.[55]

By contrast, conversations in cease-fire areas generally place transitional justice concerns "on the backburner," as the executive director of the TBBC put it. The TBBC, as previously discussed, provides aid to the refugee camps and has closely coordinated with cross-border groups to assist IDPs for more than two decades. "While TJ is an issue" she said, three others prevent it from moving to the forefront of national reconciliation conversations: the fragility of the cease-fire process, the pressing livelihood concerns of the refugees and IDPs, and the refusal of the Tatmadaw to withdraw from brown areas where its troops are busily hardening their military positions.[56] The director of the Salween Institute for Public Policy, a prominent think tank, agreed. "The most pressing issue in their [the Karen leaders] minds is to get a reasonable deal with the government, so they will wait and address the livelihood needs of ordinary people in the meantime." "But no one," he said, "is willing to say forget it. Many want to see a legal process."[57]

ND-Burma's director, who represents a dozen plus fact-finding organizations, most of them in southeastern Myanmar, that participate in its human rights documentation project, offers a somewhat different view. "Most of the victims just want acknowledgment of what happened and for the perpetrators to apologize to them." However, he emphasized, "We need to start not with victim forgiveness, but perpetrator acknowledgement. Only then can we work together."[58] Acknowledgment, in his eyes, is thus a fundamental precondition for national reconciliation in which official, public apologies play a crucial part. In the meantime, ND-Burma continues to build its centralized human rights archive, which draws on the spot reporting of its member organizations, the contents of which may one day inform the creation of a criminal case file for litigation. A critical gap exists within ND-Burma's archive, however, and this points to a pervasive evidentiary problem that several of the participants in the international accountability workshop in Washington, D.C., flagged.

The KHRG, the premier fact-finding organization in southeastern Myanmar, continues to keep ND-Burma somewhat at arm's length. The former Burma project coordinator for the International Center for Transitional Justice offered me several explanations when I asked her why this was the case. Two stand out. "First, it is because they are very good at what they do and don't need the [ND-Burma] network to add value. They have funding and documentation capacity already," she said. "The second concerns different histories. It is KHRG's feeling that Karen State was never really part of Burma. So, they believe Karen take care of Karen.[59] Nonparticipation in ND-Burma is not limited to KHRG, however. Many other Karen groups also document violations, either directly or indirectly, as part of their program activities: KORD, CIDKP, THWEE Community Development Network, and the Karen Environmental and Social Action Network, among others. But like KHRG, none of them participate in the ND-Burma human rights archive project either.

The absence of Karen-related information in ND-Burma's archive is symptomatic of the broader nationwide problem mentioned in the introduction—namely, documentation archipelagos. (Tatmadaw records, maintained by the Defense Services Historical Research Institute, are essential to overcoming this fragmentation as well, but are closed to human rights research.)

A "complete" archive is, of course, a utopian project, and even if possible, for security reasons would not be the safest approach for protecting victims, witnesses, and other sources from retaliation in the future. But the fragmentation continues to significantly constrain efforts to write a more comprehensive history of human rights "fact" production in Myanmar. This obstacle remains the case even in KNU-delineated Karen State, which is the best-documented conflict region in the country. Information asymmetry is not limited to conflict-affected areas, however. Such asymmetry extends nationwide. ("There is lots of information regarding human rights outside the country and very little inside for the ordinary person," a Burman activist told me. "It is hard to convince people in the city that the government and the military commit such abuses in ethnic areas.")[60] This asymmetry will need to be overcome if transitional justice initiatives that need the support of the ethnic majority are to be successful.

———

Sustained engagement with archives as the subject of analysis, a running theme in this book, did not originate with Jacques Derrida. But his highly influential book, *Archive Fever*, which helped drive this epistemological and methodological turn across multiple disciplines, created fertile ground for scholars to reflect on their own research experiences.[61] Long-standing and often romanticized tropes (e.g., the struggle to overcome hindrances to access, the serendipitous discovery of previously unexamined documents, and ruminations on the tactile pleasures of physically handling historical materials) were no longer accepted at face value.[62] Instead, scholarly attention began to more fully take into account the implications of what philosopher Jacques Rancière called the "double absence" that lies at the heart of historiography. "The status of history," he wrote, "depends on the treatment of this twofold absence of the 'thing itself' that is *no longer there*—that is in the past, and that never was—because it never was *such as it was told*."[63] Other scholars investigated a different absence: sentiments, long dismissed as irrelevant to the documentation of historical facts, became increasingly recognized as being critical to shaping them.[64] These two strands of investigation (there were many others) signaled the emergence of a broader "structure of feeling," one in which growing numbers of scholars argued that archives were not simply repositories of knowledge, but also an important site of its creation.[65]

My analysis of human rights fact-finding, a subfield that is only just beginning to grapple with social theory, has pursued a different line of inquiry, albeit one that is also strongly influenced by it as applied to archival studies. My process-oriented approach has centered on "fact" production before, within, and after "the archive." In the course of doing so, I have faced the challenge of writing and unwriting this history, having participated in many of the same knowledge practices during my more than two decades of engagement with human rights issues in Myanmar. "The field [was] both within and without myself" as a result, to again quote legal anthropologist Annelise Riles.[66] Her insight, that the "distance between data and method in the ethnographic imagination of information" may narrow to nearly nothing in bureaucratic contexts, applies here.[67] I leave it to the reader to decide the degree to which I have succeeded in delineating when and how this occurs.

I must also answer a broader question here that I have so far avoided. Namely, how do human rights archives differ, if at all, from archives as conventionally understood? Anne Gilliland, who studies how archival systems and practices can support human rights in postconflict settings, asserts that "all archives are human rights archives."[68] I do not share Gilliland's position, which by virtue of including everything risks excluding nothing from an archive. Michelle Caswell, who positions her scholarship and practice at the intersection of archival studies, social justice, and human rights, provides a somewhat narrower definition. According to Caswell, "human rights archive" is an umbrella term that encompasses the records perpetrators produce; the evidence others gather for use in trials, tribunals, and truth commissions; and accounts from "survivors, victims' family members, and communities to memorialize the dead and forge collective memory of past injustice."[69] Caswell's definition is still quite expansive, but her fundamental point regarding human rights archives holds. It is impossible to separate the violence and its effects on human life from the documentary record, the archive in which it is preserved, the means used to mobilize this information, the ends to which it is put, and its reception by others.[70]

This impossibility raises further questions about how to archive with the potential needs of the future in mind, a task that requires the responsible stewardship of materials, not just custody of them.[71] As the previous section demonstrated, discussions regarding transitional justice in Myanmar remain in their initial stages, with little attention devoted so far to the many challenges that stewardship will pose. John Ciorciari, the senior legal adviser to the Documentation Center of Cambodia, an organization that safeguards records related to the Khmer Rouge period, has identified some of the key issues to consider, which again are relevant to all post–mass atrocity contexts. His questions underscore the trade-offs that need to be made, as the right to truth and the duty to record can be at odds with one another, especially in postconflict settings where limited resources make it difficult to make progress on both fronts simultaneously. Should, for example, the prompt dissemination of records be prioritized over the need to collect, systematize, and preserve them for historical purposes, in addition to legal ones? Who should have access to these records, and how can privacy concerns be protected at the same time? In what ways can the materials be used to promote accountability and reconciliation? Finally, how might efforts achieve both goals, often unproductively framed as a stark either/or choice between achieving justice or maintaining the peace?[72]

Ciorciari's questions, which have no easy answers, underscore the complex ethical quandaries that archivists face when they want to democratize "the archive." "There is no political power without control of the archives," argues Jacques Derrida. "Effective democratization," he declares, "can always be measured by this essential criterion: the participation in and access to the archive, its constitution, and its interpretation."[73] Such efforts currently go by a variety of names. "Archival activism" and "activist archiving" are two common ones.[74] "Self-determination in archiving" for the purposes of greater community autonomy is a third.[75] Regardless of terminology and the differences that distinguish these approaches, all of them call for greater inclusivity in determining what is recorded, how, and with what purposes in mind.[76]

The goal of democratizing the archive, while laudable in my view, raises epistemological obstacles, in addition to ethical ones. Human rights "facts," while often mobilized for adjudicatory purposes, have a more fundamental goal, one that links back to what the UN Commission on Human Rights (now Human Rights Council) defined as the "right to truth" with regard to serious violations of human rights law. (In 2006, the commission stated that the "right to truth" was "an inalienable and autonomous right, linked to the duty and obligation of the State to protect and guarantee human rights, to conduct effective investigations and to guarantee effective remedy and reparations.")[77] Fact-finding, which is one way of making the "right to truth" possible, is fundamentally concerned with documenting "what happened." But "what happened," when expressed in idiomatic form, is not always intelligible to influential actors in a position to take action in response to the stated "facts." The cultural specificity of "what happened" typically needs to be stripped away to recast separate incidents into patterns, such as crimes against humanity, that are then communicated through the frameworks and procedures that international law provides.[78] The process of decontextualization (the removal of idiomatic expression and interpretation) followed by recontextualization (the addition of legalistic expression and interpretation) arguably impoverishes our understanding of how affected populations understand the meaning of what reportedly took place.[79] It does so by making the recontextualized descriptions intellectually inaccessible to the people who experienced and/or witnessed the violations. Conflicts between the resulting "social truth"; "judicial truth," if legal proceedings occur; and "state truth," which may or may not accept a degree of responsibility for the violence, are often the result.[80] Unfortunately, the long history of preemptive violence in Myanmar, which has produced conflicting social, judicial, and state "truth" claims, promises to continue to hamper any efforts to reconcile them in the foreseeable future and, especially, in a manner that promotes transitional justice—which, it should be noted, is far from a universal desire.

The book chapters have examined what these competing truths look like in the form of enslaved bodies via forced labor, starved bodies as a result of the use of food as a weapon of war, executed bodies as part of willful killings and indiscriminate attacks on civilians, and investigative bodies to determine whether these actions qualified as widespread and systematic crimes against humanity and, in some instances, war crimes. My process-oriented account of the investigative decisions made, field methods employed, analytical practices utilized, and advocacy strategies applied has highlighted a fundamental and largely overlooked issue that connected all of these various bodies. Specifically, the praxis of fact-finding, even in its most basic forms, contains embedded within it a range of epistemological, methodological, and ethical quandaries that warrant careful, well-reasoned, and informed decisions and subsequent critical self-reflection. As I have demonstrated, when these decisions are fully taken into account as they shape data collection and processing, publication, and advocacy, an inescapable and unsettling conclusion presents itself. Human rights "facts"—the determination of what occurred, who bears responsibility for it, and what kinds of action are recommended in response—are quite often fashioned rather than found. The implications of this conclusion are profound, particularly given ongoing technological developments in fact-finding, such as the accelerating use of remote sensing, digital crowdsourcing, open-source intelligence gathering, and big data analytics, including machine learning.[81] The time has come to not only grapple with how these developments are transforming human rights documentation both for better *and* for worse in the present. It is also time to reexamine how "fact" production has shaped the crimes that already exist in archival form, if we are to understand and thus avoid eliding the dynamics of this process in the future.

Epilogue

"Major, violent upheaval is not easily put to rest," Bridget Conley, the research director of the World Peace Foundation, has observed. "One must ask: when, for whom, by what measure, and how does an ending become possible?"[1] As this epilogue discusses, answers to these important questions remain complicated and uncertain in KNU-delineated Karen State, as well as the country's southeast more generally. The general consensus is that human security, particularly in terms of civilian protection, has improved.[2] "We don't worry everyday about being attacked," a former Karen IDP explained. "We know there is a lull and that lines of communication have improved. The KNLA do not go into white zones and the Tatmadaw do not go into black zones. But things could change very quickly."[3] Not surprisingly, the modest improvements in human security have contributed to a broader shift in civilian attitudes, according to Steve Marshall, a former ILO liaison officer, who was based in Yangon. A separate Karen IDP told him on a visit to a cease-fire zone, "Whoever breaks the ceasefire is the enemy." The statement, which the IDP directed at KNU and government representatives at a public meeting, "was very strong," Marshall explained. "It told the KNU and government officials that they could meet separately if they wished and craft an otherwise beautiful agreement, but if it did not involve the villagers and they decided it did not work for them, it would be a problem in the future."[4]

The improvements in human security have not eradicated conflict-related problems, however. Instead, the status quo has given rise to "cold" rather than "hot" conflicts in many places, which are reflective of the "interim arrangements" currently in place. The concept of interim arrangements, although now widely used in official circles, is a contested one, meaning different things to different actors. Despite these differences in interpretation, the concept accurately conveys the liminal nature of "governance functions, administrative authority, and service delivery systems" in these zones, a result of the continued absence of a comprehensive political and economic settlement to the armed conflicts.[5]

At present, the Tatmadaw seeks to limit the ability of the NSAGs to continue to govern, administer, and provide services in former "black areas," that is, places that were under their exclusive control when the cease-fires were reached. These areas have yet to be officially demarcated, however, so tensions exist between the armed parties over where the areas begin and end in geographic terms.[6] The absence of a code of conduct with which to "co-define" the day-to-day monitoring of the cease-fire and to handle violations of it based on mutually agreed upon protocols compounds this problem further.[7] At the same time, the NSAGs are attempting to extend their influence into former brown areas to serve the ethnic populations in them that they claim to represent. Doing so offers a key means for the NSAGs to rebuild support for their legitimacy with populations they lost touch with as their territorial control fragmented under Tatmadaw pressure and factional splits resulting from separate cease-fire agreements. The competition between the armed groups, including the Tatmadaw, also has significant implications for the development agendas of donors, service providers, NGOs, and private sector actors with regard to agricultural livelihoods and job creation, land and natural resource management, health and education, and many other issues. Civilians are thus caught in the middle of this competition and must struggle to reconstitute their lives in a context characterized by conflicting "policies," double taxation among them.[8]

PREPARATION NOT PLANNING

The fluid nature of the interim arrangements in cease-fire areas poses significant problems for the large-scale return of refugees as well. Between 2005 and 2011, the main focus of humanitarian debate concerning durable solutions for refugees was on the third-country resettlement. (The vast majority of those resettled were Karen, who primarily relocated to the United

States.) The 2012 cease-fire between the Tatmadaw and the KNU changed the conversation, as it opened up the long-delayed possibility of repatriation, UNHCR's preferred option for a durable solution to the protracted conflict. Questions regarding who gets to return when, where, and upon whose say so remain highly politically charged. Myanmar government officials have long wanted the IDP issue to be resolved before discussing large-scale refugee returns. But NSAGs, such as the KNU, maintain a quite different position. Their leaders also want refugees to return, but only to areas under their territorial control.[9] Yet NSAG leaders are also cognizant of the fact that if the camps in Thailand completely close, they will lose one of the few means of keeping the still unresolved conflicts a topic of international attention and concern. Karen CBOs, by contrast, immediately adopted a refugee-centered approach and issued a position paper after the cease-fire agreement was reached detailing the preconditions that would have to be met before UNHCR and other international humanitarian organizations should begin to assist voluntary repatriation.[10]

Despite the Karen CBOs' calls for caution, donors immediately and dramatically reduced funding to the camps by shifting a significant percentage of aid to "inside" the country. "Every man and his dog had to get into Burma," remarked one humanitarian worker, who noted that camp residents regarded the shift in aid as direct pressure on them to get ready to return.[11] (In a rare public critique, the Karen Women's Organization publicly accused TBBC, which oversees the distribution of aid to refugees in the camps, of "taking our meals to Burma.")[12] The cut in food rations, which were already insufficient prior to this point, became a significant push factor for refugees, many of whom regularly risked their official status with the UN by working illegally outside the camps to earn the income necessary to supplement their meager diets. (TBBC's standard rations allocation in 2018 was the equivalent of 1,319 kcal per person/day, whereas the World Health Organization recommends an average of 2,100 kcal/day.)[13] By contrast, modest improvements to the security situation in cease-fire areas became a pull factor for the then-estimated 239,000 IDPs across southeastern Myanmar who wanted to resume a more stable life "in the open."[14] Both factors, which have grown stronger in the intervening years, will make it difficult for any actors, beyond the refugees and IDPs themselves, to dictate the process of return and reintegration.[15]

I spoke with the senior coordinator for the UN High Commissioner for Refugees (UNHCR) in Thailand about these dynamics in 2014, two years after the Tatmadaw-KNU cease-fire went into effect. Our conversation chiefly concerned the question of what a "voluntary, safe, and dignified" return of refugees would entail in the view of the UNHCR, as well as the views different stakeholders held on it.[16] According to him, all of the stakeholders, including the royal Thai government, which had a vested interest in closing down the refugee camps for strategic reasons, agreed that the still uncertain security situation made it too soon to discuss a concrete "plan." Instead, the concept of "preparedness" dominated conversations among the stakeholders involved in humanitarian issues as part of a broader effort to initiate a shift from a relief focus to a development one.[17] "One of the things we've done is advised all of our staff not to use the word 'return . . .' to avoid confusion and anxiety." "In fact, the best returns," he continued, "are the ones that we can barely keep up with because people are voting with their feet. Because they are doing things on their own rather than relying on us. So, this return, when it happens, is not likely to be a classic one. Instead, I believe it will be more self-assisted, spontaneous." When I asked about the implications of such a return for UNHCR, he explained, "There will have to be lots of local negotiations within the various armed groups' areas of control. The situation will look very messy. Things will be hard for this reason. Because all of the ceasefire agreements are different, local conditions will vary."[18]

The messiness, which has not abated since then, has significant implications for organizations tasked with monitoring different aspects of the return and reintegration process. As of mid-2021, more than ninety-one thousand refugees, the vast majority of them Karen, still resided in the camps in Thailand. (During the prior three years, only a few thousand refugees had chosen to participate in the "facilitated return" process supported by UNHCR but led by the governments of Myanmar and Thailand.)[19] Some of the challenges to their large-scale return are logistical due to the rugged terrain and the very limited number of all-season roads that traverse the area, which will force many of the returnees to walk deep into the mountains. The lack of adequate travel infrastructure will consequently make it quite difficult to ensure both that international protection standards are met and that new arrivals are properly credentialed with national ID cards after they reach their destination.[20] Other challenges are connected to start-up costs. Refugees traveling with resettlement start-up funds risk outright theft and/or "taxation" by soldiers on all sides of the armed conflict, so aid distribution would likely need to occur at designated reception centers, such as churches and schools.[21] But a cash allowance will not be sufficient, according to Reverend Robert Htwe, chair of the Karen Refugee Committee. "The refugees need supplies for two years [one year to subsist on until the next year's crop is harvested]. But no one . . . wants to provide it. If there is no food, how can they survive?"[22]

FRAGMENTATION OF SOURCES

Still other challenges reflect the realities on the ground when IDPs and refugees begin to resettle in sizable numbers. There is not sufficient arable land to accommodate all of those who want it, and land mine contamination of what is vacant will remain a serious problem for the foreseeable future.[23]

Moreover, the influx of private sector actors, many of them with Tatmadaw connections, into cease-fire areas to extract natural resources will make it impossible to resolve land conflicts in a way that favors sustainable livelihoods, due to the current legal framework, which largely does not recognize the customary practices that Karen communities and other "ethnic nationalities" use.[24]

Finally, the security situation, while improved, is far from stable in places. During 2018, Tatmadaw and KNU/KNLA forces engaged in fifty-seven skirmishes, primarily in Papun District of government-delineated Karen State, and one of the larger clashes temporarily displaced more than two thousand people.[25] According to the Myanmar Peace Monitor, the situated deteriorated further in 2019, as the total number of credibly documented skirmishes exceeded one hundred.[26] Given the destabilizing effects of the 2021 coup, such skirmishes are likely to increase in the future. But refugees, by leaving the camps, lose their protected status, which means that they cannot return to them should they come to fear for their safety.[27] For all these reasons, secondary migrations by returnees, particularly by those who grew up in the camps and have no experience farming in remote areas, are likely to move in one of three directions: to towns inside Myanmar, to export-processing zones along the border, and into the informal economy in Thailand. All three of these destinations will make monitoring reintegration and providing postreturn start-up assistance an impossible task.[28]

The multifaceted issues that will affect how and where IDPs and refugees resettle will also pose problems for human rights fact finders who want to

FIGURE 6. Land mine education poster. SOURCE: Photo by Ken MacLean.

document past crimes. The documentation of the crimes against humanity and war crimes that reportedly occurred during the Northern Offensive in KNU-delineated Karen State is a case in point.

The fact that a cohort of people fled the same conflict area during roughly the same period and found sanctuary in the same cluster of refugee camps made it possible for the IHRC field researchers to easily and cost-effectively collect testimonies regarding the offensive. According to IHRC, the many similarities they identified across the individual testimonies led them to conclude that sufficient prima facie evidence existed for the ICC to issue an arrest warrant for three senior commanders for crimes the sources said the officers' subordinates committed. The eventual closing of these camps and the departure of their residents to different locations will fragment this conflict cohort, which will make it exponentially more difficult for future researchers to gather additional testimonies should they wish to augment IHRC's existing case file.[29]

Tragically, large-scale preemptive violence by the Tatmadaw has produced two new conflict cohorts in recent years. In both cases, the geopolitics of international borders has fundamentally shaped what it is possible to know about each of them. One border limits fact-finding, whereas the other facilitates it, and the difference has important implications.

In 2011, the Tatmadaw broke a seventeen-year cease-fire agreement with the Kachin Independence Organization (KIO), one of the country's best-trained and best-equipped NSAGs, when its combat battalions launched their largest military offensive since the Northern Offensive in KNU-delineated Karen State. The armed conflict soon spread throughout not just large parts of Kachin State, but also the northern part of Shan State, where several other NSAGs became involved as well. A decade later, the conflict drags on, with nearly 100,000 people languishing in squalid IDP camps, many of them close to the Chinese border.[30] The Chinese government has consistently blocked access to IDPs from its side of the border, which has sharply limited the ability of fact finders to gather testimonies about past crimes, as well as to document new ones. (By contrast, the Thai government tolerated the cross-border NGOs for decades, which is why an extensive body of documentation exists on the evolving human rights situation and changing nature of humanitarian needs in southeastern Myanmar.) The Myanmar government restricted access to the conflict areas in Kachin and Shan States several years later, and it completely ceased to grant travel authorizations to the UN and its humanitarian partners in mid-2015. The government expanded the ban in 2016 to prevent all international humanitarian organizations from delivering relief supplies, including food, to IDPs in zones that the Tatmadaw did not control. The situation today remains dire, and human rights documentation about what is happening is very limited.

The crisis in the north has since been overshadowed by a much larger one to the southwest, and its transborder nature permits human rights documentation in a manner that the crisis in Kachin and Shan States does not. In 2017, Tatmadaw battalions initiated "clearance operations," as the Tatmadaw referred to them, targeting Rohingya Muslims in Rakhine State, which borders Bangladesh. (The government maintains that Rohingya are "Bengalis" and thus illegal migrants to Myanmar who can and should be forced out.) The clearance operations drove nearly 750,000 Rohingya to seek refuge in and around the already existing refugee settlements of Kutupalong and Nayapara in Bangladesh's Cox's Bazar District. (There, they joined approximately 250,000 other Rohingya who had fled prior waves of ethnic cleansing, some dating back to the early 1990s.) The dramatic exodus, which was photographed extensively and spatially plotted using satellite imagery, was of massive proportions, and it prompted urgent and widespread calls for international action.

The humanitarian response to the Rohingya crisis, while significant, remains insufficient given the current scale of need and the likelihood that the massive displacement will be protracted in nature.[31] But the camps, by virtue of their location in Bangladesh, have provided a base of operations for the documentation of the mass atrocities that drove Rohingya communities across the border, however. A new archival formation, based on the rapidly growing number of NGO and UN-sponsored fact-finding reports, is currently taking shape—replete with verbatim, redactions, and citations like the ones examined in this book. But unlike the earlier CoI campaign (2003–2011), which sought to designate the country as a "threat to peace and security," the focus now is squarely on the issue of genocide.[32]

In early 2020, the International Court of Justice, the primary judicial organ of the United Nations, took an unprecedented step and ordered the Myanmar government to "take all measures within its power" to prevent further actions that "meet the legal definition of genocide," and to preserve evidence about alleged genocidal acts.[33] Myanmar, which is a party to the Genocide Convention, is legally bound to comply with the court's provisional order. The government denied the charges but has since submitted its first report to the ICJ detailing what it has done to protect the Rohingya. The security situation has arguably worsened for the estimated 600,000 Rohingya who remain in Myanmar, however. Many of them now find themselves caught up in the escalating conflict between the Tatmadaw and the Arakan Army, an NSAG that claims to fight on behalf of the ethnic Rakhine, many of whom actively participated in mass atrocities against Rohingya during the 2017–2018 "clearance operations." Documenting violations perpetrated against Rohingya civilians and providing them with humanitarian assistance has only become more difficult as a result.

A final comment on the (often unfulfilled) promise of fact-finding, which is all the more urgent given the number of human rights crises globally. Report writers (like academics writing about them) occupy a privileged "gatekeeper" position in the process of human rights "fact" production, deciding what is documented and how it is represented to others. But it is almost always unclear to ordinary people what happens to the information they have provided to fact finders after the report is published, especially as it only rarely contributes to a clearly measurable positive impact on their lives afterward. The limited understanding of how the advocacy process works and what is reasonable to expect of it is not a new issue in Myanmar. (Nor is the issue to limited to Myanmar; it is, sadly, universal.)[34] The problem has existed since fact finders first began to interview people in large numbers regarding human rights violations in the country in the early 1990s. But report fatigue, the result of contributing to fact-finding report after fact-finding report for years with little to no substantive change resulting from it, has grown worse recently. This situation is, to a significant degree, due to the unmet expectations that the "transition" to a quasi-civilian elected government (now dissolved following the 2021 coup) would meaningfully respond to people's long-standing desires for peace, justice, and accountability, though the meanings of these terms, as the examples I have provided indicate, are not always clear or in alignment with one another.[35] Closer attention to the dynamics of "fact" production as well as our ethical responsibilities to our sources provides a critical reminder for those of us who want to help support domestic efforts to achieve these desired outcomes. As part of this effort, we need to more effectively explain the possibilities and limits of fact-finding, reporting, and advocacy to those communities directly affected by violence and not just to representatives of what is euphemistically referred to as the "international community." It is my hope that this book will contribute to these long-overdue and much-needed conversations.

NOTES

NOTES ON TERMINOLOGY

1. Dittmer (2010), 1–20.
2. Duffield (2008), 6.
3. Myanmar Information Management Unit (2020).

INTRODUCTION

The epigraph is from American Law Institute, "Model Code of Evidence" (1942), cited in Ramcharan (2014), 42.

1. ERI was cocounsel to the plaintiffs in the precedent-setting case against Unocal.
2. Becker (2017), 5. Emphasis in original.
3. Mégret (2016), 38.
4. I am grateful to reviewer 2, who expressed the point more clearly than I originally did.
5. Mégret (2016), 18–21.
6. The phrasing comes from Mégret (2016), 27. See also Lubet (2017).
7. Alston and Knuckey (2016).
8. Mégret (2016), 27–48.
9. Ramcharan (2014), 221–41.
10. Mégret (2016), 32–33.
11. Goodman, Tomlinson, and Richland (2014), 453.
12. Ibid.
13. Cohen (2001).
14. Wilkinson (2011).
15. Human Rights Watch (2019), 4.
16. American Association for the Advancement of Science (2018).

17. Senior Program Associate, Geospatial Technologies Project (Interview 22 February 2019).

18. Myanmar-China Pipeline Watch Committee (2016).

19. Weingartner (2012).

20. The phrasing is inspired by Annelise Riles's (2004, xiii) examination of "informational practices" in the UN context.

21. Van Maanen and Pentland (1994), 53.

22. Bell (2009), 5; Teitel (2014).

23. Montgomery (1996); Bickford (2007).

24. International Bar Association (2015).

25. Ibid., 1.

26. HURIDOCS (2017). See also International Center for Transitional Justice (2009a).

27. Ball (2016).

28. Archivists for Human Rights (2016).

29. Swisspeace (2013); Caswell (2014b).

30. Harris (2014), 216.

31. Stoler (2002), 93–95.

32. Trouillot (1995), 26.

33. Ibid., 2. See also Trace (2002).

34. See, for example, Carter (2006); Caswell (2014a); Gates-Madsen (2016).

35. White (1990). See also McClennan and Slaughter (2009).

36. Mawani (2012), 342.

37. Montgomery (1996, 2004).

38. Weld (2014).

39. For a related example, see Le Caisne (2018).

40. Montgomery (2004), 24.

41. Trouillot (1995).

42. Weld (2014), 6, 9–13.

43. Ketelaar (2002).

44. Mnookin (2001), 165.

45. McKemmish et al. (2005), 128.

46. Ibid., 402.

47. Gilliland and McKemmish (2014).

48. Wood et al. (2014), 410-11; Gorham, Taylor, and Jaeger (2016).

49. Price (2009).

50. Steedman (2011), 321; Mawani (2012), 337 (notable exceptions); Foucault (1972), 126 ("historical events").

51. Foucault (1972), 126.

52. Eichorn (2008), 7.

53. McKemmish (2005), 15.

54. Papailias (2005), 3.

55. Ibid., 4.

56. IHRC (2009), 93–102.

57. Ibid.

58. United Nations General Assembly (2015).

59. Pedersen (2007); Woods (2011).

60. Barany (2018); Associated Press journalist and Pulitzer Prize winner (interview 30 April 2019).

61. Confidential source no. 3 (interview 22 February 2019).

62. Action Committee for Democracy and Development advocacy coordinator (interview 2 July 2019); Myint Kyaw, Myanmar Press Council joint secretary (interview 1 July 2019).

63. Moe Htet Nay, Nyan Linn Thit Analytica (interview 10 July 2019).

64. See Verisk Maplecroft's annual *Political Risk Atlas* reports (Verisk Maplecroft 2016).

65. Transparency International (2018).

66. National Resource Governance Institute (2018); Revenue Watch researcher (interview 10 June 2014).

67. Freedom House (2020).

68. Merry (2016), 21.

69. Ibid., 22.

70. Anna Lindh, Human Rights Prize winner and member of the Women's League of Burma (interview 14 July 2017).

71. Crouch (2019).

72. Htet Naing Zaw (2018).

73. McCarthy (2019).

74. Burma News International (2016).

75. Taylor (2017).

76. Journalist (interview 15 June 2014).

77. Center for Peace and Conflict Studies (2015, 2016).

78. Internal Displacement Monitoring Centre (2015).

79. Duffield (2008), 6.

80. Membe (2001), 67.

81. On the production and preservation of protest ephemera, see Lee (2016).

82. The Endangered Archives Program (https://eap.bl.uk) provides support for this very task. To quote the cofounder, the program "captures forgotten and still not written histories, often suppressed or marginalized. It gives voice to the voiceless: it opens a dialogue with global humanity's multiple pasts. It is a library of history still waiting to be written."

83. *Democratic Voice of Burma* editor in chief (interview 5 July 2019).

84. Online Burma/Myanmar Library (2019).

85. ILO (1998a), para. 259.

86. For access policies, see United Nations High Commissioner for Refugees (2019).

87. Alston and Gillespie (2012), 1093.

88. Sunstein (2006), 7.

89. Alston and Gillespie (2012), 1093.

90. Achille Mbembe, "The Power of the Archive and Its Limits," in Hamilton et al. (2002), 21.

91. Richards (1993).

92. Cooley and Ron (2002), 5.

93. Han Gyi, director of the Network for Human Rights Documentation-Burma (interview 25 June 2013).

94. Head of the Myanmar Program for the International Center for Transitional Justice (interview 3 July 2013).

95. Archival materials related to the history of the armed forces and its organization are exceptions. See Callahan (2005); Maung Aung Myoe (2009).

96. See, for example, KHRG (2001).

97. Dudai (2006), 790.

98. For guidelines, see González-Quintana (2009).

99. Free Expression Myanmar, "New National Records and Archives Law Preserves Government Secrecy" (email communication, 12 March 2020).

100. Constitution of the Republic of the Union of Myanmar (Naypidaw, 2008).

101. de Lang (2012).

102. Gilliland and McKemmish (2014), 81.

103. Feldman and Ticktin (2010), 3.

104. Ibid., 6.

105. Luban (2004), 91.

106. Crimes Against Humanity Initiative (2012).

107. Sadat (2013).

108. ICC (2011), 12.

109. The UN Human Rights Council, UN General Assembly, UN Security Council, and UN Secretary-General all possess the authority to issue a resolution establishing such a CoI. Myanmar is not party to the ICC, but the court can assume jurisdiction if the UN Security Council decides to refer the case to it. See this book's conclusion.

110. Ambos (2011), 284–86.

111. Robinson (1999), 47.

112. Murphy (2015), para. 128.

113. Mettraux (2011).

114. Merry (2011), S85.

115. Evans (2005), 1047.

116. Ibid., 1052.

117. Tomlins and Comaroff (2011), 1063.

118. Ibid.

119. Bruch (2011), 368.

120. Derrida (1992), 6.

121. Benjamin (1996).

122. Marcus (2010), 358.

123. For related discussion, see Matelski (2014); Morgenbesser and Weiss (2018).

124. MacLean (2013).

125. Jones (2014), 60.

126. Riles (2004), 20.

127. Ibid., 191n29.

128. Verdery (2018), xiii.

129. Myanmar country specialist, Fortify Rights (personal email communication, 21 January 2020).

130. Program officer for the Open Society Institute (interview 10 July 2017).

131. In 2015, the All Burma Students Democratic Front, which maintained an armed wing, released a report prepared by its Truth and Justice Committee titled "Dignity." It detailed the abuses that some of its members had committed during the 1990s. No other NSAG has released a similar report.

132. Feldman (1991), 12.z

133. Taussig (1999), 5.

134. See, for example, Shan Human Rights Foundation and Shan Women's Action Network (2014). For the first significant study on this issue, see Apple (1998).

135. Morris (2010). Disagreements about whether to prioritize retributive or restorative justice are one example.

136. IHRC Clinic Database, interview nos. 89, 124, and 128.

137. On KNU-delineated maps, these townships include Lu Thaw, Daw Pha Kho, Htaw Ta Htoo, Mu, Ler Doh, and Hsaw Hti. The boundaries of these administrative units roughly correspond with Hpapun, northern Thandaung, southern Thandaung, Mone, Kyaukgyi, and Shwe Gyin Townships on government-delineated ones, respectively.

138. Interview expert no. 3.

139. Retired colonel U Ye Htut, deputy director general in the Ministry of Information and a former Tatmadaw field commander who coordinated many offensive operations for Light Infantry Division No. 22 against the KNLA from the 1980s until 2005. United States Embassy Rangoon (Burma) (2006a).

140. Interview expert no. 3.

141. MacLean (2018a), 74n27; TBBC (2008b), 30. This figure does not include people who fled to other places in Myanmar or across the border into Thailand.

142. Myanmar Information Management Unit (2019). The figure is based on 2011 HMIS data. No data on the 2005–2008 period are currently available.

143. Burma Medical Association and Back Pack Health Worker Team (2010).

144. Free Burma Rangers (2008), 27–38.

CHAPTER 1. PACIFYING BODIES

The epigraph is from Carter (2006), 216.

1. Kaplan (2002), 344.

2. John Wigmore, summarized in Meehan (2006), 137.

3. People who put NSAG abuses on a par with those of the Tatmadaw, as promilitary spokespersons sometimes do, are "guilty of making a false equivalency par excellence" [Name withheld], international legal observer of the 21st Century Panglong Conference peace negotiations (interview 6 July 2017).

4. Phrasing drawn from Smith and Jones (2015), 1–28.

5. Jackson (2008).

6. Finn and Momani (2017), 383.

7. Cooper (2019), 18–24.

8. Wilkinson (1992), 228–29. See also Blakeley (2012).

9. By this I mean the state bueacracy was subservient to the Tatmadaw, both ideologically and in terms of policy, as its officers held all key government positions.

10. Scott (2009), 13.

11. Massumi (2015), 5–19.

12. Ibid., 6.

13. Ibid., 13.

14. Ibid.

15. Scott (1998).

16. International Crisis Group (2001).

17. Starn (1991).

18. This is not a new phenomenon. See Aung-Thwin (2001).

19. Rajah (2001); Gravers (2006).

20. Ibid., 11.

21. Retired KNU judge, KNLA Brigade 3 headquarters (interview 9 July 2017).

22. Karen Peace Support Initiative director (interview 30 June 2017).

23. MacLean (2008).

24. Jolliffe (2015).

25. Nordstrom (2000), 38.

26. Statista (2018); Thiha Ko Ko (2019).

27. See, for example, Japan International Cooperation Agency (2013).

28. Myanmar Peace Support Initiative consultant (interview 11 June 2014).

29. Saw Greh Moo (2013).

30. The Border Consortium partnership director (interview 7 July 2017).

31. Burma Relief Center director (interview 29 May 2014). See also Jolliffe (2014), 23–31.

32. Aung-Thwin (1985). See also Beckett (2019).

33. See, for example, Durand (1915); Heyland (2004); Crosthwaite (1912); Ni Ni Myint (1983); Adas (1983); Ghosh (2000); Aung-Thwin (2008).

34. Aung-Thwin (1985).

35. Trouillot (1995), 26.

36. *Telegraphic Correspondence* (1886), 7.

37. Tinker (1983b), xi.

38. Callahan (2003), 123; Tinker (1983b), xxvii.

39. Thawnghmung (2012), 93–105; Smith (1999), 472n112.

40. Quoted in Callahan (2003), 122.

41. Ibid., 145–71.

42. Maung Aung Myoe (2009), 17.

43. Clinical Expert Declaration No. 1, para. 81, in IHRC (2014b), 25. See also Clinical Expert Declaration No. 2, David Eubank (1 August 2012), para. 63, in IHRC (2014b). The expert is a former US Army officer with a deep understanding of ethnic armed conflict in Myanmar. He founded the Free Burma Rangers, which provides humanitarian relief in conflict-affected areas.

44. Meehan (2006), 138–39.

45. Jones (2006).

46. Clarified Document (CD) 993, Military Strategy and Tactics in Counterinsurgency (Colonel Kyin Win), DSHMRI, 1, cited in Maung Aung Myoe (2009), 18–19.

47. CD 105 (14), Report Submitted by the General Staff Office at the 1959 Tatmadaw Conference, DSHMRI, cited in Maung Aung Myoe (2009), 43.

48. CD 341 (2), Reports by the General Staff Office at the 1962 Tatmadaw Conference, DSHMRI, cited in Maung Aung Myoe (2009).

49. CD 880 (10), Report of the General Staff Office at the 1964 Tatmadaw Conference, DSHMRI, cited in Maung Aung Myoe (2009).

50. Smith (1999), 259.

51. Maung Aung Myoe (2009), 27.

52. Ibid., 24–25. See also Nakanishi (2013), 234.

53. Selth (2002), 78.

54. Smith (1999), 263.

55. Ibid., 260.

56. Ibid., 262–63.

57. Ibid., 262.

58. Maung Aung Myoe (2009), 27.

59. IHRC (2014a).

60. Clinic Expert Declaration, expert 1, para. 83; Clinic Expert Declaration, expert 2, paras. 94–98; Clinic Expert Declaration, expert 3, para. 43; and Clinic Expert Declaration, expert 4, para. 31, all cited in IHRC (2014b), 25–26.

61. Smith (1999), 259.

62. Ibid., 25. IHRC Clinical Expert Declaration, expert 1 (interview 4 August 2012). The expert is an academic who has studied the Myanmar Defense Services and the human rights violations associated with the Tatmadaw's military operations.

63. Human Rights Council (2018), 15, para. 76.

64. Harriden (2002); Gravers (2015).

65. Cheesman (2002).

66. Rajah (2002).

67. Thawnghmung (2008).

68. South (2007); Horstmann (2011).

69. Keenan (2011), 3.

70. Smith (1999), 170.

71. Ibid., 172–74.

72. Cusano (2001).

73. Clinical Expert Declaration No. 2, David Eubank (1 August 2012), para. 45.

74. The most frequently stated estimate places the current total number at between three thousand and four thousand troops, but again the KNLA has not confirmed this figure publicly.

75. Quoted in Jolliffe (2014), 10.

76. Jolliffe (2016), 37; Holland (1991).

77. Jolliffe (2014), 6.

78. These areas roughly correspond with government-delineated Taungoo, Papun, and Nyaunglebin Districts, respectively.

79. Jolliffe (2016), 3.

80. The Border Consortium (2014), 31–32. TBC did not conduct another IDP survey until 2018.

81. KHRG (2016). For a position paper coauthored by leaders representing affected communities, see Transnational Institute (2019).

82. Border Guard Forces largely consist of former insurgent groups that now operate under the Tatmadaw's Regional Military Commands.

83. The Border Consortium (2014), 10.

84. Lutz (2019).

85. Guha (1998).

86. Tilly (1975), 42. See also Gallant (1999).

87. Callahan (2005).

88. Massumi (2015), 13.

89. Smith (1991), 100–101.

90. The Border Consortium (2013), 18.

91. The figures mentioned do not include IDPs in Rakhine, Kachin, and Shan States.

92. Martin and Lynch (2009), 244. Emphasis in original.

93. Bentham (1827), 17–18. Emphasis added.

94. Carter (2006), 216.

95. Trouillot (1995), 26.

CHAPTER 2. ENSLAVING BODIES

The epigraph is from Inoue (2018), 221.

1. Bauman and Briggs (2003), 212–13.

2. Inoue (2018), 218.

3. Ibid., 220.

4. Ibid., 219.

5. Urban (1996), 21.

6. Forced labor is a violation of *jus cogens* peremptory norms. A peremptory norm is a fundamental principle of international law from which no derogation is permitted, meaning that states cannot justify a prohibited practice—in this case, forced labor—by citing domestic laws or customs.

7. Horsey (2011), 15.

8. Ibid.

9. Wilkinson (2011), 5.

10. Horsey (2011), 20.

11. Ibid., 20–23.

12. On the source material, see ILO (1998b), para. 259.

13. ILO (1998b), para. 538. See also ICC (2011), 5n11.

14. ILO (1998b), para. 539.

15. MacLean (2007).

16. Ministry of Home Affairs (2000). The military regime, then known as the State Law and Order Restoration Council (SLORC), promulgated Secret Directive No. 82 on 27 April 1995 and Secret Directive No. 125 on 2 June 1995, respectively.

17. David Eubank, Founder of Free Burma Rangers (interview 1 August 2012), para. 31–32.

18. ILO (2018).

19. InterPares (2020).

20. KHRG (2012a).

21. [Name withheld], KHRG fact-finding coordinator (interview 2 August 2012).

22. [Names withheld], KHRG advocacy coordinators nos. 1, 2, and 3 (interviews 6 June 2014).

23. Inoue (2018), 220.

24. KHRG (2000a).

25. KHRG (2000b).

26. KHRG (2002, 2003).

27. KHRG (2007b; 2011a; 2013).

28. KHRG (2006); Human Rights Watch and KHRG (2011); KHRG (2011b).

29. Tin Maung Maung Than (2001), 169.

30. Maung Aung Myoe (1998).

31. Selth (2002), 136.

32. Callahan (2007), 36; Keenan and Saw Tah Doh Moo (2010).

33. It was common for battalions to seize farmland and/or orchards from villagers, who were then required to plant, tend, and harvest crops for them.

34. Orders 135, 80, and 99, respectively, KHRG (2002); Order no. 178, KHRG (2002), Set 2001-A.

35. Order 222, KHRG (2002), Set 2000-A.

36. Order 47, KHRG (2000b).

37. Only one order referenced the ban on forced labor out of a data set of more than fifteen hundred orders. No. 328, after providing a lengthy list of demands, stated, "This is not covered by *loq ah pay* [forced labor order] 1/99." KHRG (2002), 8.

38. KHRG (2000b, 2003, 2007b).

39. KHRG (2000b), 3–4.

40. Traditionally, a *fonds* consists of records originating from the same source. In this case, the situation is reversed: the same "record" (a type of order) originating from multiple sources (Tatmadaw officers).

41. Order 121, KHRG (2003), Set 2003-A.

42. Ibid. Orders 12, 13. See also Order 17.

43. Ward (2015), 299.

44. Verdery (1996), 19-35.

45. Interview no. 51, ERI (March 2002) (on file with author).

46. Horsey (2011), 15.

47. ILO (1998a), para. 131 and 112.

48. TBBC (2002).

49. The policy shift toward the large-scale use of convict porters, confirmed by the director-general of the Prison Service in 2002, appears to have been an attempt to exploit an exemption in the ILO Convention, which permits forced labor when it is part of a prison sentence. Horsey (2011), 233n2.

50. KHRG (2005), 5.

51. KHRG (2006, 2011b); Human Rights Watch and KHRG (2011).

52. KHRG (2006), 5. Hundreds of them are known to have died during the offensive as a direct result of exhaustion, illness, and summary execution. MacLean (2018), 52n172.

53. Human Rights Watch and KHRG (2011), 7.

54. KHRG (2006), 15–16.

55. Inoue (2018), 221.

56. KHRG (2011), 32–33.

57. Bennett (2010), xvi.

58. Ibid., 6.

59. MacLean (2016), 83.

60. TBBC (2007b), 47.

61. Eubank (interview 2012), para. 32; Mae Tao Clinic assistant deputy director of operations and prosthetics (interview 3 June 2014).

62. Humanitarian demining expert (interview 31 May 2014).

63. KHRG (2012b); Halo Trust national country representative (interview 4 July 2017).

64. Eubank (interview 2012), para. 65.

65. Henckaerts and Doswald-Beck (2005), 280–86; Rome Statute Articles 7 and 8 (ICC 1998).

66. Dudai (2009), 252.

67. KHRG (2011b), 65.

68. Ibid., 28.

69. Ibid., 126–27.

70. Human Rights Watch and KHRG (2011), 37. One informant, a KNU judge in Brigade area 3, explained the fear to me as a "big death" because land mine incidents "affect not just the victim, but the entire family" (interview 9 July 2017).

71. Root (2016), 355.

72. KHRG (2011b), 27; Satterthwaite and Simeone (2016), 340.

73. Merry (2011), S85.

74. ILO (2011), para. 26.

75. Ibid., para. 26.

76. ILO liaison officer (interview 13 June 2014).

77. Cook (1993), 32.

78. Ibid.

79. For details on the conditions that must be met, see Articles 25 and 28 of the Rome Statute (1998).

80. Erosion does not mean erasure. Villagers engaged in a wide variety of everyday forms of resistance to soldiers' demands. A discussion of these tactics is beyond the scope of this book, however.

81. KHRG (2007b), 4.

82. Ibid., 4.

83. Inoue (2018), 221.

84. Van Wyke (2013), 548.

CHAPTER 3. STARVING BODIES

The epigraph is from Wiktionary (2020).

1. Redfield (2006).

2. Fassin (2007), 499.

3. Conley (2017), 18. Emphasis in original.

4. Pinchevski (2011), 253.

5. Back Pack Health Worker Team (2006), 39.

6. IHRC Clinical Database interview no. 103.

7. Curtis (2006), 4.

8. Marcus (2003), 245, fn. 1.

9. ICC (2011), Article 7(1)(c) and 8(2)(b)(xxv), 6, 32.

10. Marcus (2003), 247.

11. Butler (2007).

12. International Criminal Court Assembly of State Parties (2019).

13. Pejic (2001), 1097.

14. Ibid., 1098.

15. TBBC (2004b), 12.

16. Back Pack Health Worker Team (2006), 32, 44, and 65.

17. "Chronology for Karens in Burma" (2017).

18. Ibid.

19. CIDKP secretary and KNU joint secretary (interview 5 July 2017); CIDKP relief coordinator Brigade 3 area (interview 8 July 2017).

20. Karen Environmental and Social Action Network staff (interview 3 June 2003).

21. TBBC Deputy Executive Director (interview 29 May 2013).

22. Burma Border Consortium (2004), 114.

23. Vismann (2008), 7.

24. CIDKP 2008-12 (7 May 2008), on file with author.

25. House of Commons International Development Committee (2007), 8.

26. Poovey (1998), 172.

27. One basket of paddy is approximately equivalent to 21 kg (45 lbs) of paddy or 32 kg (70 lbs) of milled rice.

28. Karen speakers often colloquially refer to the Tatmadaw as the SPDC (State Peace and Development Council), the name of the military regime in power at that time.

29. 1 *viss* equals 1.6 kg or 3.5 lbs.

30. MacLean (2018a), 553–59.

31. Periodically, mobile medics traveled with the teams to create health profiles and provide basic care to IDPs.

32. ERA Distribution Summary (2 September 2008), contained in KORD-2008-2012 (on file with author).

33. The KNLA obtained sophisticated communications equipment from an unknown Australian source during the early 2000s. Prior to this point, they used two-way radios and were not able to intercept Tatmadaw communications when they jumped frequencies. The new equipment allowed KNLA troops to "channel jump, listen in, and transcribe information" about Tatmadaw plans and field operations. The Tatmadaw reportedly did not realize the KNLA had this capacity until around 2008. Burma Center for Ethnic Studies director (interview 18 June 2013).

34. Lampland (2010), 378.

35. Ibid., 384.

36. Curtis (2006), 14.

37. Carifio and Perla (2009), 407.

38. Ibid.

39. Ehrenberg (1978), 95.

40. TBBC (2002), 6.

41. Of this reported total, nearly one-third of the IDPs counted were in KNU-delineated Karen State: 99,765 people in Tatmadaw-controlled relocation sites and 96,469 in hiding or temporary settlements. TBBC (2002), 1-2.

42. Ibid., 12.

43. Ibid., 8.

44. Ashley South, former TBBC consultant (interview 18 October 2017).

45. TBBC (2006b), 21.

46. TBBC (2007b), 23.

47. TBBC (2008b), 19.

48. By contrast, refugees are described in generic terms as "people in strife" (*baw ba kaw ba keh*). Burma Relief Centre consultant (personal communication, 19 December 2006).

49. A formal phrase exists in Burmese to convey the official definition of an IDP (*pyi twin nay yar shwayt pyaung khan ya tu myar*), but very few people beyond experts would understand it. The phrase, "hide and run villagers" (*ywar pone ywar shaung*), which British Broadcasting Corporation (BBC) reporters often use, is easier to grasp. Ardeth Thawnghmung (personal communication, 13 February 2018).

50. Keenan and Nan Mu Chaung Ku (2011).

51. Duncan McArthur, TBBC Burma program director (interview 29 May 2013).

52. Cited in Levi and Hagan (2012), 25.

53. Conley (2017), 37.

54. *Agence France-Presse* (2006a).

55. Ibid., 4.

56. Ehrenberg (1978), 87.

57. Merry (2016), 31.

58. Agamben (1998).

59. Small-scale skirmishes have characterized the fighting since this final offensive and the 2012 cease-fire that followed. These skirmishes were not "ideologically driven," however. "Rather, they were over territorial control and resources." UNHCR senior coordinator (interview 4 June 2014).

CHAPTER 4. KILLING BODIES

The epigraph is from Feldman (1991), 14.

1. Conley (2017), 21. Emphasis in original.

2. Ibid., 19.

3. KSWDC-2005-03 reproduced in MacLean (2018a), 583.

4. Several notable exceptions exist. The problematics of working with the torture testimonies is one area in which considerable psychoanalytical work has been done, as severe trauma often resists or entirely escapes coherent narrativization. How ideological positions and cultural assumptions shape what constitutes acceptable forms of narration with regard to asylum claims is another area.

5. Bucholtz (2000), 1439.

6. Ibid.

7. Sternberg (1982), 150.

8. Stoler (1992), 151–52.

9. Ibid., 179.

10. Rule 153: Command Responsibility for Failure to Prevent, Repress, or Report War Crimes," https://ihl-databases.icrc.org/customary-ihl/eng/docs/v1_cha_chapter 43_rule153, in ICRC (2018).

11. "Rule 1: The Principle of Distinction between Civilians and Combatants," https://ihl-databases.icrc.org/customary-ihl/eng/docs/v1_cha_chapter1_rule1, in ICRC (2018).

12. "Article 4," https://ihl-databases.icrc.org/applic/ihl/ihl.nsf/Comment.xsp ?action=openDocument&documentId=18E3CCDE8BE7E2F8C12563CD0042A50B, in ICRC (2018).

13. Articles 13–18 in United Nations Commission on Human Rights (1978/2018).

14. Kinsella (2011), 4.

15. Rome Statute, Article 8(2)(e)(i).

16. ICC (2020).

17. May (2005).

18. IHRC (2006).

19. Melzer (2009).

20. "Humanitarian Engagement with Non-state Armed Actors" (2005).

21. Brouwer and van Wijk (2013); Horstmann (2011).

22. This is not meant to suggest that the KNU/KNLA did not commit abuses. Fact-finding organizations have documented many cases in which the NSAG demanded forced labor, employed child soldiers, carried out extrajudicial executions, and so on. "You have to do that kind of human rights documentation," explained one prominent activist. "But I worry that the main perpetrator [i.e., Tatmadaw] will be equalized because it is the armed forces' strategy to state that they are not only ones committing violations even though they are by far the primary offenders." Women's League of Burma director (interview 14 July 2017).

23. Anderson (2011), 219.

24. IHRC Clinic Database interview no. 69. The statement is likely a modification of the proverb: "On account of one fish, the whole boatload went bad."

25. Free Burma Rangers (2008), 13; TBBC (2006b), 21; (2007b), 23; and (2008b), 19.

26. MacLean (2018b), 19n27.

27. IHRC (2014b). Willful killings are a war crime under Article 8 2(a)(i) of the Rome Statute.

28. ICC (2011), 5–42; IHRC (2014b), 1–2, 7.

29. Under Article 28(a) of the Rome Statute, command responsibility requires that "1) the commanders exercised effective command and control over those who committed the crimes; 2) the commander knew or should have known that the crimes were being committed or about to be committed; and 3) the commander failed to take all necessary and reasonable measures . . . to prevent or repress [the commission of crimes] or to submit the matter to the competent authorities for investigation and prosecution."

30. IHRC (2014a), 3, 7–8. Myanmar is not party to the Rome Statute, but it provides "a recognized framework for analyzing violations of international criminal law" according to IHRC (6n6).

31. Global Justice fellow with Harvard Law School's Human Rights Program and principal researcher (interview 28 June 2017). Unless indicated, all of the quotes are excerpted from this interview.

32. IHRC (2014a), 15–20. The *fonds* reproduced in MacLean (2018b) also contain dozens of references to successful and attempted willful killings that took place between 2003 and 2008. The details corroborate the claims IHRC, FBR, and KHRG made regarding willful killings: namely, unarmed civilians, including the elderly and the very young, were targeted during the Tatmadaw operations.

33. United Nations Office for the Coordination of Humanitarian Affairs (2018a).

34. IHRC (2014a).

35. Burma News International (2013a).

36. Fuller (2014).

37. Ibid.
38. White (1981), 19.
39. Walsh (2007), 39.
40. Dudai (2006).
41. Boutruche (2016), 131.
42. Ronald Rosenthal, quoted in ibid., 138.
43. Lundy and McGovern (2008).
44. KHRG (1999), interview nos. 2, 12, 19, 20, 21, 29, 30, and 36.
45. Ibid., interview no. 21. Emphasis added.
46. Ibid., interview no. 1. Emphasis added.
47. Ibid., interview no. 32. Emphasis added.
48. Ibid., interview no. 2. Emphasis added.
49. Taussig (1987), xiii.
50. KHRG (1999), 11.
51. Ibid., 52.
52. Ibid., 28–29.
53. Ibid., 24, interview no. 30.
54. Ibid., 34, interview no. 8.
55. Ibid., 12.
56. KHRG (1999), 13–16, 18, interview nos. 1, 20, 30, and 50.
57. IHRC Clinic Database, interview no. 11.
58. Ibid., interview nos. 52, 86, 133, 142, and 146. Interview nos. 61 and 67 also refer to incidents in which troops cut off the heads of their victims. Short Pants units are known to remove heads, whereas ordinary Tatmadaw soldiers generally do not, making the former the more likely perpetrators if past patterns hold true.
59. Ibid., interview no. 52.
60. Ibid., interview no. 142.
61. IHRC (2014a), 72–73.
62. IHRC Clinic Database, interview no. 146. Villagers without cash commonly paid with chickens or rice.
63. KHRG (2000a), order no. 1.
64. IHRC Clinic Database, interview no. 146.
65. Ibid., interview no. 100.
66. Ibid.
67. Ibid.
68. IHRC Clinic Database, interview no. 146. See also interview no. 109.
69. Ibid., interview no. 109. See also interview nos. 47, 52, 80, 86, 111, and 150.
70. Ibid., interview no. 80.
71. IHRC (2014a), 27.
72. Ibid., 16n28–36.
73. Ibid., 14.
74. Ibid., 14.
75. TBBC (2006b), 36.

76. Checchi (2018), 4.

77. Free Burma Rangers (2008), 19.

78. Checchi (2018), 7.

79. IHRC Clinic Database, interviews nos. 16, 27, 58, 118, and 119, for example. Accounts of torture, by contrast, were always recounted in great detail.

80. Ibid., interview no. 38. See also interview no. 120.

81. Ibid., interview no. 115. The informant was thirty-seven years old at the time of interview in 2012. See also interview no. 51.

82. Ibid., interview no. 17.

83. Ibid., interview no. 118.

84. Villages, such as Shah Si Boh, Klaw Mi Der, and Mwee Loh, in western Toungoo District, were considered brown zones, as were the towns of Bawgaligyi and Thandaung in the mountains. The Tatmadaw regarded everything outside of these areas as black areas. Clinic Expert Declaration No. 2 (interview 1 August 2012), para. 95.

85. TBBC field coordinator (interview 2 June 2014).

86. IHRC Clinic Database, interview no. 69. See also interview nos. 98, 100, 115, and 139.

87. Ibid., interview nos. 51, 120, 139, and 146.

88. Ibid., interview no. 68. The soldier was not operational during the Northern Offensive. Interviews with other (former) soldiers support his statement. IHRC Expert Declaration, expert 1, para. 84.

89. IHRC Clinic Database, interview no. 68.

90. IHRC (2014a), 18. IHRC Clinic Database, interview nos. 68, 90, 98, 125, 152, 156, 157, 160, and 161.

91. IHRC Clinic Database, interview no. 90.

92. IHRC (2014a), 26.

93. Ibid., 60–65.

94. Cassese and Gaeta (2013), 368.

95. Smith (1999), 100–101.

96. Conley (2017), 21. Emphasis in original.

97. Ibid., 19.

98. Hühn (1997), 452. Emphasis in original.

99. Segal (2010).

100. See, for example, Free Burma Rangers (2008) and MacLean (2018a).

101. Dudai (2009).

102. IHRC (2014a), 16n28–36.

CHAPTER 5. INVESTIGATING BODIES

The epigraph is from Mawani (2012), 350.

1. Drucker (2008), 123.

2. Genette (1997), 2. Emphasis in original.

3. Garritzen (2012), 407.

4. Ibid., 42.

5. Mawani (2012): 341.

6. Dudai (2006).

7. Ibid., 784.

8. Ibid.

9. Ibid., 787.

10. Barad (2007).

11. See, for example, Mutua (2001).

12. See, for example, Selth (2008).

13. Silverstein (1976).

14. For an overview, see United Nations Library (2020).

15. Butler (1997), 13.

16. Evans (1995), 214.

17. Ibid., 219.

18. Ibid.

19. Johannsson (2009), 309–10.

20. Ibid., 318.

21. National Coalition Government of the Union of Burma and Burma UN Service (2003), 15.

22. Ibid., 16.

23. United Nations Security Council (2019).

24. United Nations Commission on Human Rights (2003).

25. DLA Piper Rudnick Gray Cary (2005).

26. Ibid., foreword.

27. Ibid., 44.

28. Garritzen (2012), 420.

29. United Nations Security Council (2019).

30. DLA Piper Rudnick Gray Cary (2005), foreword.

31. Ibid., 58.

32. Bruch (2011), 336.

33. United Nations Security Council (2008), 539–40.

34. United Nations Security Council (2015).

35. Pedersen (2007); Jones (2008).

36. United Nations Security Council (2008), 540.

37. United Kingdom of Great Britain and Northern Ireland and United States of America (2007).

38. United Nations Office of the High Commissioner for Human Rights (2006b).

39. Jennifer Quigley, director, US Campaign for Burma (interview 1 August 2014).

40. During this period, the government of Myanmar blocked ILO-led efforts to conduct a CoI regarding the pervasive use of forced labor throughout the country. See Horsey (2011).

41. International Justice Resource Center ([2008] 2020).

42. United Nations Security Council (2007), 540.

43. United Kingdom of Great Britain and Northern Ireland and United States (2007), 2.

44. Amnesty International (2008); TBBC (2008b); Women's League of Burma (2010); Irish Center for Human Rights (2010); Physicians for Human Rights (2011); Partners in Relief and Development (2011).

45. Public International Law and Policy Group (2008); International Federation for Human Rights, ALTSEAN-Burma, and Burma Lawyers' Council (2009); International Federation for Human Rights and Burma Lawyers' Council (2009); International Bar Association (2011).

46. IHRC (2009).

47. US Campaign for Burma director (interview 1 August 2014).

48. IHRC (2009), iv–v.

49. US Campaign for Burma director (interview 1 August 2014).

50. IHRC (2009), 6.

51. Ibid., 93–100. The report, although it focused on UN documentation, was researched and written during the Northern Offensive in KNU-delineated Karen State. The analysis informed the clinic's fact-finding efforts, discussed in the previous chapter.

52. IHRC (2009), 4.

53. "HLS Human Rights Program Issues New Report on Abuses in Burma" (2009).

54. International Federation for Human Rights, ALTSEAN-Burma, and Burma Lawyers' Council (2009); International Federation for Human Rights and Burma Lawyers' Council (2009).

55. International Federation for Human Rights, ALTSEAN-Burma, and Burma Lawyers' Council (2009), 37–44.

56. Alt-ASEAN director and FIDH general secretary (interview 19 May 2014).

57. US Campaign for Burma director (interview 1 August 2014). See also Nice and Stevenson (2010).

58. Quintana (2010).

59. Ibid., 2, 19.

60. Ibid., 2.

61. Ibid., 29.

62. Ibid., 29.

63. "Statement by His Excellency U Wunna Maung Lwin" (2010), 1.

64. Ibid., 3–4.

65. United Nations Human Rights Council (2007). Emphasis added.

66. "Statement by His Excellency U Wunna Maung Lwin" (2010), 4.

67. Genette and Maclean (1991), 266.

68. Cohen (1996), 522; (2001), 7–9, 25–37.

69. Cohen (2001), 1. For a contrasting view, see Center for Peace and Conflict Studies (2010).

70. "Statement by His Excellency U Wunna Maung Lwin" (2010), 2. For a contrasting view, see International Bar Association (2012); Cheesman (2015).

71. "Statement by His Excellency U Wunna Maung Lwin" (2010), 2–3. For a contrasting view, see International Crisis Group (2013).

72. "Statement by His Excellency U Wunna Maung Lwin" (2010), 4. For a contrasting view, see United Nations Human Rights Council (2010).

73. Tonkin (2011).

74. His recent statements are available at "Network Myanmar" (2020).

75. UN General Assembly (2011).

76. Quintana (2010), 29, para. 121.

77. Ibid., 29, para. 122.

78. Jennifer Q. Quigley, US Campaign for Burma director (interview 1 August 2014).

79. See, for example, Selth (2008).

80. The United Nations' Human Rights Council is not compliant with the Paris Principles, however, and former officials who defended the previous regime's human rights record supervise its activities. Hkun Okker, Burma Lawyers' Council general secretary (interview 1 June 2014).

81. IHRC (2009), 101–2; US Campaign for Burma director (interview 1 August 2014); Burma Partnership director (interview 4 June 2014).

82. US Campaign for Burma director (interview 1 August 2014).

83. Grafton (1997), 24.

84. Ibid., 23.

85. Moon (2012), 877.

86. Ibid., 877–78.

87. Ibid., 880.

88. Evans (2005).

89. Bruch (2011), 350.

90. Ibid., 884–85. See, for example, Maill (2008); Waldorf (2012).

91. Farmer (1997).

92. IHRC (2009), 93–102.

93. United Nations General Assembly (2015).

94. Foucault (1972).

95. David Chandler, "Semiotics for Beginners," http://visual-memory.co.uk/daniel/Documents/S4B/sem02a.html (accessed 22 March 2016).

96. Mégret (2016), 43. For related discussion, see Combs (2010).

97. United Nations Human Rights Council (2018), 7, para. 29.

98. Cohen (1996), 522.

CONCLUSION

The epigraph is from Mégret (2016), 37.

1. Sikkink (2017), 3. For related discussion, see Brown (2004).

2. See, such as, Hopgood (2013); Moyn (2012); Posner (2014).

3. Sikkink (2017), 31.

4. Ibid., 21.

5. See, for example, Evans (2005); Mutua (2001); Orford (2003), 158–85.

6. For related discussion, see Lubet (2017). His recommendations, however, are not readily applicable to human rights fact-finding, where an experiment-based approach to replication is not always possible or advisable.

7. Finnegan (2011), 95–96, 98; "What Is an Author" (1977), 113–38.

8. Sternberg (1982), 107.

9. Finnegan (2011), 4.

10. Inoue (2018), 219.

11. TBBC (2008b), 1.

12. Ibid.

13. Shohat (1995), 173.

14. TBBC (2008b), 23.

15. Ibid., 3.

16. Ibid.

17. Finnegan (2011), ch. 5.

18. Quintana (2010), 21. Emphasis added.

19. Ibid. Emphasis added.

20. Gilbert (1977).

21. Inoue (2018), 221.

22. The Declassification Project, launched in 2013 at Columbia University, is behind this effort.

23. Abel (2012), 3.

24. Herzfeld (2009), 135.

25. Mnookin (2001), 165.

26. KHRG (2001), 5.

27. IHRC (2009), iv–v.

28. IHRC (2014b), 27.

29. Ibid., 47.

30. McKemmish and Upward (1991), 19.

31. Duranti (1995), 7–8.

32. International Standards Organization (2020).

33. Kastenhofer (2015).

34. Rhoads (1966), 207. Emphasis in original.

35. See also Van Maanen and Pentland (1994), 53.

36. Mégret (2016), 27.

37. Vismann (1999), 284.

38. All quotes in this section, unless otherwise noted, are taken from the author's meeting notes.

39. For details on Tatmadaw command structures and their utilization during military operations, see IHRC (2014a), 21–29.

40. Pyidaungsu Institute for Peace and Dialogue researcher (interview 28 May 2014).

41. International Center for Transitional Justice, Myanmar project coordinator (interview 22 July 2017); International Center for Transitional Justice, Myanmar project coordinator (interview 3 June 2013).

42. Transnational Institute (2017).

43. Director, the Border Consortium, Yangon Office (interview 11 June 2014).

44. Myanmar Peace Support Initiative (2014); Euro-Burma Office, Myanmar research and analysis consultant (interview 18 June 2013).

45. Paung Sie Facility (2019). Paung Sie, which means "living and working together in harmony," was renamed Peace Support Fund in 2017.

46. The Assistance Association for Political Prisoners (AAPP) has long maintained an impressive museum about political prisoners on the Thai side of the Myanmar border, and it has built a modest one in Yangon. AAPP has also supported the construction of a monument in Shan State for prodemocracy protestors killed in 1988, and it is involved in negotiations with officials in Bago Region to do the same.

47. Margueritta Hpeh, Open Society Institute Burma Project member (interview 10 July 2017). See also Tan (2012); Dukalskis (2015).

48. Alt-Asean and FIDH director (interview 22 July 2017).

49. International Center for Transitional Justice (2009a), (2014), 6–14.

50. International Center for Transitional Justice, (former) Burma Project staff (interview 22 July 2017).

51. ND-Burma (2018).

52. The viewpoints presented are indicative rather than comprehensive, however. Quite simply, what people affected by state repression and state-sponsored violence desire in terms of justice, broadly defined, will remain unknown until large-scale surveys are carried out.

53. AAPP human rights officer and AAPP staff and 2007 Saffron Revolution activist (interview 5 June 2014).

54. AAPP deputy in charge of foreign affairs (interview 30 June 2017).

55. I am grateful to the reviewer who reminded me of this point.

56. Thai-Burma Border Consortium executive director (interview 29 May 2013). Her colleague, who oversees the documentation of IDP realities and needs across southeastern Myanmar, added that progress on transitional justice would need to be sequenced when the time comes. "It should start with paralegal access to justice in conflict-affected areas to address current perpetrators, and at a later date, address pass atrocities. But justice delayed is justice denied," he stressed during the same interview.

57. Salween Institute for Public Policy director (interview 15 June 2014).

58. ND-Burma director (interview 19 July 2017). See also Center for Peace and Conflict Studies (2018).

59. International Center for Transitional Justice, Burma project coordinator (interview 22 July 2017).

60. Name and position withheld (interview 22 February 2019).

61. Alston and Gillespie (2012), 1093.

62. Steedman (2002); Burton (2005); Dirks (2015).

63. Rancière (1994), 63. Emphasis in original.

64. Stoler (2010); Eichorn (2013); Cvetkovich (2003).

65. Williams (1961).

66. Riles (2004), 20.

67. Ibid., 191n29.

68. Ibid., 209. See also Adami (2007), 215.

69. Caswell (2014b), 208.

70. Wood et al. (2014), 398.

71. Caswell (2013).

72. Ciorciari (2012), 1. See also Wood et al. (2014).

73. Derrida (1996), 4n1.

74. Lee (2016).

75. Evans et al. (2015), 337–68.

76. Flinn and Alexander (2015), 329–35. See also Caswell and Cifor (2016). They argue that it is necessary to shift human rights archives away from a narrowly legalistic focus to a more inclusive ethics of care to address a broader array of social justice concerns beyond the courtroom.

77. United Nations Office of the High Commissioner for Human Rights (2006), 1.

78. Mégret (2016), 34.

79. Saunders (2008).

80. Accatino and Collins (2016); Ciorciari and Heindel (2016).

81. Land and Aronson (2018); Dubberley, Koenig, and Murray (2020).

EPILOGUE

1. Conley (2017), 1.

2. See Rudolf and Schmitz-Pranghe (2018), 22.

3. Anonymous source, journalist (personal communication, 15 June 2014).

4. ILO liaison officer, Yangon (interview 13 June 2014).

5. South et al. (2018), 6.

6. KNU Joint Secretary and Central Committee member (interview 2 June 2017).

7. International Center for Transitional Justice, Myanmar program head (interview 3 June 2013); Burma Center for Ethnic Studies director (interview 18 June 2013).

8. KNU Joint Secretary and Central Committee member (interview 2 June 2017).

9. Progressive Voice (formerly Burma Partnership) staff (interview 14 July 2017).

10. "Karen Community-Based Organizations' Position on Refugees Return to Burma" (11 September 2012). Copy on file with author.

11. The Border Consortium field coordinator (interview 2 June 2014).

12. The Border Consortium director, Yangon (interview 11 June 2014). The sharp decline in funding affected not only humanitarian aid, but also assistance to a large number of other CBOs and CSOs involved in human rights trainings. United

Nationalities League for Democracy administrator (2001–2008) and Ethnic Nationalities Council senior staff member (interview 27 May 2014).

13. The Border Consortium (2020).

14. Office for the Coordination of Humanitarian Affairs (2012). A 2018 survey indicated that more than seventy-two thousand IDPs in eastern Bago Region and Kayin State have yet to resettle, in large part because of fears that the cease-fire will not hold. The Border Consortium (2018), 14–17; CIDKP staff member, KNU Brigade 3 area (interview 9 July 2017).

15. The Border Consortium executive director (interview 29 May 2013); International Organization for Migration regional program coordinator (interview 19 May 2014); UNHCR senior field coordinator (interview 12 July 2017); Progressive Voice researcher (interview 14 July 2017).

16. For broader discussion, see Vungsiriphisal, Chusri, and Supang Chantavanich (2014). The situation has yet to markedly improve. Rudolf and Schmitz-Pranghe (2018).

17. The conversations informed a "living document" that could be quickly transformed into a plan. Committee for the Coordination of Services to Displaced Persons in Thailand and United Nations High Commissioner for Refugees (2013).

18. UNHCR senior coordinator for Thailand (interview 4 June 2014).

19. Harrison (2019).

20. Norwegian Refugee Council program managers (interview 3 July 2017).

21. The Border Consortium partnerships coordinator (interview 7 July 2017).

22. Karen Refugee Committee chairperson (interview 15 July 2017).

23. Halo Trust country representative (interview 4 July 2017).

24. Myanmar Peace Support Initiative consultant (email communication 13 June 2017). See also Human Rights Watch (2016); KHRG (2018).

25. Shan Herald Agency for News (2018).

26. Wansai (2019). A KNU source provided the figure, which has not yet been independently verified.

27. UNHCR senior field coordinator (interview 12 July 2017).

28. The monitoring concerns, which are legitimate, reflect a specific point of view, namely that of the humanitarian agencies involved. The agency of IDPs and refugees and their resilience are important factors that also need to be taken into account.

29. For an overview, see Combs (2018).

30. United Nations Office for the Coordination of Humanitarian Affairs (2018b).

31. United Nations High Commissioner for Refugees (2020).

32. United Nations Human Rights Council (2018), 1.

33. *UN News* (2020).

34. Siméant and Taponier (2014).

35. See, for example, KHRG (2019).

BIBLIOGRAPHY

Abel, Jonathan. *Redacted: The Archives of Censorship in Transwar Japan.* Berkeley: University of California Press, 2012.

Accatino, Daniela, and Cath Collins. "Truth, Evidence, Truth: The Deployment of Testimony, Archives, and Technical Data in Domestic Human Rights Trials." *Journal of Human Rights Practice* 8 (2016): 81–100.

Adami, Tom. "Who Will Be Left to Tell the Tale? Recordkeeping and International Criminal Jurisprudence." *Archival Science* 7, no. 3 (2007): 213–21.

Adas, Michael. "Bandits, Monks, and Pretender Kings: Patterns of Peasant Resistance and Protest in Colonial Burma, 1826–1941." In *Power and Protest in the Countryside: Studies of Rural Unrest in Asia, Europe, and Latin America,* edited by Robert Weller and Scott Guggenheim, 75–105. Durham, NC: Duke University Press, 1983.

Agamben, Giorgio. *Homo Sacer: Sovereign Power and Bare Life.* Translated by Daniel Heller-Roazen. Palo Alto, CA: Stanford University Press, 1998.

Agence France-Presse. "Medical Charity Pulls French Staff from Myanmar." 30 March 2006a.

———. "Myanmar Rebel Group Issues Plea to Military Rulers." 3 May 2006b.

All Burma Students Democratic Committee. "Dignity: The Report of the Truth and Justice Committee." 2015. http://thedignityreport.blogspot.com.

Alston, Philip. "Reconceiving the UN Human Rights Regime: Challenges Confronting the New UN Human Rights Council." *Melbourne Journal of International Law* 7 (2006): 1–40.

Alston, Philip, and Colin Gillespie. "Global Human Rights Monitoring, New Technologies, and the Politics of Information." *European Journal of International Law* 23, no. 4 (2012): 1089–1123.

Alston, Philip, and Sarah Knuckey. "The Transformation of Human Rights Fact-Finding: Challenges and Opportunities." In *The Transformation of Human Rights*

Fact-Finding, edited by Philip Alston and Sarah Knuckey, 3–24. Oxford: Oxford University Press, 2016.

ALTSEAN-Burma. "Military Budget." www.altsean.org/Reports/BN%202017%202015%20tatmadaw.php.

Ambos, Kai. "Crimes against Humanity and the International Criminal Court." In *Forging a Convention for Crimes against Humanity,* edited by Leila Nadya Sadat, 279–304. Cambridge: Cambridge University Press, 2011.

American Association for the Advancement of Science. "Geospatial Evidence in International Human Rights Litigation." Washington, DC: American Association for the Advancement of Science, 2018.

Amnesty International. "Crimes against Humanity in Eastern Burma." London: Amnesty International, 2008.

———. "Myanmar: Remaking Rakhine State." London: Amnesty International, 2018.

Anderson, Ben. "Facing the Future Enemy: US Counterinsurgency Doctrine and the Pre-Insurgent." *Theory, Culture, and Society* 28, no. 7 (2011): 216–40.

Apple, Betsy. "School for Rape: The Burmese Military and Sexual Violence." Chiang Mai, Thailand: EarthRights International, 1998.

Archivists for Human Rights. "Records of the UN War Crimes Commission to Open to the Public for the First Time." 15 November 2014. https://archivistsforhuman rights.blogspot.com/2014/11/records-of-un-war-crimes-commission.html.

Asad, Talal. "What Do Human Rights Do? An Anthropological Inquiry." *Theory & Event* 4, no. 4 (2000): 137–51.

Asian Human Rights Commission. "People's Tribunal on Food Scarcity and Militarization in Burma." Hong Kong: Asian Human Rights Commission, 1999.

Aung, Htet. "The USDA Role under the Constitution." www2.irrawaddy.com/print _article.php?art_id=17436.

Aung-Thwin, Maitrii. "British Counter-insurgency Narratives and the Construction of a Twentieth Century Burmese Rebel." PhD diss., University of Michigan, 2001.

———. "Structuring Revolt: Communities of Interpretation in the Historiography of the Saya San Rebellion." *Journal of Southeast Asian Studies* 39, no. 2 (2008): 297–317.

Aung-Thwin, Michael. "British 'Pacification' of Burma: Order without Meaning." *Journal of Southeast Asian Studies* 16, no. 2 (1985): 245–62.

Back Pack Health Worker Team. "Chronic Emergency: Health and Human Rights in Eastern Burma." Chiang Mai, Thailand: BPHWT, 2006.

Bagshaw, Simon, and Diane Paul. "Protect or Neglect: Toward a More Effective United Nations Approach to the Protection of Internally Displaced Persons." Geneva: Brookings Institute and UN Office for the Coordination of Humanitarian Affairs, 2004.

Ball, Patrick. "The Bigness of Big Data: Samples, Models, and the Facts We Might Find When Looking at Data." In *The Transformation of Human Rights Fact-Finding,* edited by Philip Alston and Sarah Knuckey, 425–40. Oxford: Oxford University Press, 2016.

Barad, Karen. *Meeting the Universe Halfway: Quantum Physics and the Entanglement of Matter and Meaning.* Durham, NC: Duke University Press, 2007.

Barany, Zoltan. "Burma: Suu Kyi's Missteps." *Journal of Democracy* 29, no. 1 (2018): 5–19.

Bassiouni, M. Cherif. *Crimes against Humanity in International Criminal Law.* 2nd rev. ed. The Hague: Kluwer Law International, 1999.

Bauman, Richard, and Charles Briggs, *Voices of Modernity: Language Ideologies and the Politics of Inequality.* Cambridge: Cambridge University Press, 2003.

Becker, Howard. *Evidence.* Chicago: University of Chicago Press, 2017.

Beckett, Ian. "The Campaign of the Lost Footsteps: The Pacification of Burma, 1885–95." *Small Wars and Insurgencies* 30, nos. 4–5 (2019): 994–1019.

Bell, Christine. "Transitional Justice, Interdisciplinarity and the State of the 'Field' or 'Non-Field.'" *International Journal of Transitional Justice* 3, no. 1 (2009): 5–27.

Benjamin, Walter. *Illuminations.* Edited by Hannah Arendt. Translated by Harry Zohn. New York: Schocken Books, 1968.

———. "Critique of Violence." In *Walter Benjamin: Selected Writings,* Vol. 1, *1913–1926,* edited by Marcus Bullock and Michael Jennings, 236–52. Cambridge, MA: Harvard University, 1996.

Bennett, Jane. *Vibrant Matter: A Political Ecology of Things.* Durham, NC: Duke University Press, 2010.

Bentham, Jeremy. *Rationale of Judicial Evidence.* Edited by J. S. Mill. Vol. 1. London: Hunt and Clarke, 1827.

Bickford, Louis. "Unofficial Truth Projects." *Human Rights Quarterly* 29 (2007): 994–1035.

Blakeley, Ruth. "State Violence as State Terrorism." In *The Ashgate Research Companion to Political Violence,* edited by Marie Breen-Smyth, 63–78. London: Ashgate, 2012.

The Border Consortium. "Poverty, Displacement, and Local Governance in South East Burma/Myanmar." Bangkok: TBC, 2013.

———. "Protection and Security Concerns in South East Burma/Myanmar." Bangkok: TBC, 2014.

———. "Human Security in Southeastern Myanmar." Bangkok: TBC, 2018.

———. "Food Assistance." Accessed 23 March 2020. www.theborderconsortium.org/what-we-do/thailand/food-assistance/.

Boutruche, Théo. "The Relationship between Fact-Finders and Witnesses in Human Rights Fact-Finding." In *The Transformation of Human Rights Fact-Finding,* edited by Philip Alston and Sarah Knuckey, 131–53. Oxford: Oxford University Press, 2016.

Brouwer, Jelmer, and Joris van Wijk. "Helping Hands: External Support for the KNU Insurgency in Burma." *Small Wars & Insurgencies* 24, no. 5 (2013): 835–56.

Brown, Wendy. "'The Most We Can Hope For . . .' Human Rights and the Politics of Fatalism." *South Atlantic Quarterly* 103, nos. 2–3 (2004): 451–63.

Bruch, Elizabeth. "Is International Law Really Law? Theorizing the Multi-dimensionality of Law." *Akron Law Review* 44, no. 2 (2011): 343–73.

Bucholtz, Mary. "The Politics of Transcription." *Journal of Pragmatics* 32, no. 10 (2000): 1439–65.

Burma Border Consortium. "Internally Displaced People and Relocation Sites in Eastern Burma." Bangkok: BBC, 2002.

———. "Twenty Years on the Border." Bangkok: BBC, 2004.

Burma Medical Association and Back Pack Health Worker Team. "Diagnosis Critical: Health and Human Rights in Eastern Burma." Chiang Mai: BMA and BPHWT, 2010.

Burma News International. *Deciphering Myanmar's Peace Process: A Reference Guide.* Chiang Mai, Thailand: Myanmar Peace Monitor, 2013a.

———. *Economics of Peace and Conflict.* Chiang Mai, Thailand: Myanmar Peace Monitor, 2013b.

———. *Deciphering Myanmar's Peace Process: A Reference Guide.* Chiang Mai, Thailand: Myanmar Peace Monitor, 2016.

Burton, Antoinette, ed. *Archive Stories: Facts, Fictions, and the Writing of History.* Durham, NC: Duke University Press, 2005.

Butler, Daniel. "Enforced Starvation: Exploring Individual Criminal Responsibility for State-Induced Famines." Human Rights Law Commentary. Nottingham, UK: University of Nottingham, 2007. www.nottingham.ac.uk/hrlc/documents/publications/hrlcommentary2007/enforcedstarvation.pdf.

Butler, Judith. "Further Reflections on Conversations of Our Time." *Diacritics* 27, no. 1 (1997): 13–15.

Callahan, Mary. *Making Enemies: War and State Building in Burma.* Ithaca, NY: Cornell University Press, 2005.

———. "Of Kyay-Zu and Kyet-Su: The Military in 2006." In *Myanmar: The State, Community, and the Environment,* edited by Monique Skidmore and Trevor Wilson, 36–53. Canberra: Australian National University, 2007.

Carifio, James, and Rocco Perla. "A Critique of the Theoretical and Empirical Literature of the Use of Diagrams, Graphs, and Other Visual Aids in the Learning of Scientific-Technical Content from Texts and Instruction." *Interchange* 40, no. 4 (2009): 403–36.

Carol, Brittany, and Isaac Baker. "Grid: A Methodology Integrating Witness Testimony and Satellite Imagery for Documenting Mass Atrocities." *Genocide Studies and Prevention: An International Journal* 8, no. 3 (2014): 49–61.

Carter, Rodney. "Of Things Said and Unsaid: Power, Archival Silence, and Power in Silence." *Archivaria* 61 (2006): 215–33.

Cassese, Antonio. *The Oxford Companion to International Criminal Justice.* Oxford: Oxford University Press, 2013.

Cassese, Antonio, and Paola Gaeta. *Cassese's International Criminal Law.* 3rd ed. Oxford: Oxford University Press, 2013.

Caswell, Michelle. "Using Classification to Convict the Khmer Rouge." *Journal of Documentation* 68, no. 2 (2012): 162–84.

———. "Rethinking Inalienability: Trusting Nongovernmental Archives in Transitional Societies." *American Archivist* 76, no. 1 (2013): 113–34.

———. *Archiving the Unspeakable: Silence, Memory, and the Photographic Record in Cambodia.* Madison: University of Wisconsin Press, 2014a.

———. "Defining Human Rights Archives." *Archival Science* 14, nos. 3–4 (2014b): 207–13.

Caswell, Michelle, and Marika Cifor. "From Human Rights to Feminist Ethics: Radical Empathy in the Archives." *Archivaria* 81 (Spring 2016): 23–43.

Center for Peace and Conflict Studies. "2010 Myanmar Elections: Learning and Sharing the Future." Siam Riep, Cambodia: CPCS, 2010.

———. "We Want Genuine Peace: Voices of Communities from Myanmar's Ceasefire Areas." Phnom Penh, Cambodia: CPCS, 2015.

———. "Peace Is Living with Dignity: Voices of Communities from Myanmar's Ceasefire Areas 2016." Phnom Penh, Cambodia: CPCS, 2016.

———. "We Want Our Communities Back, No More Fighting and Violence: Voices of Communities from Myanmar's Ceasefire Areas from 2017–2018." Siam Reap, Cambodia: Centre for Peace and Conflict Studies, 2018.

Chakrabarty, Dipesh. "*Subaltern Studies* and Postcolonial Historiography." *Nepantla: Views from the South* 1, no. 1 (2000): 9–32.

Chandler, David. "Semiotics for Beginners." Accessed 22. March 2016. http://visual-memory.co.uk/daniel/Documents/S4B/sem02a.html.

Checchi, Francesco. *Estimation of Population Mortality in Crisis-Affected Populations: Guidance for Humanitarian Coordination Mechanisms*. Geneva: World Health Organization, 2018.

Cheesman, Nick. "Seeing 'Karen' in the Union of Myanmar." *Asian Ethnicity* 3, no. 2 (2002): 199–220.

———. *Opposing the Rule of Law: How Myanmar's Courts Make Law and Order*. Cambridge: Cambridge University Press, 2015.

Chin, Charlene. "Myanmar Launches Digital Identities for Citizens." GovInsider. 11 January 2017. https://govinsider.asia/innovation/myanmar-launches-digital-identities-for-citizens/.

"Chronology for Karens in Burma." Accessed 28 September 2017. www.mar.umd.edu/chronology.asp?groupId=77504.

Ciorciari, John. *Archiving Memory after Mass Atrocities*. Austin, TX: The Bernard and Audre Rappoport Center for Human Rights and Justice, 2012.

Ciorciari, John, and Anne Heindel, "Victim Testimony in International and Hybrid Criminal Courts: Narrative Opportunities, Challenges, and Fair Trial Demands." *Virginia Journal of International Law* 56, no. 2 (2016): 2–74.

Clark, Ann Marie, and Kathryn Sikkink. "Information Effects and Human Rights Data: Is the Good News about Increased Human Rights Information Bad News for Human Rights Measures?" *Human Rights Quarterly* 35, no. 3 (2010): 539–68.

Cohen, Stanley. "Government Responses to Human Rights Reports: Claims, Denials, and Counterclaims." *Human Rights Quarterly* 18, no. 3 (1996): 517–43.

———. *States of Denial: Knowing about Atrocities and Suffering*. New York: Polity Press, 2001.

Combs, Nancy. *Fact-Finding without Facts: The Uncertain Evidentiary Foundation of International Criminal Convictions*. Cambridge: Cambridge University Press, 2010.

————. "Deconstructing the Epistemic Challenges to Mass Atrocity Prosecutions." *Washington and Lee Law Review* 75, no. 1 (2018): 223–300.

Committee for the Coordination of Services to Displaced Persons in Thailand and United Nations High Commissioner for Refugees. "Strategic Framework for Durable Solutions 2013/2014." Version 5.0. Bangkok: CSSDPT and UNHCR, 2013.

Committee on the Judiciary, House of Representatives. "Federal Rules of Evidence." Washington, DC: US Government Printing Office, 2015.

Conley, Bridget. "What Counts at the End? Questioning Consensus in the Construction of Mass Atrocity Narratives." *Global Responsibility to Protect* 9, no. 1 (2017): 15–37.

Cook, Terry. "The Concept of Archival Fonds and the Post-custodial Era: Theory, Problems, and Solutions." *Archivaria* 35 (Spring 1993): 24–37.

Cooley, Alexander, and James Ron. "The NGO Scramble: Organizational Insecurity and the Political Economy of Transnational Action." *International Security* 27, no. 1 (2002): 5–39.

Cooper, Davina. *Feeling like a State: Desire, Denial, and the Recasting of Authority*. Durham, NC: Duke University Press, 2019.

Cotula, Lorenzo and Margaret Vidar. "The Right to Food in Emergencies." Rome: Food and Agriculture Organization, 2002.

Crimes Against Humanity Initiative. "Proposed International Convention on the Prevention and Punishment of Crimes against Humanity." St. Louis, MO: Washington University School of Law, 2012.

Crosthwaite, Sir Charles. *The Pacification of Burma*. London: Edward Arnold, 1912.

Crouch, Melissa. *The Constitution of Myanmar: A Contextual Analysis*. Oxford: Hart Publishing, 2019.

Curtis, Bruce. "Textual Economies and the Presentation of Statistical Material: Charts, Tables, and Texts in 19th Century Public Education." *Canadian Journal of the History of Science, Technology, and Medicine* 29, no. 1 (2006): 3–28.

Cusano, Chris. "Burma Displaced Karens: Like Water on the Khu Leaf." In *Caught between Borders: Response Strategies of the Internally Displaced*, edited by Mark Vincent and Brigitte Refslund, 139–71. London: Pluto Press, 2001.

Cvetkovich, Ann. *An Archive of Feelings: Trauma, Sexuality, and Lesbian Public Cultures*. Durham, NC: Duke University Press, 2003.

Davis, Kevin, Angelina Fisher, Benedict Kingsbury, and Sally Engle Merry, eds. *Governance by Indicators: Global Power through Classification and Rankings*. Oxford: Oxford University Press, 2012.

Daw Mya Sein. *The Administration of Burma*. Oxford: Oxford University Press, 1973.

de Lang, Niki Esse. "The Establishment and Development of the Myanmar National Human Rights Commission and Its Conformity with International Standards." *Asia-Pacific Journal on Human Rights and the Law* 1 (2012): 1–41.

Derrida, Jacques. "Force of Law: The 'Mystical Foundation of Authority.'" In *Deconstruction and the Possibility of Justice*, edited by Drucilla Cornell, Michael Rosenfeld, and David Gray Carlson, 3–67. London: Routledge, 1992.

————. *Archive Fever: A Freudian Impression.* Translated by Eric Prenowitz. Chicago: University of Chicago Press, 1998.

Devereux, Stephen. *Theories of Famine.* London: Harvester Wheastsheaf, 1993.

Dirks, Nicholas. *Autobiography in the Archive.* New York: Columbia University Press, 2015.

Dittmer, Lowell. *Burma or Myanmar: The Struggle for National Identity.* Edited by Lowell Dittmer. Singapore: World Scientific, 2010.

DLA Piper Rudnick Gray Cary. "Threat to Peace: A Call for UN Security Council to Act in Burma." Washington, DC: DLA Piper Rudnick Gray Cary, 2005.

Dopplick, Renee. "Famine and International Criminal Law under the Rome Statute." *Inside Justice.* 17 April 2009. www.insidejustice.com/intl/2009/04/27/famine _rome_statute/.

Drucker, Johanna. "Graphic Devices: Narration and Navigation." *Narrative* 16, no. 2 (2008): 121–39.

Du Bois, John. "Self-Evidence and Ritual Speech." In *Evidentiality: The Linguistic Code of Epistemology,* edited by Wallace Chafe and Johanna Nicholas, 313–36. Norwood, NJ: Ablex, 1986.

Dubberley, Sam, Alexa Koenig, and Daragh Murray, eds. *Digital Witness: Using Open Source Information for Human Rights Investigation, Documentation, and Accountability.* Oxford: Oxford University Press, 2020.

Dudai, Ron. "Advocacy with Footnotes: The Human Rights Report as Literary Genre." *Human Rights Quarterly* 28, no. 3 (2006): 783–95.

————. "Can You Describe This? Human Rights Reports and What They Tell Us about the Human Rights Movement." In *Humanitarianism and Suffering,* edited by Richard Wilson and Richard Brown, 245–65. Cambridge: Cambridge University Press, 2009.

Duffield, Mark. "On the Edge of 'No Man's Land': Chronic Emergency in Myanmar." Working Paper No. 01-08. Bristol: University of Bristol, 2008.

Dukalskis, Alexander. "Transitional Justice in Burma/Myanmar: Cross-National Patterns and Domestic Context." *Irish Studies in International Affairs,* no. 26 (2015): 1–15.

Durand, Mortimer Sir. *The Life of Field-Marshal Sir George White, V.C.* London: William Blackwood and Sons, 1915.

Duranti, Luciana. "Reliability and Authenticity: The Concepts and Their Implications." *Archivaria* 39 (Spring 1995): 5–10.

EarthRights International. "More of the Same: Forced Labor Continues in Burma (October 2000–September 2001)." Chiang Mai, Thailand: ERI, 2001.

————. "We Are Not Free to Work for Ourselves: Forced Labor and Other Human Rights Abuses in Burma (January 2002–May 2002)." Chiang Mai, Thailand: ERI, 2002.

Edkins, Jenny. "The Criminalization of Mass Starvations: From Natural Disaster to Crime against Humanity." In *The New Famines: Why Famines Persist in an Era of Globalization,* edited by Stephen Devereux, 50–65. London: Routledge, 2007.

Ehrenberg, A. S. C. "Graphs or Tables." *Journal of the Royal Statistical Society Series D (The Statistician)* 27, no. 2 (1978): 87–96.

Eichorn, Kate. "Archival Genres: Gathering Texts and Reading Spaces." *Invisible Culture: An Electronic Journal for Visual Culture* 12 (Spring 2008): 1–10.

———. *The Archival Turn in Feminism: Outrage in Order.* Philadelphia: Temple University Press, 2013.

European Court of Auditors. "EU Assistance to Myanmar/Burma Special Report 04." Brussels: European Union, 2018.

Evans, Cedric. "Concept of Threat to Peace and Humanitarian Concerns: Probing the Limits of Chapter VII of the U.N. Charter." *Transnational Law and Contemporary Problems* 5 (1995): 213–26.

Evans, Joanne, Sue McKemmish, Elizabeth Daniels, and Gavan McCarthy. "Self-Determination and Archival Autonomy." *Archival Science* 15, no. 4 (2015): 337–68.

Evans, Tony. "International Human Rights Law as Power/Knowledge." *Human Rights Quarterly* 27, no. 3 (2005): 1046–68.

Farmer, Paul. "On Suffering and Structural Violence: A View from Below." In *Social Suffering*, edited by A. Kleinman, V. Das, and M. Lock, 261–84. Berkeley: University of California Press, 1997.

Fassin, Didier. "Humanitarianism as a Politics of Life." *Public Culture* 19, no. 3 (2007): 499–520.

Federated Trade Unions of Burma. "Field Mission Reports September 2001." Mae Sot, Thailand: FTUB, 2001.

Feldman, Allen. *Formations of Violence: The Narrative of the Body and Political Terror in Northern Ireland.* Chicago: University of Chicago Press, 1991.

Feldman, Ilana, and Miriam Ticktin, eds. *In the Name of Humanity: The Government of Threat and Care.* Durham, NC: Duke University Press, 2010.

Finn, Mellisa, and Bessma Momani. "Building Foundations for the Comparative Study of State and Non-state Terrorism,'" *Critical Studies on Terrorism* 10, no. 3 (2017): 379–403.

Finnegan, Ruth. *Why Do We Quote? The Culture and History of Quotation.* Cambridge: Open Book Publishers, 2011.

Fitzgerald, Lt. Colonel T. O. *Bush Warfare: Notes from Lectures.* London: Macmillan, 1918.

Flinn, Andrew, and Ben Alexander. "'Humanizing an Inevitably Political Craft': Introduction to the Special Issue on Archiving Activism and Activist Archiving." *Archival Science* 15, no. 4 (2015): 329–35.

Fortify Rights. "Policies of Persecution: Ending Abusive State Policies against Rohingya Muslims in Myanmar." Bangkok: Fortify Rights, 2014.

Foucault, Michel. *The Archaeology of Knowledge.* Translated by A. Sheridan. London: Tavistock, 1972.

Frank, Jerome. *Courts on Trial: Myth and Reality in American Justice.* Princeton, NJ: Princeton University Press, 1973.

Free Burma Rangers. "A Campaign of Brutality: Report and Analysis of Burma Army Offensive and Ongoing Attacks against the People of Northern Karen State, Eastern Burma." Chiang Mai: FBR, 2008.

Freedom House. "Myanmar." In *Freedom in the World 2019*. New York: Freedom House, 2020. https://freedomhouse.org/report/freedom-world/2019/myanmar.

Fuller, Thomas. "Report Cites Evidence of War Crimes in Myanmar." *The New York Times*, 5 November 2014.

Furnivall, J. S. *Colonial Policy and Practice: A Comparative Study of Burma and Netherlands India*. Cambridge: Cambridge University Press, 2014.

Gallant, Thomas. "Brigandage, Piracy, Capitalism, and State Formation: Transnational Crime from a Historical World-Systems Perspective." In *States and Illegal Practices*, edited by Joshua Heyman, 25–61. London: Berg Publishers, 1999.

Garritzen, Elise. "Paratexts and Footnotes in Historical Narrative: Henry Biaudet and Scholarly and Nationalistic Ambitions of Historical Research, 1902–1915." *Scandinavian Journal of History* 37, no. 4 (2012): 407–29.

Gates-Madsen, Nancy. *Trauma, Taboo, and Truth-Telling: Listening to Silences in Postdictatorship Argentina*. Madison: University of Wisconsin Press, 2016.

Genette, Gérard. *Paratexts: Thresholds of Interpretation*. Translated by Jane Lewin. Cambridge: Cambridge University Press, 1997.

Genette, Gérard, and Marie Maclean, "Introduction to Paratext." *New Literary History* 22, no. 2 (1991): 261–72.

Gewirth, Alan. "The Epistemology of Human Rights." *Social Philosophy and Policy* 1, no. 2 (1984): 1–24.

Ghaddar, J. J. "The Spectre in the Archive: Truth, Reconciliation, and Indigenous Archival Memory." *Archivaria* 82 (Fall 2016): 3–26.

Ghosh, Parimal. *Brave Men of the Hills: Resistance and Rebellion in Burma, 1825–1932*. Honolulu: White Lotus, 2000.

Gilbert, Nigel. "Referencing as Persuasion." *Social Studies of Science* 7, no. 1 (1977): 113–22.

Gilliland, Anne, and Sue McKemmish. "The Role of Participatory Archives in Furthering Human Rights, Reconciliation, and Recovery." *Atlanti* 24, no. 1 (2014): 79–88.

Global Protection Cluster Working Group. "Handbook for the Protection of Internally Displaced Persons." Geneva: Global Protection Cluster, 2010.

González-Quintana, Antonio. "Archival Policies in the Protection of Human Rights." Paris: International Council on Archives, 2009.

Goodman, Jane, Matt Tomlinson, and Justin Richland. "Citational Practices: Knowledge, Personhood, and Subjectivity." *Annual Review of Anthropology* 43 (2014): 449–63.

Gorham, Ursula, Natalie Greene Taylor, and Paul Jaeger, eds. *Perspectives on Libraries as Institutions of Human Rights and Social Justice*. Bingley, UK: Emerald Group Publishing Limited, 2016.

Grafton, Anthony. *The Footnote: A Curious History*. Cambridge, MA: Harvard University Press, 1997.

Gravers, Michael, ed. *Exploring Ethnic Diversity in Burma*. Singapore: Nordic Institute of Asian Studies, 2006.

———. "Disorder as Order: The Ethno-nationalist Struggle of the Karen in Burma/Myanmar—a Discussion of the Dynamics of Ethnicized Civil War and Its Historical Roots." *Journal of Burma Studies* 19, no. 1 (2015): 27–78.

Green, Maria. "What We Talk about When We Talk about Indicators: Current Approaches to Human Rights Measurement." *Human Rights Quarterly* 23, no. 4 (2001): 1062–97.

———. "Myanmar: The Politics of Rakhine State." Brussels: ICG, 2014.

Guha, Ranajit. *Dominance without Hegemony: History and Power in Colonial India.* Cambridge, MA: Harvard University Press, 1998.

———. *Elementary Aspects of Peasant Insurgency in Colonial India.* Durham, NC: Duke University Press, 1999.

Hamilton, Carolyn, Verne Harris, Jane Taylor, Michele Pickover, Graeme Reid, and Razia Saleh, eds. *Refiguring the Archive.* New York: Springer, 2002.

Haraway, Donna. "Situated Knowledges: The Science Question in Feminism and the Privilege of Partial Perspective." *Feminist Studies* 14, no. 3 (1988): 575–99.

Harriden, Jessica. "Making a Name for Themselves: Karen Identity and the Politicization of Ethnicity in Burma." *Journal of Burma Studies* 7 (2002): 84–144.

Harris, Verne. "Antonyms of Our Remembering." *Archival Science* 14, nos. 3–4 (2014): 215–29.

Harrison, Jennifer. "After Decades in Thailand, Myanmar Refugees Head Home." UNHCR. 29 July 2019. www.unhcr.org/en-us/news/stories/2019/7/5d3822dc4 /decades-thailand-myanmar-refugees-head-home.html.

Henckaerts, Jean-Marie, and Louise Doswald-Beck. *International Humanitarian Law,* Vol. 1. Cambridge: Cambridge University Press, 2005.

———. *Customary International Humanitarian Law,* Vol. 1, *Rules.* Cambridge: Cambridge University Press, 2009.

Herzfeld, Michael. "The Performance of Secrecy: Domesticity and Privacy in Public Spaces." *Semiotica* 1 (2009): 135–62.

Heyland, Colonel. "Notes on Cavalry Employed in Upper Burma from October 1886 to October 1887." *SOAS Bulletin of Burma Research* 2, no. 1 (2004): 29–38.

"HLS Human Rights Program Issues New Report on Abuses in Burma." 28 May 2009. http://today.law.harvard.edu/hls-human-rights-program-issues-new-report-on -abuses-in-burma/.

Holland, Eugene. "Deterritorializing 'Deteritorialization',: From the 'Anti-Oedipus' to 'A Thousand Plateaus'." *SubStance* 20, no. 3 (1991): 55–65.

Holt, Elizabeth. "Reporting and Reacting: Concurrent Responses to Reported Speech." *Research on Language and Social Interaction* 33, no. 4 (2000): 425–54.

Hong, Emily. "Scaling Struggles over Land and Law: Autonomy, Investment, and Inter-legality in Myanmar's Borderlands." *Geoforum* 82 (2017): 225–36.

Hopgood, Stephen. *Debating the Endtimes of Human Rights.* Ithaca, NY: Cornell University Press, 2013.

Horsey, Richard. *Ending Forced Labor in Myanmar: Engaging a Pariah Regime.* London: Routledge, 2011.

Horstmann, Alexander. "Ethical Dilemmas and Identifications of Faith-Based Humanitarian Organizations in the Karen Refugee Crisis." *Journal of Refugee Studies* 24, no. 3 (2011): 513–32.

Horton, Guy. *Dying Alive: A Legal Assessment of Human Rights Violations in Burma*. Chiang Mai, Thailand: Images Asia, 2005.

House of Commons International Development Committee. "DFID Assistance to Burmese Internally Displaced People and Refugees on the Thai-Burma Border: Responses to the Committee's Tenth Report of Session 2006–07." London: The Stationery Office, Ltd., 2007.

Houtman, Gustaaf. *Mental Culture in Burmese Crisis Politics: Aung San Suu Kyi and the National League for Democracy*. Tokyo: Tokyo University of Foreign Studies, 1999.

Howe, Paul, and Stephen Devereux. "Famine Intensity and Magnitude Scales: A Proposal for an Instrumental Definition of Famine." *Disasters* 28, no. 4 (2004): 353–72.

———. "Famine Scales: Towards an Instrumental Definition of 'Famine.'" In *The New Famines: Why Famines Persist in an Era of Globalization*, edited by Stephen Devereux, 27–49. London: Routledge, 2007.

Htet Naing Zaw. "Defense Ministry Asks for Budget Increase." *The Irrawaddy*, 17 January 2018. www.irrawaddy.com/news/burma/defense-ministry-asks-budget-increase .html.

Hühn, Peter. "The Detective as Reader: Narrativity and Reading Concepts in Detective Fiction." *MFS Modern Fiction Studies* 33, no. 3 (1997): 451–66.

Hull, Stephen. "The 'Everyday Politics' of IDP Protection in Karen State." *Journal of Current Southeast Asian Affairs* 28, no. 2 (2009): 7–21.

Human Rights Information and Documentation Systems International (HURIDOCS). "Resource Library: Resources for Information Management and Preservation." Accessed 22 February 2017. www.huridocs.org/our-manuals/.

Human Rights Watch. "Burma: Q&A on an International Commission of Inquiry." 2011. www.hrw.org/news/2011/03/24/burma-q-international-commission-inquiry.

———. "'All You Can Do Is Pray': Crimes against Humanity and Ethnic Cleansing of Rohingya Muslims in Burma's Arakan State." New York: Human Rights Watch, 2013.

———. "'The Farmer Becomes the Criminal': Land Confiscation in Burma's Karen State." New York: Human Rights Watch, 2016.

———. "Human Rights Watch, Inc. and Subsidiaries: Consolidated Financial Report (June 30, 2019)." New York: Human Rights Watch, 2019.

Human Rights Watch and KHRG. "Dead Man Walking: Convict Porters on the Front Lines in Eastern Burma." New York: HRW, 2011.

"Humanitarian Engagement with Non-State Armed Actors: The Parameters of Negotiated Armed Access." Humanitarian Practice Network Paper No. 51. London: Chatham House, 2005.

"ICC Pre-Trial Chamber I Rules that the Court May Exercise Jurisdiction Over the Alleged Deportation of the Rohingya People from Myanmar to Bangladesh." International Criminal Court. 6 September 2018. www.icc-cpi.int/Pages/item.aspx?name =pr1403.

Inoue, Miyako. "Word for Word: Verbatim as Political Technologies." *Annual Review of Anthropology* 47 (2018): 217–32.

Internal Displacement Monitoring Centre. "Myanmar IDP Figure Analysis." March 2015. www.internal-displacement.org/south-and-south-east-asia/myanmar/figures-analysis.

Internal Displacement Monitoring Centre and Norwegian Refugee Council. "Internal Displacement: Global Overview of Trends and Developments in 2010." Geneva: Internal Displacement Monitoring Centre and Norwegian Refugee Council, 2010.

Internal Displacement Monitoring Centre and UN Office for the Coordination of Humanitarian Affairs. "Guidance on Profiling Internally Displaced Persons." Geneva: UNOCHA, 2008.

International Bar Association, Human Rights Institute. "Justice for Burma: The Establishment of a UN Commission of Inquiry into International Crimes." London: IBAHRU, 2011.

———. "The Rule of Law in Myanmar: Challenges and Prospects." London: International Bar Association, 2012.

———. "Guidelines on International Human Rights Fact-Finding Visits and Reports by Non-Governmental Organizations." London: International Bar Association, 2015.

International Center for Transitional Justice. "Documenting Truth." New York: ICTJ, 2009a.

———. "Impunity Prolonged: Burma and Its 2008 Constitution." New York: ICTJ, 2009b.

———. "Navigating Paths to Justice in Myanmar's Transition." New York: ICTJ, 2014.

International Coalition for the Responsibility to Protect. "Navigating Paths to Justice in Myanmar's Transition." Accessed 7 September 2021. www.ictj.org/publication/navigating-paths-justice-myanmars-transition.

International Committee of the Red Cross (ICRC). "IHL Database: Customary IHL." Accessed 4 April and 13 July 2018. https://ihl-databases.icrc.org/customary-ihl/eng/docs/home.

———. "The Principle of Distinction between Civilians and Combatants Rule 1." IHL Database. Accessed 7 September 2021. https://ihl-databases.icrc.org/customary-ihl/eng/docs/v1_rul_rule1#:~:text=The%20Principle%20of%20Distinction%20between%20Civilians%20and%20Combatants,-Related%20Practice&text=Rule%201.,distinguish%20between%20civilians%20and%20combatants.&text=State%20practice%20establishes%20this%20rule,and%20on-international%20armed%20conflicts.

International Criminal Court (ICC). "Rome Statute of the International Criminal Court." The Hague: ICC, 1998.

———. "Elements of Crimes." The Hague: ICC, 2011.

———. "About the ICC." Accessed 25 August 2020. www.icc-cpi.int/about.

International Criminal Court Assembly of State Parties. "Report on the Working Group on Amendments." 3 December 2019. https://asp.icc-cpi.int/iccdocs/asp_docs/ASP18/ICC-ASP-18-32-ENG.pdf.

International Crisis Group. "Myanmar: The Military Regime's View of the World." Brussels: ICG, 2001.

———. "The Dark Side of Transition: Violence against Muslims in Myanmar." Brussels: ICG, 2013.

———. "Counting the Costs: Myanmar's Problematic Census." Brussels: ICG, 2014.

International Federation for Human Rights, ALTSEAN-Burma, and Burma Lawyers' Council. "International Crimes in Burma: The Urgent Need for a Commission of Inquiry." Paris: International Federation for Human Rights, 2009.

International Federation for Human Rights and Burma Lawyers' Council. "Advancing Human Rights and Ending Impunity in Burma: Which External Leverages?" Bangkok: FIDH, 2009.

International Human Rights Clinic at Harvard Law School (IHRC). "Preliminary Findings and Conclusions on the Material Support for Terrorism Bar as Applied to the Overseas Resettlement of Refugees from Burma." Cambridge, MA: IHRC, 2006.

———. "Crimes in Burma." Cambridge, MA: IHRC, 2009.

———. "Policy Memorandum: Preventing Indiscriminate Attacks and Willful Killings of Civilians by the Myanmar Military." Cambridge, MA: IHRC, March 2014a.

———. "Legal Memorandum: War Crimes and Crimes against Humanity in Eastern Myanmar." Cambridge, MA: IHRC, November 2014b.

International Justice Resource Center. "UN Human Rights Council." Accessed 8 December 2020. https://ijrcenter.org/un-human-rights-council/#:~:text=The %20Council%27s%20mandate%20is%20to,%2C%20and%20make%20recommen dations%20thereon.

International Labour Organization (ILO). "Convention Concerning Forced or Compulsory Labor, 1930 (No. 29)." Geneva: ILO, 1930.

———. "Forced Labor in Myanmar (Burma) Report of the Commission of Inquiry Appointed under Article 26 of the Constitution of the International Labor Organization to Examine the Observance by Myanmar of the Forced Labor Convention, 1930 (No. 29)." Geneva: ILO, 1998a.

———. "Report of the Commission of Inquiry Appointed under Article 26 of the Constitution of the International Labor Organization to Examine the Observance of the Forced Labor Convention, 1930 (No. 29)." Geneva: ILO, 1998b.

———. "Speech of the Myanmar Minister for Labor to the International Labor Conference, 9 June 1998 (Provisional Record)." Geneva: ILO, 1998c.

———. "Measures Recommended by the Governing Body under Article 33 of the Constitution: Implementation of Recommendations Contained in the Report of the Commission of Inquiry Entitled Forced Labor in Myanmar (Burma) Provisional Record 88th Session." Geneva: International Labor Conference, 2000.

———. "Developments Concerning the Question of the Observance by the Government of Myanmar of the Forced Labor Convention, 1930 (No. 29)." Geneva: ILO, 2011.

———. "Forced Labor Complaints Mechanism." Accessed 24 October 2018. www.ilo .org/yangon/complaints/lang--en/index.htm.

———. "Individual Case (CAS)—Discussion: 2019, Publication: 108th ILO Session (2019), Forced Labour Convention, 1930 (No. 29)—Myanmar (Ratification: 1955)." 2019.

www.ilo.org/dyn/normlex/en/f?p=NORMLEXPUB:13100:0::NO::P13100
_COMMENT_ID:4000332.

International Standards Organization. "ISO 15489 Records Management." Accessed 13 February 2020. https://committee.iso.org/sites/tc46sc11/home/projects/published /iso-15489-records-management.html.

InterPares. "Kevin Malseed: Telling the Stories of Displaced People in Burma." Accessed 30 March 2020. https://interpares.ca/voice/kevin-malseed-telling-stories-displaced -people-burma.

Irish Center for Human Rights. "Crimes against Humanity: The Situation of the Rohingyas." Galway, Ireland: ICGR, 2010.

Jackson, Richard. "The Ghosts of State Terror: Knowledge, Politics, and Terrorism Studies." *Critical Studies on Terrorism* 1, no. 3 (2008): 377–92.

Japan International Cooperation Agency. "Preparatory Survey for the Integrated Regional Development for Ethnic Minorities in South-East Myanmar." Yangon: JICA, 2013.

Johannsson, Patrik. "The Humdrum Use of Ultimate Authority: Defining and Analyzing Chapter VII Resolutions." *Nordic Journal of International Law* 78 (2009): 309–42.

Jolliffe, Kim. "Ethnic Conflict and Social Services in Myanmar's Contested Regions." Yangon: Asia Foundation, 2014.

———. "Ethnic Armed Conflict and Territorial Administration in Myanmar." Yangon: Asia Foundation, 2015.

———. "Ceasefires, Governance, and Development: The Karen National Union in Times of Change." Yangon: Asia Foundation, 2016.

Jones, Anthony. *The History and Politics of Counterinsurgency.* Lexington: University of Kentucky Press, 2006.

Jones, Graham. "Secrecy." *Annual Review of Anthropology* 43 (2014): 53–69.

Jones, Lee. "ASEAN's Albatross: ASEAN's Burma Policy—from Constructive Engagement to Critical Disengagement." *Asian Security* 4 (2008): 271–93.

Kaplan, Sam. "Documenting History, Historicizing Documentation: French Military Officials' Ethnological Reports on Cilicia." *Comparative Studies in Society and History* 44, no. 2 (2002): 344–69.

Karen Human Rights Group (KHRG). "Death Squads and Displacement." Mae Sot, Thailand: KHRG, 1999.

———. "SPDC & DKBA Orders to Villages: Set 2000-A." Mae Sot, Thailand: KHRG, 2000a.

———. "SPDC & DKBA Orders to Villages: Set 2000-B." Mae Sot, Thailand: KHRG, 2000b.

———. "Abuse under Orders: The SPDC & DKBA Armies through the Eyes of Their Soldiers." Mae Sot, Thailand: KHRG, 2001.

———. "Forced Labor Orders since the Ban: A Compendium of SPDC Order Documents Demanding Forced Labor since November 2000." Mae Sot, Thailand: KHRG, 2002.

————. "SPDC & DKBA Orders to Villages: Set 2003-A." Mae Sot, Thailand: KHRG, 2003.

————. "Commentary: Seeing through the Smoke of Ceasefires." Mae Sot, Thailand: KHRG, 2005.

————. "Less Than Human: Convict Porters in the 2005–2006 Northern Karen State Offensive." Mae Sot, Thailand: KHRG, 2006.

————. "The Limits of the New ILO Mechanism and Potential Misrepresentation of Forced Labor in Burma." Mae Sot, Thailand: KHRG, 2007a.

————. "Shouldering the Burden of Militarization: SPDC, DKBA, and KPF Order Documents and Forced Labor since September 2006." Mae Sot, Thailand: KHRG, 2007b.

————. "Village Agency: Rural Rights and Resistance in a Militarized Karen State." Mae Sot, Thailand: KHRG, 2008.

————. "Self-Protection under Strain: Targeting of Civilians and Local Responses in Northern Karen State." Mae Sot, Thailand: KHRG, 2010.

————. "Civilian and Military Order Documents: March 2008 to July 2011." Mae Sot, Thailand: KHRG, 2011a.

————. "From Prison to Front Lines: Analysis of Convict Porter Testimony 2009–2011." Mae Sot, Thailand: KHRG, 2011b.

————. "Field Documentation Philosophy." Mae Sot, Thailand: KHRG, 2012a.

————. "Uncertain Ground: Landmines in Eastern Burma." Mae Sot, Thailand: KHRG, 2012b.

————. "Civilian and Military Order Documents: November 2009 to July 2013." Mae Sot, Thailand, 2013.

————. "Ongoing Militarization in Southeast Myanmar." Mae Sot, Thailand: KHRG, 2016.

————. "'Development without Us': Village Agency and Land Confiscations in Southeast Myanmar." Mae Sot, Thailand: KHRG, 2018.

————. "Beyond the Horizon: Local Perspectives on Peace, Justice, and Accountability in Southeast Myanmar." Mae Sot, Thailand: Karen Human Rights Group, 2019.

————. "Locally Defined Northern and Central Karen Districts." Accessed 7 September 2021. https://khrg.org/maps.

Karen Office for Relief and Development. "ERA Request Summary." Chiang Mai, Thailand: TBC archive, 2008.

Kastenhofer, Julia. "The Logic of Archival Authenticity: ISO 15489 and the Varieties of Forgeries in Archives." *Archives and Manuscripts* 43, no. 3 (2015): 166–80.

Keck, Stephen. "Involuntary Sight-Seeing: Soldiers as Travel Writers and the Construction of Colonial Burma." *Victorian Literature and Culture* 43, no. 2 (2015): 389–407.

Keenan, Paul. *Saw Ba U Gyi.* Mae Sot, Thailand: Karen History and Cultural Preservation Society, 2011.

Keenan, Paul, and Nan Mu Chaung Ku. "Karen—Dta Bee Dta Ber." 27 May 2011. Document on file with author.

Keenan, Paul, and Saw Tah Doh Moo. "Life in Burma's Relocation Sites." Chiang Mai, Thailand: Ethnic Nationalities Council, 2010.

Ketelaar, Eric. "Archival Temples, Archival Prisons: Modes of Power and Production." *Archival Science* 2 (2002): 221–38.

———. "Recordkeeping and Societal Power." In *Archives: Recordkeeping in Society*, edited by Sue McKemmish, Michael Piggott, Barbara Reed, and Frank Upward, 277–98. Wagga Wagga, Australia: Center for Information Studies, 2005.

Kinsella, Helen. *The Image before the Weapon: A Critical History of the Distinction between Combatant and Civilian.* Ithaca, NY: Cornell University, 2011.

Kramer, Tom. "The United Wa State Party: Narco-Army of Ethnic Nationalist Party." Washington, DC: East-West Center, 2007.

Kuwali, Dan. "Old Crimes, New Paradigms: Preventing Mass Atrocity Crimes." In *Mass Atrocity Crimes: Preventing Future Outrages*, edited by Robert Rotberg, 25–54. Cambridge, MA: Brookings Institution Press, World Peace Foundation, and Harvard Kennedy School Program on Intrastate Conflict, 2010.

Lampland, Martha. "False Numbers as Formalizing Practices." *Social Studies of Science* 40, no. 3 (2010): 377–404.

Land, Molly, and Jay Aaronson, eds. *New Technologies for Human Rights Law and Practice.* Cambridge: Cambridge University Press, 2018.

Landmine Monitor. "Myanmar/Burma Country Report." Geneva: International Campaign to Ban Landmines, 2017.

Law, John. *After Method: Mess in Social Science Research.* Hove, UK: Psychology Press, 2004.

Le Caisne, Garance. *Operation Caesar: At the Heart of the Syrian Death Machine.* Translated by David Watson. London: Polity Press, 2018.

Lee, Doreen. *Activist Archives: Youth Culture and the Political Past in Indonesia.* Durham, NC: Duke University Press, 2016.

Levi, Ron, and John Hagan. "Lawyers, Humanitarian Emergencies, and the Politics of Large Numbers." In *Lawyers and the Construction of Transnational Justice*, edited by Yves Dezalay and Bryant Garth, 13–47. London: Routledge, 2012.

Litner, Bertil. *The Rise and Fall of the Communist Party.* Ithaca, NY: Cornell University Press, 1990.

Luban, David. "A Theory of Crimes against Humanity." *Yale Journal of International Law* 29 (2004): 85–167.

Lubet, Steven. *Interrogating Ethnography: Why Evidence Matters.* Oxford: Oxford University Press, 2017.

Lundy, Patricia, and Mark McGovern. "Whose Justice? Rethinking Transitional Justice from the Bottom Up." *Journal of Law and Society* 35, no. 2 (2008): 265–92.

Lutz, Catherine. "The Military Normal: Feeling at Home with Counterinsurgency in the United States." In *Militarization: A Reader*, edited by Roberto González, Hugh Gusterson, and Gustaaf Houtman, 157–62. Durham, NC: Duke University Press, 2019.

MacLean, Ken. "Lawfare and Impunity in Burma since the 2000 Ban on Forced Labor." *Asian Studies Review* 36 (June 2007): 189–206.

——. "Sovereignty after the Entrepreneurial Turn: Mosaics of Control, Commodified Spaces, and Regulated Violence in Contemporary Burma." In *Taking Southeast Asia to Market: Commodities, Nature, and People in the Neoliberal Age*, edited by Joseph Nevins and Nancy Lee Peluso, 140–57. Ithaca, NY: Cornell University Press, 2008.

——. *The Government of Mistrust: Illegibility and Bureaucratic Power in Socialist Vietnam*. Madison: University of Wisconsin Press, 2013.

——. "Humanitarian Mine Action in Myanmar and the Mismanagement of Risk." *Focaal: Journal of Global and Historical Anthropology* 74 (2016): 83–96.

——. "Famine Crimes: Military Operations, Forced Migration, and Chronic Hunger in Eastern Burma/Myanmar (2006–2008)." Occasional Paper. Worcester, MA: Clark University, 2018a.

——. "The Rohingya Crisis and the Practices of Erasure." *Journal of Genocide Research* 20, no. 3 (2018b): 83–95.

Maill, Zinaida. "Effects of Invisibility: In Search of the 'Economic' in Transitional Justice." *International Journal of Transitional Justice* 2, no. 3 (2008): 266–91.

Malseed, Kevin. "Networks of Noncompliance: Grassroots Resistance and Sovereignty in Militarized Burma." *Journal of Peasant Studies* 36, no. 2 (2009): 365–91.

Mamdani, Mahmood. *Citizen and Subject: Contemporary Africa and the Legacy of Late Colonialism*. Princeton, NJ: Princeton University Press, 1996.

Marcus, David. "Famine Crimes in International Law." *American Journal of International Law* 97, no. 2 (2003): 245–81.

Marcus, George. "Experts, Reporters, Witnesses: The Making of Anthropologists in States of Emergency." In *Contemporary States of Emergency: The Politics of Military and Humanitarian Interventions*, edited by Didier Fassin and Mariella Pandolfi, 163–202. New York: Zone Books, 2010.

Marston, Daniel. "Lost and Found in the Jungle: The Indian and British Army Jungle Warfare Doctrines for Burma, 1943–1945, and the Malayan Emergency, 1948–1960." In *Big Wars and Small Wars*, edited by Hew Strachan, 81–114. London: Routledge, 2006.

Martin, Aryn, and Michael Lynch. "Counting Things and People: The Practices and Politics of Counting." *Social Problems* 56, no. 2 (2009): 243–66.

Massumi, Brian. "Potential Politics and the Primacy of Preemption." In *Ontopower: War, Powers, and the State of Perception*, 1–19. Durham, NC: Duke University Press, 2015.

Matelski, Maaike. "On Sensitivity and Secrecy: How Foreign Researchers and Their Local Contacts in Myanmar Deal with Risk Under Authoritarian Rule." *Journal of Burma Studies* 18, no. 1 (2014): 59–82.

Maung Aung Myoe. "'Building the Tatmadaw': The Organizational Development of the Armed Forces in Myanmar, 1948–1998." SDC Working Paper No. 327. Canberra: Australian National University, 1998.

——. *Building the Tatmadaw: Myanmar Armed Forces since 1948*. Singapore: Institute of Southeast Asian Studies, 2009.

Mawani, Renisa. "Law's Archive." *Annual Review of Law and Social Science* 8 (October 2012): 337–65.

May, Larry. "Killing Naked Soldiers: Distinguishing between Combatants and Non-combatants." *Ethics & International Affairs* 19, no. 3 (2005): 39–53.

McArtan, Brian, and Kim Jolliffe. "Ethnic Armed Actors and Justice Provision in Myanmar." Yangon: Asia Foundation, 2016.

McCarthy, Gerard. *Military Capitalism in Myanmar: Examining the Origins, Continuities, and Evolution of "Khaki Capital".* Singapore: Institute of Southeast Asian Studies, 2019.

McClennan, Sophia, and Joseph Slaughter. "Introducing Human Rights and Literary Forms: Or, the Vehicles and Vocabularies of Human Rights." *Comparative Literature Studies* 46, no. 1 (2009): 1–19.

McKemmish, Sue. "Traces: Document, Record, Archive, Archives." In *Archives: Record-keeping in Society*, edited by Sue McKemmish, Michael Piggott, Barbara Reed, and Frank Upward, 1–20. Wagga Wagga, Australia: Center for Information Studies, 2005.

McKemmish, Sue, Michael Piggott, Barbara Reed, and Frank Upward, eds. *Archives: Recordkeeping in Society*. Wagga Wagga, Australia: Center for Information Studies, 2005.

McKemmish Sue, and Frank Upward, "The Archival Document: A Submission to the Inquiry into Australia as an Information Society." *Archives and Manuscripts* 19, no. 1 (1991): 17–32.

Meehan, Jennifer. "Towards an Archival Concept of Evidence." *Archivaria* 61 (Spring 2006): 127–46.

Mégret, Frédéric. "Do Facts Exist, Can They Be 'Found,' and Does It Matter?" In *The Transformation of Human Rights Fact-Finding*, edited by Philip Alston and Sarah Knuckey, 27–48. Oxford: Oxford University Press, 2016.

Melzer, Nils. *Interpretive Guidance on the Notion of Direct Participation in Hostilities under International Humanitarian Law.* Geneva: International Committee of the Red Cross, 2009.

Membe, Achille. *On the Postcolony.* Berkeley: University of California Press, 2001.

Merry, Sally Engle. "Measuring the World: Indicators, Human Rights, and Global Governance." *Current Anthropology* 52, supplement 3 (2011): S83–S95.

———. *The Seductions of Quantification: Measuring Human Rights, Gender Violence, and Sex Trafficking.* Chicago: University of Chicago Press, 2016.

Mettraux, Guénaël. *International Crimes and the Ad Hoc Tribunals.* Oxford: Oxford University Press, 2006.

———. "The Definition of Crimes against Humanity and the Question of a 'Policy' Element." In *Forging a Convention for Crimes against Humanity*, edited by Leila Nadya Sadat, 142–76. Cambridge: Cambridge University Press, 2011.

Ministry of Home Affairs, ed. "Order Directing Not to Exercise Powers under Certain Provisions of the Towns Act, 1907, and the Village Act, 1907 (14 May)." Yangon: Ministry of Home Affairs, 1999.

———. "Order Supplementing Order No. 199 (27 October)." Yangon: Ministry of Home Affairs, 2000.

Mnookin, Jennifer. "Scripting Expertise: The History of Handwriting Evidence and the Judicial Construction of Reliability." Public Law and Legal Theory Research Paper Series. University of Virginia Law School, 2001.

Mongia, Radhika. "Impartial Regimes of Truth." *Cultural Studies* 18, no. 5 (2004): 749–68.

Montgomery, Bruce. "Archiving Human Rights: A Paradigm for Collection Development." *Journal of Academic Librarianship* 22, no. 2 (1996): 87–97.

———. "Fact-Finding by Human Rights Non-Governmental Organizations: Challenges, Strategies, and the Shaping of Archival Evidence." *Archivaria* 58 (Fall 2004): 21–51.

Moon, Claire. "What One Sees and How One Sees: Human Rights Reporting, Representation, and Action." *British Journal of Sociology* 46, no. 5 (2012): 876–90.

Morgan, Major C. B. *Hints on Bush Fighting.* London: McMillan, 1899.

Morgenbesser, Lee, and Meredith Weiss. "Survive and Thrive: Field Research in Authoritarian Southeast Asia." *Asian Studies Review* 42, no. 3 (2018): 385–403.

Morris, Rosalind, ed. *Reflections on the History of an Idea: Can the Subaltern Speak?* New York: Columbia University Press, 2010.

Moyn, Samuel. *The Last Utopia: Human Rights in History.* Cambridge, MA: Harvard University Press, 2012.

Mullany, Luke, Adam Richards, Catherine Lee, Voravit Suwanvanickiij, Cynthia Maung, Mahn Mahn, Chris Beyrer, and Thomas Lee. "Population-Based Survey Methods to Quantify Associations between Human Rights Violations and Health Outcomes among Internally Displaced Persons in Eastern Burma." *Journal of Epidemiology & Community Health* 61, no. 10 (2007): 908–14.

Murphy, Sean. "First Report of the Special Rapporteur on Crimes against Humanity." United Nations International Law Commission. UN Doc. A/CN.4/680. Geneva: UN International Law Commission, 2015.

Mutua, Makau. "Savages, Victims, and Saviors: The Metaphor of Human Rights." *Harvard International Law Journal* 42, no. 1 (2001): 201–45.

Myanmar-China Pipeline Watch Committee. "In Search of Social Justice Along the Myanmar-China Oil and Gas Pipeline." Yangon: Myanmar-China Pipeline Watch Committee, 2016.

"Myanmar Foreign Direct Investment." Trading Economics. Accessed 21 September 2021. https://tradingeconomics.com/myanmar/foreign-direct-investment#:~:text=Foreign%20Direct%20Investment%20in%20Myanmar%20averaged%20507.09%20USD%20Million%20from,Million%20in%20June%20of%202016.

Myanmar, Government of. "Constitution of the Republic of the Union of Myanmar." Naypyidaw: Government of Myanmar, 2008.

Myanmar Information Management Unit. "Kayin." Accessed 20 May 2019. www.themimu.info/states_regions/kayin.

———. "Place Codes (Pcodes)." Accessed 6 January 2020. http://themimu.info/place-codes.

Myanmar Peace Support Initiative. "Lessons Learned from MPSI's Work Supporting the Peace Process in Myanmar—March 2012 to March 2014." Yangon: MPSI, 2014.

"Myanmar Says International Criminal Court Has No Jurisdiction in Rohingya Crisis." Reuters, 7 September 2018. www.reuters.com/article/us-myanmar-rohingya-icc /myanmar-says-international-criminal-court-has-no-jurisdiction-in-rohingya-crisis -idUSKCN1LN22X.

Myon Myint. "Final Report of the Inquiry Commission on Sectarian Violence in Rakhine State." Naypyidaw: Republic of the Union of Myanmar, 2013.

Nakanishi, Yoshiro. *Strong Soldiers, Failed Revolution: The State and Military in Burma, 1962–1988.* Singapore: National University Press, 2013.

National Coalition Government of the Union of Burma and Burma UN Service. "The Crisis in Burma: An Agenda for the United Nations Security Council." Washington, DC: Burma Fund, 2003.

National Coalition Government of the Union of Burma and PILPG. "Justice in Burma." Oxford: Oxford University, 2008.

National Resource Governance Institute. "Myanmar's Performance on the Resource Governance Index 2018." 2018. www.resourcegovernance.org/our-work/country /myanmar.

ND-Burma. "You Cannot Ignore Us: Victims of Human Rights Violations in Burma from 1970–2017 Outline Their Desires for Justice." Chiang Mai, Thailand: ND-Burma, 2018.

Nelson, Diane. "Reckoning the After/Math of War in Guatemala." *Anthropological Theory* 10, nos. 1–2 (2010): 87–95.

"Network Myanmar." Accessed 31 July 2020. www.networkmyanmar.org.

Ni Ni Myint. *Burma's Struggle against British Imperialism, 1885–1895.* Rangoon: The Universities Press, 1983.

Nice, Sir Geoffrey, QC, and Julianne Kerr Stevenson. "UN Inaction on Burma War Crimes 'Unjustifiable.'" *Democratic Voice of Burma,* 20 September 2010.

Nikken, Pedro, and Geoffrey Nice. "What the U.N. Can't Ignore in Burma." *Washington Post,* 2 June 2009.

Nordstrom, Carolyn. "Shadows and Sovereigns." *Theory, Culture, and Society* 17, no. 4 (2000): 35–54.

Norwegian Refugee Council and Internal Displacement Monitoring Centre. "2017 Global Report on Internal Displacement." ReliefWeb. 22 May 2017. http://reliefweb .int/report/world/2017-global-report-internal-displacement-grid-2017.

Norwegian Refugee Council and UN Office for the Coordination of Humanitarian Affairs. "Guidance on Profiling Internally Displaced Persons." Geneva: OCHA, 2008.

Office for the Coordination of Humanitarian Affairs. "Myanmar: Humanitarian Snapshot—November 2012." Geneva: OCHA, 2012.

Online Burma/Myanmar Library. Home page. Accessed 5 December 2019. www .burmalibrary.org.

Orford, Anne. *Reading Humanitarian Interventions: Human Rights and the Use of Force in International Law.* Cambridge: Cambridge University Press, 2003.

Papailias, Penelope. *Genres of Recollection: Archival Poetics and Modern Greece*. London: Palgrave Macmillan, 2005.

Parmar, Parveen, Jade Benjamin-Chung, Linda Smith, Saw Nay Htoo, Sai Laeng, Aye Lwin, and Mahn Mahn. "Health and Human Rights in Eastern Myanmar Prior to Political Transition: A Population-Based Assessment Using Multi-staged Household Cluster Sampling." *BMC International Health and Human Rights* 14 (2014). https://bmcinthealthhumrights.biomedcentral.com/articles/10.1186/1472-698X-14-15.

Partners in Relief and Development. "Crimes in Northern Burma: Results from a Fact-Finding Mission to Kachin State." Denver, CO: PRD, 2011.

Paung Sie Facility. "Our Goal." Accessed 22 April 2019. www.paungsiefacility.org/about.html.

Pedersen, Morton. *Promoting Human Rights in Burma: A Critique of Western Sanctions Policy*. Boulder, CO: Rowman & Littlefield, 2008.

Pejic, Jelena. "The Right to Food in Situations of Armed Conflict: The Legal Framework." *International Review of the Red Cross* 83, no. 844 (2001): 1097–1109.

Physicians for Human Rights. "Life under the Junta: Evidence of Crimes against Humanity in Burma's Chin State." New York: PHR, 2011.

Pinchevski, Amit. "Archive, Media, Trauma." In *On Media Memory*, edited by Motti Neiger, Oren Myers, and Eyal Zandberg, 253–64. London: Palgrave Macmillan, 2011.

Poovey, Mary. *A History of the Modern Fact: Problems of Knowledge in the Sciences of Wealth and Society*. Chicago: Chicago University Press, 1998.

Posner, Eric. *The Twilight of Human Rights*. New York: Oxford University Press, 2014.

Price, Kenneth. "Edition, Project, Database, Archive, Thematic Research Collection: What's in a Name?" *Digital Humanities Quarterly* 3, no. 3 (2009). www.digitalhumanities.org/dhq/vol/3/3/000053.html#.

Public International Law and Policy Group. *Justice in Burma*. Oxford: Oxford University Press, 2008.

Quintana, Tomás Ojea. "Human Rights Situations that Require the Council's Attention: Progress Report of the Special Rapporteur on the Situation of Human Rights in Myanmar." UN Doc. A/HRC/13/48. 10 March 2010. www2.ohchr.org/english/bodies/hrcouncil/docs/13session/A-HRC-13-48.pdf.

Rajah, Ananda. "Burma: Protracted Conflict, Governance, and Non-traditional Security Issues." Singapore: Institute of Defense and Strategic Studies, 2001.

———. "A 'Nation of Intent' in Burma: Karen Ethno-Nationalism, Nationalism, and Narrations of Nation." *Pacific Review* 15, no. 4 (2002): 517–37.

Ramcharan, Bertrand, ed. *International Law and Fact-Finding in the Field of Human Rights*. Leiden: Brill Nijhoff, 2014.

Rancière, Jacques. *The Names of History: On the Poetics of Knowledge*. Minneapolis: University of Minnesota Press, 1994.

Redfield, Paul. "A Less Modest Witness: Collective Advocacy and Motivated Truth in a Medical Humanitarian Movement." *American Ethnologist* 35, no. 1 (2006): 3–28.

"Report of the Preparatory Commission for the International Criminal Court, Addendum, Part II, Finalized Draft Text of the Elements of Crimes." Geneva: United Nations, 2000.

Rhoads, James. "Alienation and Thievery: Archival Problems." *American Archivist* 29, no. 2 (1966): 197–208.

Richards, Thomas. *The Imperial Archive: Knowledge and the Fantasy of Empire.* London: Verso, 1993.

Riles, Annelise. *The Network Inside Out.* Ann Arbor: University of Michigan Press, 2004.

———. *Documents: Artifacts of Modern Knowledge.* Ann Arbor: University of Michigan Press, 2006.

Robertson, Craig. "A Documentary Regime of Verification: The Emergence of the US Passport and the Archival Problematization of Identity." *Cultural Studies* 23, no. 3 (2008): 1–26.

Robinson, Darryl. "Defining 'Crimes against Humanity' at the Rome Conference." *American Journal of International Law* 93, no. 1 (1999): 43–57.

Root, Brian. "Numbers Are Only Human: Lessons from Human Rights Practitioners from the Quantitative Literacy Movement." In *The Transformation of Human Rights Fact-Finding,* edited by Philip Alston and Sarah Knuckey, 355–76. Oxford: Oxford University Press, 2016.

Rudolf, Markus, and Clara Schmitz-Pranghe. "Beyond Aid: The Continuous Struggle to Cope with Displacement in Myanmar and Thailand." Bonn: Bonn International Center for Conversion, 2018.

Sadat, Leila Nadya. "Crimes against Humanity in the Modern Age." *American Journal of International Law* 107 (2013): 334–77.

Satterthwaite, Margaret, and Justin Simeone. "A Conceptual Roadmap for Social Science Methods in Human Rights Fact-Finding." In *The Transformation of Human Rights Fact-Finding,* edited by Philip Alston and Sarah Knuckey, 321–53. Oxford: Oxford University Press, 2016.

Saunders, Rebecca. "Lost in Translation: Expressions of Human Suffering, the Language of Human Rights, and the South African Truth and Reconciliation Commission." *SUR—International Journal on Human Rights* 5, no. 9 (2008): 51–69.

Saw Greh Moo. "Caught in a Two-Front War in Post-ceasefire Karen State." *Karen News,* 18 July 2013. http://karennews.org/2013/07/caught-in-a-two-front-war-in-post-ceasefire-karen-state.html/.

Scheffer, David. "Why the ICJ Is Trying to Protect Myanmar's Rohingya." Center for Foreign Relations. 24 January 2020. www.cfr.org/article/why-icj-trying-protect-myanmars-rohingya.

Scott, James. *Seeing Like a State: How Certain Schemes to Improve the Human Condition Have Failed.* New Haven, CT: Yale University Press, 1998.

———. *The Art of Not Being Governed: An Anarchist History of Upland Southeast Asia.* New Haven, CT: Yale University Press, 2009.

Segal, Eyal. "Closure in Detective Fiction." *Poetics Today* 31, no. 2 (2010): 153–213.

Seligman, Steven. "Politics and Principle at the UN Human Rights Commission and Council (1992-2008)." *Israel Affairs* 17, no. 4 (2011): 520–41.

Selth, Andrew. *Burma's Armed Forces: Power without Glory.* Norwalk, CT: Eastbridge, 2002.

———. "Even Paranoids Have Enemies: Cyclone Nargis and Myanmar's Fears of Invasion." *Contemporary Southeast Asia* 30, no. 3 (2008): 379–402.

Seshadri, Kalpana Rahita. "When Home Is a Camp: Global Sovereignty, Biopolitics, and Internally Displaced Persons." *Social Text* 26, no. 1 (2008): 29–58.

Seybolt, Taylor, Jay Aronson, and Baruch Fischhoff. *Counting Civilian Casualties: An Introduction to Recording and Estimating Nonmilitary Deaths in Conflict.* Oxford: Oxford University Press, 2013.

Shan Herald Agency for News. "Myanmar's Ethnic Conflict in 2018." BNI Multimedia Group. 14 December 2018. www.bnionline.net/en/news/myanmars-ethnic-armed-conflict-2018-unabated-protracted-war-and-heightened-inter-ethnic-armed.

Shan Human Rights Foundation and Shan Women's Action Network, Women's League of Burma. "Same Impunity, Same Patterns: Sexual Abuses by the Burma Army Will Not Stop Until There Is a Genuine Civilian Government." Chiang Mai, Thailand: WLB, 2014.

Shohat, Ella. "The Struggle over Representation: Casting, Coalitions, and the Politics of Identification." In *Late Imperial Culture (Postmodern Occasions)*, edited by Roman De La Campa, 166–78. London: Verso, 1995.

Shore, Cris, and Susan Wright. "Audit Culture Revisited: Rankings, Ratings, and the Reassembling of Society." *Current Anthropology* 56, no. 3 (2015): 421–44.

Sikkink, Kathryn. *Evidence for Hope: Making Human Rights Work in the 21st Century.* Princeton, NJ: Princeton University Press, 2017.

Silverstein, Michael. "Shifters, Linguistic Categories, and Cultural Description." In *Meaning in Anthropology*, edited by Keith Basso and Henry Shelby, 11–55. Albuquerque: University of New Mexico Press, 1976.

Siméant, Johanna, and Susan Taponier. "Interpreting the Rise of International 'Advocacy.'" *Humanity: An International Journal of Human Rights, Humanitarianism, and Development* 5, no. 3 (2014): 323–43.

Simon-Skjodt Center for the Prevention of Genocide. "'They Want Us All to Go Away': Early Warning Signs of Genocide in Burma." Washington, DC: US Holocaust Memorial Museum, 2015.

Smith, M. L. R., and David Martin Jones. *The Political Impossibility of Modern Counterinsurgency: Strategic Problems, Puzzles, and Paradoxes.* New York: Columbia University Press, 2015.

Smith, Martin. *Burma: Insurgency and the Politics of Ethnicity.* New York: Zed Books, 1999.

South, Ashley. "Karen Nationalist Communities: The 'Problem' of Diversity." *Contemporary Southeast Asia* 29, no. 1 (2007): 55–76.

———. "The Politics of Protection in Burma: Beyond the Humanitarian Mainstream." *Critical Asian Studies* 44, no. 2 (2012): 175–204.

South, Ashley, Tim Schroeder, Kim Jolliffe, Mi Kun Chan Mon, Sa Shine, Susanne Kempel, Axel Schroeder, and Naw Wah Shee Mu. *Between Ceasefires and Federalism: Exploring Interim Arrangements in the Myanmar Peace Process.* Yangon, Myanmar: Covenant Consultancy Co., Ltd., 2018.

Starn, Orin. "Missing the Revolution: Anthropologists and the War in Peru." *Cultural Anthropology* 6, no. 1 (1991): 63–91.

"Statement by His Excellency U Wunna Maung Lwin, Ambassador and Permanent Representative/Leader of the Myanmar Delegation to the 13th Session of the Human Rights Council." 26 March 2010. www.burmalibrary.org/docs08/Mmr Statement_on_L-15.pdf.

Statista. "Foreign Direct Investment New Inflows in Myanmar from 2013 to 2017." Accessed 2 October 2018. www.statista.com/statistics/607842/myanmar-foreign -direct-investment-net-inflows/.

Steedman, Carolyn. *Dust: The Archive and Cultural History.* New Brunswick, NJ: Rutgers University Press, 2002.

———. "After the Archive." *Comparative Critical Studies* 8, nos. 2–3 (2011): 321–40.

Steinburg, David. *Burma's Road toward Development: Growth and Ideology under Military Rule.* Boulder, CO: Westview Press, 1981.

———. "The State, Power, and Civil Society in Burma-Myanmar: The Status and Prospects of Pluralism." In *Burma Myanmar: Strong Regime Weak State?*, edited by Morton Pedersen and R. J. May, 91–122. Adelaide: Crawford Publishing House, 2000.

Sternberg, Meir. "Proteus in Quotation-Land: Mimesis and the Forms of Reported Discourse." *Poetics Today* 3, no. 2 (1982): 107–56.

Stoler, Ann. "Perceptions of Protest: Defining the Dangerous in Colonial Sumatra." *American Ethnologist* 12, no. 4 (1985): 642–58.

———. "'In Cold Blood': Hierarchies of Credibility and the Politics of Colonial Narratives." *Representations*, no. 37 (1992): 151–89.

———. "Colonial Archives and the Arts of Governance." *Archival Science* 2, nos. 1–2 (2002): 87–109.

———. *Along the Archival Grain: Epistemic Anxieties and Colonial Common Sense.* Princeton, NJ: Princeton University Press, 2010.

Sunstein, Cass. *Infotopia: How Many Minds Produce Knowledge.* Oxford: Oxford University Press, 2006.

Swisspeace. "Archives in Human Rights and Dealing with the Past—a Collection of Resources." Bern, Switzerland: Swisspeace, 2013.

Tan, Audrey. "Myanmar's Transitional Justice: Addressing a Country's Past in a Time of Change." *Southern California Law Review* 8, no. 6 (2012): 1643–84.

Taussig, Michael. *Shamanism, Colonialism, and the Wild Man: A Study in Terror and Healing.* Chicago: University of Chicago Press, 1987.

———. *Defacement: Public Secrecy and the Labor of the Negative.* Palo Alto, CA: Stanford University Press, 1999.

Taylor, Robert. *The State in Myanmar.* Honolulu: University of Hawaii Press, 2009.

———. "Myanmar's Military and the Dilemma of Federalism." *ISEAS Perspective* 7 (2017). www.iseas.edu.sg/images/pdf/ISEAS_Perspective_2017_7.pdf.

Tee Noo. "I Do Need Peace." *Transnational Literature* 6, no. 2 (2014): 2–3.

Teitel, Ruti. *Globalizing Transitional Justice*. Oxford: Oxford University Press, 2014.

Telegraphic Correspondence relating to Military Executions and Dacoity in Burmah. Vol. C. 4960. London: House of Commons Parliamentary Papers, 1886.

Thai-Burma Border Consortium (TBBC). "Internally Dispersed People and Relocation Sites in Eastern Burma." Bangkok: TBBC, 2002.

———. "Internal Displacement and Reclaiming the Right to Rice in Eastern Burma." Bangkok: TBBC, 2003a.

———. "Reclaiming the Right to Rice: Food Security and Internal Displacement in Eastern Burma." Bangkok: TBBC, 2003b.

———. "ERA Financial Tracker." Unpublished. TBBC, 2004a.

———. "Internal Displacement and Vulnerability in Eastern Burma." Bangkok: TBBC, 2004b.

———. "ERA Financial Tracker." Unpublished. TBBC, 2005a.

———. "Internal Displacement and Protection in Eastern Burma." Bangkok: TBBC, 2005b.

———. "ERA Financial Tracker." Unpublished. TBBC, 2006a.

———. "Internal Displacement in Eastern Burma 2006." Bangkok: TBBC, 2006b.

———. "ERA Financial Tracker." Unpublished. TBBC, 2007a.

———. "2007 Survey of Internal Displacement in Eastern Burma." Bangkok: TBBC, 2007b.

———. "ERA Financial Tracker." Unpublished. TBBC, 2008a.

———. "Internal Displacement and International Law in Eastern Burma." Bangkok: TBBC, 2008b.

———. "Protracted Displacement and Militarization in Eastern Burma." Bangkok: TBBC, 2009.

———. "Protracted Displacement and Chronic Poverty in Eastern Burma/Myanmar." Bangkok: TBBC, 2010.

———. "Displacement and Poverty in South East Burma/Myanmar." Bangkok: TBBC, 2011.

Thawnghmung, Ardeth Maung. *The Karen Revolution in Burma: Diverse Voices, Uncertain Ends*. Honolulu: East-West Center, 2008.

———. *The 'Other' Karen in Myanmar: Ethnic Minorities and the Struggle without Arms*. New York: Lexington Books, 2012.

Thiha, Amira. "Understanding the Tatmadaw's 'Standard Army' Reforms." *Frontier Myanmar*. 22 June 2017. https://frontiermyanmar.net/en/understanding-the-tatmadaws-standard-army-reforms.

Thiha Ko Ko. "FDI Forecast to Remain Flat at US$5.8B in Fiscal 2019–20." *Myanmar Times*, 3 October 2019. www.mmtimes.com/news/fdi-forecast-remain-flat-us58b-fiscal-2019-20.html.

Tilly, Charles. *The Formation of Nation States in Western Europe*. Princeton, NJ: Princeton University Press, 1975.

Tinker, Hugh, ed. *Burma: The Struggle for Independence, 1944–48*. Vol. 1. London: Her Majesty's Stationery Office, 1983a.

———. *Burma: The Struggle for Independence, 1944–48.* Vol. 2. London: Her Majesty's Stationery Office, 1983b.

Tin Maung Maung Than. "Burma: The 'New Professionalism' of the Tatmadaw." In *Military Professionalism in Asia: Conceptual and Empirical Perspectives,* edited by Muthiah Alagappa, 163–78. Honolulu: East-West Center, 2001.

Tomlins, Christopher, and John Comaroff. "'Law as …': Theory and Practice in Legal History." *UC Irvine Law Review* 1, no. 3 (2011): 1040–79.

Tonkin, Derek. "UN Special Rapporteur Tomás Ojea Quintana and a UN Commission of Inquiry." *Myanmar Briefing Note,* no. 11 (2011). Document on file with author.

Trace, Ciaran. "What Is Recorded Is Never Simply 'What Happened': Record Keeping in Modern Organizational Culture." *Archival Science* 2 (2002): 137–59.

Trading Economics. "Myanmar Foreign Direct Investment 2012–2017." Accessed 7 September 2021. https://tradingeconomics.com/myanmar/gdp.

Transnational Institute. "Beyond Panglong: Myanmar's National Peace and Reform Dilemma." Amsterdam: Transnational Institute, 2017.

———. "Internally Displaced Persons and Refugee Right to Land." 21 August 2019. www.tni.org/files/article-downloads/position_paper_the_right_to_land_for_idps_and_refugees_english_21_august_2019.pdf.

Transparency International. "Corruption Perceptions Index 2018." 2018. www.transparency.org/country/MMR.

Trouillot, Michel-Rolph. *Silencing the Past: Power and the Production of History.* Boston: Beacon Press, 1995.

Tsuda, Takeyuki. "Is Native Anthropology Really Possible." *Anthropology Today* 31, no. 3 (2015): 14–17.

UN News. "UN Human Rights Chief Points to 'Textbook Example of Ethnic Cleansing' in Myanmar." 11 September 2017. https://news.un.org/en/story/2017/09/564622-un-human-rights-chief-points-textbook-example-ethnic-cleansing-myanmar.

———. "Secretary-General Welcomes International Court of Justice Order on the Gambia v. Myanmar Genocide Convention Case." 23 January 2020. www.un.org/press/en/2020/sgsm19946.doc.htm.

UNESCO Committee on Human Rights. "Updated Set of Principles for the Protection and Promotion of Human Rights through Action to Combat Impunity." Paris: UNESCO, 2005.

United Kingdom of Great Britain and Northern Ireland and United States of America. "UN Security Council Draft Resolution No. S/2007/14." 12 January 2007. www.responsibilitytoprotect.org/files/BurmaRes.-Jan.07.pdf.

United Nations. "Guiding Principles on Internal Displacement." Geneva: OCHA, 2004.

———. "UN Chapter I: Purposes and Principles." Accessed 7 September 2021. www.un.org/en/about-us/un-charter/chapter-1.

United Nations Commission on Human Rights. "Guiding Principles on Internal Displacement." New York: United Nations Commission on Human Rights, 1998.

———. "Commission on Human Rights Resolution 2003/12: Situation of Human Rights in Myanmar." 16 April 2003. E/CN.4/RES/2003/12.

———. "Human Rights Indicators: A Guide to Measurement and Implementation." New York: OHCHR, 2012.

———. "Protocol Additional to the Geneva Conventions of 12 August 1949 and Relating to the Protection of Victims of Non-international Armed Conflicts (Protocol II)" (entered into force 7 December 1978). Accessed 4 April 2018. www.ohchr .org/EN/ProfessionalInterest/Pages/ProtocolII.aspx.

United Nations General Assembly. "Basic Principles and Guidelines on the Right to a Remedy and Reparation for Victims of Gross Violations of International Human Rights Law and Serious Violations of International Humanitarian Law." New York: United Nations, 2005a.

———. "World Summit Outcome." New York: UN General Assembly, 2005b.

———. "Resolution Adopted by the General Assembly on 24 December 2010." UN Doc. A/RES/65/241. 21 March 2011. www.un.org/en/ga/search/view_doc.asp ?symbol=A/RES/65/241.

———. "Collected Reports to the UN General Assembly by the Special Rapporteurs on the Situation of Human Rights in Myanmar." Accessed 22 May 2015. www .burmalibrary.org/docs6/Collected_SRM_GA_reports.pdf.

United Nations High Commissioner for Refugees. "Archives and Records." Accessed 13 January 2019. www.unhcr.org/archives-and-records.html.

———. "Refugee Response in Bangladesh." 2020. https://data2.unhcr.org/en/situations /myanmar_refugees.

United Nations Human Rights Council. "5/2 Code of Conduct for Special Procedures Mandate-Holders of the Human Rights Council, Article 6(b)." 18 June 2007. www .ohchr.org/Documents/Issues/Executions/CodeOfConduct.pdf.

———. "Situation of Human Rights in Myanmar." UN Doc. A/HRC/13/L.15. 19 March 2010. www.burmalibrary.org/docs08/A-HRC-13-L.15(en).pdf.

———. "Draft Report of the Working Group on the Universal Periodic Review: Myanmar." Geneva: UNHRC, 2011.

———. "Report of the Detailed Findings of the Independent International Fact-Finding Mission in Myanmar." No. A/HRC/39/64. Geneva: Human Rights Council, 2018.

United Nations Library. "International Commissions of Inquiry, Fact-Finding Missions: Home." Accessed 5 July 2020. https://libraryresources.unog.ch/factfinding.

United Nations Office for the Coordination of Humanitarian Affairs. "Myanmar: IDP Sites in Kachin State (as of 31 March 2018)." 2 May 2018a. https://reliefweb.int/map /myanmar/myanmar-idp-sites-kachin-state-31-mar-2018.

———. "Myanmar: IDP Sites in Kachin State (as of 31 July 2018)." 21 August 2018b. https://reliefweb.int/map/myanmar/myanmar-idp-sites-kachin-state-31-july -2018-0.

United Nations Office of the High Commissioner for Human Rights. "Promotion and Protection of Human Rights: Study on the Right to Truth." Report No. E/ CN.4/2006/91. New York: Commission on Human Rights, 2006a.

———. "UN Human Rights Experts Call on Myanmar to End Counter-Insurgency Operations Targeting Civilians in Northern Karen State and Eastern Pegu Division."

16 May 2006b. https://newsarchive.ohchr.org/EN/NewsEvents/Pages/Display
News.aspx?NewsID=4095&LangID=E.

———. "Commissions of Inquiry and Fact-Finding Missions on International Human
Rights and Humanitarian Law: Guidance and Practice." New York: UNOHCR,
2015.

———. "Refugee Response in Bangladesh." 2020. https://data2.unhcr.org/en/situations
/myanmar_refugees.

———. "Refugees in Thailand." Accessed 7 September 2021. www.unhcr.org/th/en
/refugees.

United Nations Security Council. "Deliberations of 15 September 2005 (5526th meeting)." In *Repertoire of the Practice of the Security Council, 2004–2007*. New York:
Office of the High Commissioner for Human Rights, 2008.

———. "Decisions of 12 January 2007 (5619th Meeting): Rejection of a Draft Resolution." In *Repertoire of the Practice of the Security Council, 2004–2007*. New York: Office
of the High Commissioner for Human Rights, 2007.

———. "5619th Meeting (12 January 2007), Provisional Agenda." Accessed 29 April
2015. www.securitycouncilreport.org/atf/cf/%7B65BFCF9B-6D27-4E9C-8CD3
-CF6E4FF96FF9%7D/Myan%20SPV%205619.pdf.

———. "Chapter VII Resolutions and Resolutions by Year (1995–2019)." 2019.
www.un.org/securitycouncil/sites/www.un.org.securitycouncil/files/chapter_vii
_resolutions.pdf.

United States Embassy Rangoon (Burma). "Karen State: Just Another Dry Season
Offensive?" Confidential Cable, 22 June 2006a. Wikileaks ID No. 68989.

———. "Offensive in Karen State? A Cross-Border Aid Worker Offers Views." Cable
No. 06BANGKOK3799, 28 June 2006b.

———. "Burma: The KNU's Reluctant Fist." Cable No. 07RANGOON1103, 13 November 2007.

Urban, Greg. "Entextualization, Replication, and Power." In *Natural Histories of Discourse*, edited by Michael Silverstein and Greg Urban, 21–44. Chicago: University
of Chicago, 1996.

Van Maanen, John, and Brian Pentland, "Cops and Auditors: The Rhetoric of Records."
In *The Legalistic Organization*, edited by Sim Sitkin and Robert Bies, 53–90. Thousand Oaks, CA: Sage Publications, 1994.

Van Wyke, Ben. "Translation and Ethics." In *The Routledge Handbook of Translation
Studies*, edited by Carmen Millán and Franesca Bartina, 548–61. London: Routledge,
2013.

Verdery, Katherine. *What Was Socialism, and What Comes Next?* Princeton, NJ:
Princeton University Press, 1996.

———. *My Life as a Spy: Investigations in a Secret Police File*. Durham, NC: Duke
University Press, 2018.

Verisk Maplecroft. *Political Risk Atlas*. Bath, UK: Verisk Maplecroft, 2016.

Vismann, Cornelia. "Jurisprudence: A Transfer Science." *Law and Critique* 10 (1999):
279–86.

———. *Files: Law and Media Technology.* Translated by Geoffrey Winthrop-Young. Palo Alto, CA: Stanford University, 2008.

Vungsiriphisal, Premjai, Dares Chusri, and Supang Chantavanich, eds. *Humanitarian Assistance for Displaced Persons from Myanmar: Royal Thai Government Policy, and Donor, INGOs, NGO, and UN Agency Aid Delivery.* London: Springer, 2014.

Waldorf, Lars. "Anticipating the Past: Transitional Justice and Socio-economic Wrongs." *Social & Legal Studies* 21, no. 2 (2012): 171–86.

Walsh, Richard. *The Rhetoric of Fictionality: Narrative Theory and the Idea of Fiction.* Columbus: Ohio State University Press, 2007.

Walton, Matthew. "The Wages of Burman-ness: Ethnicity and Burman Privilege in Contemporary Myanmar." *Journal of Contemporary Asia* 43, no. 1 (2013): 1–27.

Wansai, Sai. "Ethnic Yearly Round-Up: Ethnic States in 2019." Myanmar Peace Monitor. 11 December 2019. www.bnionline.net/en/news/ethnic-yearly-round-ethnic -states-2019.

Ward, Geoff. "The Slow Violence of State Organized Race Crime." *Theoretical Criminology* 19, no. 3 (2015): 299–314.

Weingartner, Eric. "David Hawk on the Second Edition of Hidden Gulag." 11 July 2012. https://vtncankor.wordpress.com/2012/07/11/david-hawk-on-the-second-edition -of-hidden-gulag/.

Weld, Kristen. *Paper Cadavers: The Archives of Dictatorship in Guatemala.* Durham, NC: Duke University Press, 2014.

"What Is an Author." In *Language, Counter-Memory, Practice: Selected Essays and Interviews,* edited by Donald Bouchard, 113–38. Ithaca, NY: Cornell University Press, 1977.

White, Hayden. "The Value of Narrativity in the Representation of Reality." In *On Narrative,* edited by W. J. T. Mitchell, 1–24. Chicago: University of Chicago Press, 1981.

———. *The Content of the Form: Narrative Discourse and Historical Representation.* Baltimore, MD: Johns Hopkins University Press, 1990.

Wiktionary. "Authoritative." Accessed 17 July 2020. https://en.wiktionary.org/wiki /authoritative.

Wilkinson, Paul. "International Terrorism: New Risks to World Order." In *Dilemmas in World Politics: International Issues in a Changing World,* edited by John Baylis and Nick Rengger, 228–57. London: Clarendon Press, 1992.

Wilkinson, Stephen. "Standards of Proof in International Humanitarian and Human Rights Fact-Finding and Inquiry Missions." Geneva: Geneva Academy of International Humanitarian Law and Human Rights, 2011.

Williams, Raymond. *The Long Revolution.* London: Chatto and Windus, 1961.

Winichakul, Thongchai. *Siam Mapped: A History of the Geo-Body of a Nation.* Honolulu: University of Hawaii Press, 1997.

Women's League of Burma. "International Tribunal on Crimes against Women of Burma." Chiang Mai, Thailand: WLB, 2010.

———. "Karen Community-Based Organizations' Position on Refugees Return to Burma." 2012. www.burmalibrary.org/en/karen-community-based-organizations -position-on-refugees-return-to-burma.

Wood, Stacy, Kathy Carbone, Marika Cifor, Anne Gilliland, and Ricardo Punzalan. "Mobilizing Records: Reframing Archival Description to Support Human Rights." *Archival Science* 14 (2014): 397–419.

Woods, Kevin. "Ceasefire Capitalism: Military-Private Partnerships, Resource Concessions, and Military State-Building in the Burma-China Borderlands." *Journal of Peasant Studies* 38, no. 4 (2011): 747–70.

World Bank. "Myanmar Public Expenditure Review 2015." Washington, DC: World Bank, 2015.

INDEX

travel pass, 147–50
tribunals: former Yugoslavia, 27–28, 175, 197;
    Rwanda, 27–28, 175, 197
Trouillot, Michel-Rolph, 11, 52, 69
trust, 98, 204; betrayal, 33–34; mis-, 206;
    trustworthy, 5, 13, 33, 199
truth: commissions, 2, 7, 10, 136, 203, 205,
    210; competing, xiii, 20, 122, 164, 212; fact
    production of, 90, 162; human rights, 190,
    195, 205; legitimacy of, 136; post-truth, 9,
    180, 212; regimes of, xiii, 20; right to, 111,
    185, 211; representativeness of, 5, 141, 186;
    seeking, 8, 26; stability of, 71, 124, 136, 138,
    159; telling, 9; validity of, 9, 180, 187, 189
Tutu, Desmond, 169, 198

United National Human Rights Council, 15,
    181, 193, 211; commission of inquiry,
    179–80, 184; special rapporteur mandate,
    180–81; resolutions by, 176–78, 183, 186;
    venue for threat determination, 173
United Nations General Assembly, 15, 27,
    180; mandate, 184; resolutions on
    Myanmar, 15, 172–73, 176–77, 186
United Nations Security Council, 15, 171–72,
    174–75; Chapter VII designation, 166,
    168, 170, 193; commission of inquiry, 27,
    162, 164, 178, 187, 193; critique of, 173;
    NGO-campaign, 41, 172, 178, 198; report
    to, 167–69; resolution by, 165–67, 170, 179;
    threat to peace, 160, 166, 172
United States Campaign for Burma, 172,
    174–75, 184–85

universalism: human rights, 173, 186
utopian, 23, 209

Van Maanen, John, 8
Van Wyke, Ben, 94
verbatim: definition of, 70–71; forms of, 39,
    71, 194; politics of, 79; presentation, 77,
    90, 93, 95; quotation, 73, 75, 77, 105,
    190–91, 193; replication, 71, 78, 82, 222;
    speaking via, 69, 83, 88, 93, 119, 159;
    stability of, 70–72, 84; translation as,
    84, 94
Verdery, Katherine, 33
victim-witness: definition of, 125; position-
    ality of, 135–37
violence: communal, 35, 182, 182; preemptive,
    37, 46–47; sexual, 35, 94, 176–77, 145;
    singular v. representative, 38; slow v. fast,
    39, 71, 79–86, 89, 94

war crimes, 2, 27, 126, 193, 212, 220; allegations
    of, 89, 132, 172, 202; ICC, 129, 163, 179–81;
    IHRC legal memorandum, 159, 178
Weber, Max, 30
Weld, Katherine, 11–12
whataboutism, 34, 134
White, Hayden, 11, 135
widespread and systematic: definition of, 28;
    famine crimes, 99–101, 120; forced labor,
    39, 71–72, 85; travel restrictions, 150;
    violations against civilians, 20, 89, 133,
    175, 192, 206, 212
Wunna Maung Lwin, 180–81

Founded in 1893,
UNIVERSITY OF CALIFORNIA PRESS
publishes bold, progressive books and journals
on topics in the arts, humanities, social sciences,
and natural sciences—with a focus on social
justice issues—that inspire thought and action
among readers worldwide.

The UC PRESS FOUNDATION
raises funds to uphold the press's vital role
as an independent, nonprofit publisher, and
receives philanthropic support from a wide
range of individuals and institutions—and from
committed readers like you. To learn more, visit
ucpress.edu/supportus.